28 DAY BOOK

Across
the
Line

Al
otro
lado

Across the Line/Al otro lado

the
poetry
of
Baja
California

Edited by *Harry Polkinhorn* & *Mark Weiss*

Junction Press
San Diego
2002

Cover Art: "Tía Juana," graphite and charcoal on
board, by Hugo Crosthwaite (Rosarito, B.C.)

The translations of the poems of Heriberto Yépez
appeared in *Reversible Monuments: Contemporary
Mexican Poetry* (Port Townshend, WA: Copper Can-
yon Press, 2002), edited by Mónica de la Torre and
Michael Wiegers.

Bibliographical information on selections included
in the anthology can be found on pages 373-382,
within the biographies of the poets, and in the notes
on pages 31 and 37.

CONTENTS

FOREWORD

The poetry of Baja California is a map of the sustaining, creative function of the human imagination when confronted with extreme circumstances. The mountains, blistering deserts, and seacoast settlements scattered up and down the peninsula–what did the colonizing authorities in Mexico's large interior cities really know of this far-flung outreach except what their own baroque imaginations figured for them? As to those peoples who had been living here for centuries, members of nomadic cultures who followed the seasons, they had their own myths explaining their place in the order of things, some few of which escaped the fury of the invaders and which also appears in the living language left behind.

The task of fashioning a representative selection of the works of Baja California poets in a bilingual, English / Spanish format was undertaken because no such collection has existed. For those readers familiar with some Spanish, this collection will be especially valuable as they will be able to get an idea of what the original Spanish means by easily comparing it with the facing English rendition. The general reader will quickly gain a sense of the richness, variety, subtlety, and sweep of poetry in Baja California as it was practiced during the last half of the 20th century. The love lyric, metaphysical meditation on last things, mock epic, and political satire are just a few of the many modes taken up by Baja California's skilled poets, some of whom trace their literary roots as much to U.S. poetry as to that of their native country.

If identity formation generally proceeds along a path from the less to the more diversified, then what we see in this collection bears witness to the gradual but increasingly marked foundation of a living culture. Earlier works focused on the varied landscapes of the region, seen through the colonializing lens of the master perspective, which measures, charts, and compares for the purposes of acquisition and domination. Indigenous production must be approached with care for its ritual sacred social context, about which the non-native reader can know only a very limited amount. In our own time, the theme of the relationship between the center (Mexico City) and the provinces takes on more and more significance, often from a contestatory viewpoint. While nature writing endures, as does the love lyric, we notice a new awareness of international influences and popular mass-cultural imagery modulated by postmodern and post-structuralist ironies. Also, advances in transportation, technology, and communication have resulted in a poetry that is troubled by the energies of U.S. culture at large, perhaps to be seen here in a way that is unique in contemporary Mexican poetry. One of the most engaging features of the poetry of our time that has emerged from Baja California is that fresh and bold spirit of discovery that could only have been conferred upon a creative product by the relative youth of the social institutions and physical infrastructure of the region. The reader will see this spirit in poems that focus both on the inner world constructed by the human imagination and on the exterior world of relationships, cities, desert and mountain landscapes, and meditations on history.

I was born within yards of the U.S.-Mexico international boundary between Calexico, California, and Mexicali, Baja California, in the heart of a mixed-breed culture split and joined by the suture of the chain-link fence with its police on both sides engaged in their futile and infantile games of trying to control the spirit of life, which goes where it wants according to its own laws. Language is a strange thing. Through it, poets from both sides of the border reveal themselves to one another; through their configuration of its potential to change the sliding signifier in ways not possible if removed from the shimmering and sometimes unsettling vitality of a completely bilingual environment. They struggle with these sounds, play with them, sword-fight, sport their ways through daily life and the national literatures they claim as their mutual, nourishing backgrounds.

Yet we remain conscious of the fact that what's printed on the page has a life of its own that is different from live social interaction. The differences constitute a flattening of the imagination's reach, but by virtue of that compression something else can be achieved, the illusion of permanence. The book, so solid to the touch, such a delight to the eye, is silent, and through its silence it escapes the shredding maw, at least for a while. To compensate for its muteness, these poems ask to be read aloud, returning them to the living speech/language of a particular idiom, because what Baja California border poetry underscores perhaps more than any other quality is rootedness in a particular time and place, specificity, contingency, demanding a full presence in the here and now.

Borders are to be crossed, and that between Spanish and English involves an imaginative transformation between cultural worlds. This collection provides a bridge for that transformation and invites you to cross it.

Harry Polkinhorn

INTRODUCTION

In 1971, when I first ventured into Baja California, it took ten minutes to pass through Tijuana. Where now there is unbroken development there were a few villages and hotels along the 70 miles of coast south to Ensenada, Ensenada's streets were largely unpaved, Hussong's, its famous old bar, now at the hub of a flourishing urban center, sat on a dirt parking lot, and the pavement on Mexico 1 ran out a few miles south of town–from there almost all the way to La Paz, 700 miles south as the crow flies, and Cabo San Lucas, 100 miles further, was a dirt track. It was so bad that it used to be used for the annual Tijuana to Cabo San Lucas endurance race, one of the world's toughest off-road events. Few would have guessed that a local arts culture of extraordinary vibrancy had begun to form, as few who cross now into a very different Tijuana and Ensenada are aware of the mature culture that thrives there.

In those days and in the 300 years of Spanish, then Mexican, occupation preceding it Baja California had been the wildest part of Mexico's sparsely populated north, the last settled and the last explored, its equivalent in fact and in myth to the Wild West of the United States. Even now its deserts and mountains (it is almost entirely deserts and mountains) are virtually empty of human life, the population largely confined to several very new cities (by the standards of Mexico, many of whose cities measure their age in millennia): the four border-region cities of the state of Baja California, Tijuana (founded in 1889), Mexicali (1903), Ensenada (1870), and Tecate (1892); hundreds of miles of desert to the south, the resort cities of the state of Baja California Sur, La Paz (1811) and the smaller towns of the cape area; a couple of agricultural regions in the far north and far south; and a widely separated string of small resort towns, date palm oases, mining towns and fishing ports. One can still drive hundreds of miles of the one paved road without seeing any sign of human life except for an occasional gas station or greasy spoon. A beautiful but forbidding landscape.

That road wasn't completed until 1974. The northern half of the peninsula had only surpassed the constitutionally-mandated population of 80,000 to become the state of Baja California in 1952; Baja California Sur became the final territory of Mexico to achieve statehood in 1974.

Its distant overseers had largely ignored Baja California until then, and they continued to do so as long as they were able. As in the United States, federal aid and representation in the Chamber of Deputies, Mexico's equivalent of our House of Representatives, is proportional to population as determined by a decennial census. The PRI (Partido Revolucionario Institucional), which controlled Mexico's political life from 1938 to 2000, was not amused when the state of Baja California voted in 1958, in its first national election, for the presidential candidate of the PAN (Partido Acción Nacional), the PRI's most important rival, and census figures thereafter have been highly suspect. An educated guess would place Tijuana's population at something under 2,000,000 (it's the third or fourth largest Mexican city), Mexicali's something under 1,000,000, Ensenada's over 500,000, Tecate's between 100,000 and 200,000, and La Paz' at about 100,000.

But the north, and especially Baja California, the land of the *norteados* (the confused) and of Mexico City tabloid reports of flying saucers, has become the tail wagging the dog. After a generation of questionable PRI victories in local and state elections, the PAN won the municipal elections in Ensenada in 1986 and the gubernatorial and legislative elections in Baja California (its first state victories anywhere in Mexico) in 1989. The PAN has been in solid control of local and state governments in Baja California, and in the north as a whole, ever since, and it has been the party's most important power base. Since the establishment of *maquiladora* factories (which relieved U.S. corporations of the burdens of U.S. unions and most taxes and customs duties) beginning in the 1970s (and even more since the enactment of NAFTA, the North America Free Trade Agreement, which eliminated whatever tariffs remained on most goods passing between the United States, Mexico and Canada, in 1994), the north, and again Baja California most of all, has come to wield enormous economic power, second only to the capital's. With the PAN in control (since 2000) of the Presidential palace and the national legislature, one can expect the 2010 census to reveal an extraordinary jump in reported population.

Baja California remains in the Mexican imagination something of a stepchild, and the disdain with which the Mexico City elite has tended to view its citizens persists, as well as the distrust in the other direction, which in the past was expressed in periodic movements for independence. Norteño music, the north's country music, may have taken over the national airwaves, but Baja California is still seen as not quite "Mexican," and there's some truth to that view. Mexico is a country of very old regional cultures. The enormous growth of its urban centers in the 20th century tended, with the obvious exception of Mexico City, to draw on each city's immediate hinterland. Ties to the regional culture, and proximity to its rural or small town sources, remained. The cities of Baja California, in contrast, have very little in the way of populated hinterlands, and although almost three quarters of the poets in this anthology were born in Baja California, very few of their parents were, and almost none of their grandparents.

Missing in most Baja California cities, along with a great many other of the givens of Mexican life, is the communal cement of the *paseo*, the evening stroll of large numbers of townsfolk around a central plaza. Neither Tijuana, nor Mexicali, nor Ensenada has a central plaza. Instead of the feeling of exclusivity and belonging of the older centers, the intimate cultural habits, the musical and culinary tastes, of all the regions, ethnic and linguistic groups of Mexico, as well as of the sizeable minorities of Chinese, Russians, English and North Americans, create a cultural stew that exists nowhere else in Mexico, which defines for its children a new sense of place, moving to the frenetic rhythms of cities in a constant state of change.

And there is the special circumstance of the border. Readers of this anthology will note its frequent appearance in the poems. Attitudes towards *el otro lado* (the other side), as Mexican border residents call the U.S., are decidedly mixed. Baja California is the crossing point for most illegal immigrants to the

U.S., but illegal crossings are far outnumbered by the daily tides crossing to the north in the morning and to the south in the evening of those legally permitted to work or shop in the United States (but nonetheless subject to capricious and humiliating interrogation), and even of U.S. citizens who live in Mexico and commute northwards. The floods of Southern Californians who maintain second homes in exclusively English-speaking coastal enclaves, and the weekend invasion of young gringos intent on a cheap drunk, do little to enhance the local attitudes towards *estadounidenses* (U.S.ians).

The border crossing at Tijuana is the world's busiest, and it must also be one of the strangest. Most passages from the underdeveloped to the developed world are mediated by several crossings: one passes, for example, from Syria to Turkey to Greece to southern Italy to Germany. In Tijuana the residents of the hillside communities of shacks that spring up almost overnight to house the newest arrivals can see over the border fence into the well-ordered residential districts of San Ysidro or Chula Vista. The people in those dependencies of San Diego also speak Spanish, watch Mexican television and listen to Mexican radio, and flavor their food as Mexicans do, but they benefit from the most powerful economy the earth has ever known.

The passage from one side to the other, whether legal or illegal, is from one place to another that shares the same name–both are California, and few on the Mexican side ever forget that the other California was once Mexican. And the culture of the other California has a profound impact on the culture of Baja California.

The Mexican border towns and many of those on the U.S. side exist only because of the border and are almost completely dependent on it. Mexicali was founded by the U.S. land and irrigation company that created the Imperial Valley *al otro lado*, and its twin, Calexico (note the mirrored names), is essentially a supermarket and department store for its much larger neighbor. Tijuana began as a resort and entertainment district for Southern Californians. San Ysidro was and is its market. Ensenada, like its larger neighbors, flourished with the onset of prohibition across the line. The prosperity, and many of the problems, among them the traffic in illegal drugs and illegal immigrants, are entirely responsive to developments in the United States. If U.S. companies decided to move their factories to Asia, as some have done, the border cities would shrink drastically and revert to dependence on local tourism, and if North American tourists changed their taste in beaches the economy of La Paz and the cape region would dry up.

A graphic example is playing itself out as I write. The attack on the World Trade Center has led to a tightening of already very tight controls at the border. The result has been delays that can last three hours for those going north, a crushing inconvenience for those who must cross for work or school, and also a death-blow, if it lasts much longer, to tourism to the south (because potential tourists aren't eager to face the delay returning) and to retail trade on both sides.

It's worth noting that for many years border traffic control was casual in the extreme; people would stroll at will across the border in either direction. For awhile in the 1970s the U.S. Navy's old beach-front Border Field gunnery range, which became Border Field State Park, was known locally as Friendship Field: Mexicans and U.S. citizens would climb the low fence to stroll on each other's beaches. Now a rusty twelve-foot-tall corrugated steel fence crosses the beach and runs out to deep water to discourage migratory swimmers, and the surf casters who never catch any fish are U.S. Border Patrol agents in transparent disguise.

It should be no surprise that there's a profound ambivalence towards gringos among those on the south side of the border. That ambivalence has been one of the major themes of the poetry of Baja California. Edmundo Lizardi's long poem "Baja Times," for instance, is a disenchanted survey of the tourist culture of the entire peninsula, as seen from the perspective of a native.

The development of Baja California's poetry has paralleled its recent history. Before the 1960s there was very little–a few bits of verse by missionaries, a small amount of very minor verse by early settlers–aside from the traditional poetry of indigenous hunters and gatherers. The poetry of the extinct tribes of three quarters of the peninsula is, with all but a very few words of their languages, entirely lost to us. The extraordinary cave paintings that they left in the canyons of hundreds of miles of the mountain interior hint at what must have been lost. The remnant population, perhaps 2000, representing three languages, live in five hamlets spread across the area between Ensenada and the border. We have included versions of some of their remembered traditional poetry. Towards the end of the anthology there are also two poems by Heriberto Yépez derived from reactions of those same peoples to the changes brought by the presence of the newcomers.

We have also included two recent *corridos*. Scholars trace the origin of the corrido, Mexico's traditional folk ballad, variously to medieval Spanish and Precolumbian models. For at least the last century and a half it has functioned as both the purveyor of ancient genres, notably the outlaw ballad, and as a sort of tabloid newspaper, filled with the latest real or imagined scandals, hard news and political commentary. Often the hard news is filtered through the archetypes of the older genres. So, a drug kingpin becomes a Robin Hood. In the two recountings of very real and shocking events that we present here the heroes have become the archetypal martyrs for justice.

A modern literary culture developed very quickly in Baja California as the population began its rapid expansion. With statehood came the necessary infrastructure. There is a state "autonomous" (meaning secular) university in every Mexican state. The Universidad Autónoma de Baja California (UABC), the first of Baja California's institutions of higher learning, was founded in 1957 but wasn't fully functional until the late 1960s. There are now campuses in Mexicali, Tijuana, Ensenada and Tecate. Other universities and research institutions followed, but they have had relatively little influence on the literary culture.

For thirty years after the founding of UABC it was still impossible to get a degree in literature in Baja California, and several poets left for educations in Mexico City. Since 1986, when the Escuela de Humanidades at UABC-Tijuana was founded, degrees in literature have been available, but only in Tijuana. Before that (and still at the other campuses), literature courses were taught under the rubric of disciplines like communications sciences and human sciences (roughly, our social sciences).

The same situation prevails in Baja California Sur. UABCS in La Paz was founded in 1976, but it wasn't until 1991 that it became possible to graduate with a degree in literature.

No matter the rubric, there is no such thing as a degree in creative writing and no equivalent of our M.F.A. programs (the U.S. is one of the few countries in which such programs exist). Instead there are informal *talleres* (workshops), run by whoever can get people to come once a week and offer their work for criticism. Although they are often held at universities they are open to all, there is no course credit, no tuition, no mandatory attendance, and usually no salary for the director. They exist only because of the passion and commitment of their members, which have included most of the poets in this anthology. Some of them have nonetheless lasted for years, with membership as stable as the vagaries of life allow.

Aside from the universities talleres have been (and continue to be) held at Ensenada's Centro Social Cívico y Cultural, established in 1977, Tijuana's federally-funded Centro Cultural (1982), the Instituto de Cultura de Baja California (1989) in both cities as well as Mexicali, and at the Casas de Cultura that exist under municipal auspices in most Mexican cities, where inexpensive classes in cultural subjects are offered.

Talleres are very much like workshops on this side of the border: members submit work for the review of the group and the director. As important, the group tends to retire afterwards to a bar or coffee shop, where a lot of the cultural work gets done: literary friendships are solidified, and journals and small presses are spawned.

The first and historically most important of the talleres was the Voz de Amerindia, which met at UABC-Tijuana. From it emerged the first important literary publications in Baja California, the journal *Amerindia*, Raúl Jesús Rincón Meza's *Poemas de santo y seña para descubrir un rostro* (1974), and the anthology *Siete poetas jóvenes de Tijuana* (1974), which included Rincón Meza, Victor Soto Ferrel, Ruth Vargas Leyva, and Luis Cortés Bargalló, among others. In the years since four other regional anthologies have appeared: *Parvada. Poetas jovenes de Baja California* (1985), edited by Gabriel Trujillo Muñoz; *Baja California Sur. Otro mar otro desierto* (1991), edited by Raúl Antonio Cota; *Un camino de hallazgos. Poetas bajacalifornianos del siglo XX* (1992), edited by Trujillo Muñoz; and *Baja California. Piedra de serpiente* (1993), edited by Luis Cortés Bargalló.

Since *Amerindia* a few dozen journals have appeared in Tijuana, Mexicali, Ensenada and La Paz, and there are weekly culture supplements in all of the local papers, which often include extensive poetry selections. There are, as well, numerous small independent presses and the institutional presses of the Instituto de Cultura de Baja California, Tijuana's Instituto Municipal de Arte y Cultura,and the Fondo Editorial de Baja California. Tijuana's Centro Cultural is about to inaugurate an imprint of its own. Almost all are government subsidized. And

Tijuana has become an essential stop on the reading and lecture circuit for intellectuals and writers from all of Latin America.

There are also frequent poetry readings. It's the custom in Mexico for new books to be presented formally, several speakers delivering brief critical introductions followed by a reading. At these presentations, and at readings in general, it's not unusual to have crowds of several hundred. To a gringo this is simply astonishing.

From the Voz de Amerindia taller emerged the only poets of Baja California who can be identified as a coherent group: Rincón Meza, Soto Ferrel, Cortés Bargalló, and the younger poets Victor Hugo Limón, Gilberto Zúñiga, Manuel Romero and Horacio Ortiz Villacorta, strongly influenced by the French poets Verlaine, Mallarmé, Rimbaud (who have been integral to Latin American literature since Rubén Darío and others introduced them in the early years of the 20th century), the surrealists and the American objectivists. This group of poets tend to write lyric poems of allusive delicacy and musicality and an aesthetic detachment that is unusual in Baja California, where a great many poets, otherwise very different from each other–Francisco Morales, Rosina Conde, Luz Mercedes López Barrera, Roberto Castillo Udiarte, Juan Antonio Di Bella, Edmundo Lizardi and Heriberto Yépez among them–write poetry that is involved with and in protest against the grittier life around them.

But this is a literary culture of great diversity and sophistication, and all of the tendencies of modern Mexican and Latin American poetry are present. What differentiates it is the greater and easily-recognized influence of more recent poetry from across the border (many of the poets are prolific translators) and the presence of the border itself. And, as my coeditor Harry Polkinhorn noted, an intense investigation of place.

One of the peculiarities of the post-conquest cultures of the Americas has been their constant asking of the questions "what is this place," "who am I in this place," and "what am I doing here." There is a sense of metaphysical nakedness, not just each of us alone within our society, but alone in time as well, a heightened sense of the insecurity of things and of our own transience–abandoned by or having abandoned the former life, we or our near ancestors have built a new one amidst the evident ruins of other, unknowable cultures to which we can have no certain connection.

Mexicans in the past century have come to identify themselves with a dual heritage, unavailable to most of us to the north, as descendants of both conquered and conqueror, indigenous and invader. It's a dubious and conflicted comfort, but a comfort of sorts. Baja Californians, separated from familiar cultural and physical landscapes, and faced with the inexorable fact of their neighbor *al otro lado*, across the long scar of the fence that many refer to as "the Berlin Wall," more radically than most others in this hemisphere experience themselves as displaced, or at best provisionally situated in an unfamiliar place. They live, literally, in a liminal space–a threshold, a border. Here even the native-born experience themselves as exiles, because place exists in the dimension of time as well, and change through time has been so rapid and so extreme that the remembered place appears to have moved from beneath them. All of this enacted as if in an existential landscape, against the background of the great unpeopled, inhospitable territory beyond the cities.

This, I think, is what gives the poetry of these poets, young, most of them, as the careers of poets are measured, much of its edge: the reptilian landscape of Elizabeth Algrávez, the uneasy metaphysics of Carlos Adolfo Gutiérrez Vidal, Eduardo Arellano "in the midst of the sudden urban desolation/ that causes any man to feel himself the last of his species/ among the thousands that run with him towards their workplaces" identifying himself with the last of a prehuman race.

Baja Californians remain orphans of sorts, caught between and on the edge of the two power centers that determine their fates and that tend to render them invisible. Our goal when we began this anthology was to make them visible.

Baja Californians, and Mexicans in general, have ample reason to question the motives of the gringos who pass among them. It has been a long history of belittlement and exploitation. In commemoration of a war that Mexicans have never forgotten and we *al otro lado* scarcely remember, most Mexican cities have an Avenida de los Niños Héroes–Avenue of the Boy Heroes, the 5000 teenage cadets slaughtered by the U.S. army in the 1847 battle for Mexico City. Over Tijuana's version towers a monumental statue of Abraham Lincoln. The Good Gringo.

Despite the thousand acts of generosity that made this book possible we are aware that as outsiders we have inherited this ambivalence. Editing an anthology is not the best way to make friends, and probably none of the poets will be in total agreement with our choices, whether to include or exclude. We hope that we have succeeded in representing both the scope of the region's poetry and its best products.

Part of the task of determining who to include in a place that so many pass through has been determining who to consider Baja Californian. Cortés Bargalló, who was born and raised in Tijuana, left for school in Mexico City in 1971 and settled there permanently in 1975, put it well in an email message: "I don't think that I ever really left Tijuana–I still live in that same interminable city that never stops moving and changing." That commitment to place was our desideratum. As Javier Manríquez, resident in Mexico City since 1971, tells us of the small mining town where he was raised,

> There I lived my clarity,
> the origin of spaces
> beneath the June sun.
>
> Years go by unheeded,
> leave their stony geometry
> in the corners
> where shadows
> accumulate,

but the image burns,
transparency endures and overflows.
My names appear,
my ghosts
–your ghosts

that haven't aged
that remember me now...

("Cuaderno de San Antonio")

Mark Weiss

ACKNOWLEDGEMENTS

This collection is a testament to the spirit of cooperation and mutual assistance of many people from both sides of the border. It would not have been possible without the three groundbreaking anthologies that preceded it, Raúl Antonio Cota's *Baja California Sur. Otro mar otro desierto* (1991), Gabriel Trujillo Muñoz' *Un camino de hallazgos. Poetas bajacalifornianos del siglo XX* (1992), and Luis Cortés Bargalló's *Baja California. Piedra de serpiente* (1993).

In the decade since the earliest of these anthologies was published the poets whose work they contain have written more poems, and a new generation of poets has appeared. Defining the field and acquiring books which often are out of print or available only in their city of publication would have been impossible without the help of the poets, many of whom gave generously of their knowledge. Many gave us unpublished poems and copies of their books, as well.

We would have been unaware of several important poets without the assistance of Eduardo Arellano, Manuel Romero, Heriberto Yépez and Dante Salgado (Heriberto and Dante in particular showered us with books). They, and Gabriel Trujillo Muñoz and Carlos Adolfo Gutiérrez, have been untiring in answering our endless questions. Like others among the poets, they read and commented on the translations of their own poetry, and also on the translations of other poets; their efforts have saved us from many embarrassments.

Edgardo Moctezuma, of Moctezuma Books, Chula Vista, California, and Susie Custodia should also be mentioned here, Edgardo for his help acquiring texts and for his knowledge of the circumstances of their production, and both for their aid in understanding them.

Lastly, we wish to thank our long-suffering translators, who probably thought they would never see the finished anthology.

Harry Polkinhorn & Mark Weiss

A NOTE ON THE TEXT

To the extent that space has allowed we have avoided extracting fragments from longer texts. Many of the poets compose in sequences of independent poems, and all *fragmentos* included consist of such poems, except for those from Luis Cortés Bargalló's book-length *Al margen indomable*, and from Luz Mercedes López Barrera's long poem "Omnipresencia."

Within the limitations of space we have tried to select poems representing the range of each poet's career.

We have followed the conventions of each language in matters of punctuation.

Footnotes and broader explanatory notes follow the English versions of the poems. With few exceptions we have footnoted only references that would be more easily understood in Mexico than elsewhere.

Footnotes are indicated by an asterisk within the text.

Asterisks between lines indicate a new page in a sequence of unnamed poems.

Translators are identified by their initials. Their full names appear on pages 381 and 382.

The poets are presented in the order of their birth.

El cenzontle *(Cochimí)*

El cenzontle arriba de nosotros
arriba está cantando
es de noche y arriba el pájaro cenzontle
está cantando
el cenzontle se ha equivocado
y ahora está cantando en la noche,
lejos de amanecer

(se repite 2 veces)

es de noche
es de noche y arriba, lejos del amanecer
el cenzontle está cantando
arriba, arriba de nosotros
el cenzontle está cantando

El hombre que arrullaba a un niño *(Cochimí)*

Todos los días el hombre arrullaba al niño
el niño estaba ahí
el hombre lo tomaba en sus brazos y lo arrullaba
el niño estaba ahí llorando
todos los días el hombre arrullaba al niño
el niño estaba ahí
el niño estaba ahí llorando
todos los días el hombre arrullaba al niño
todos los días el hombre arrullaba al niño
todos los días el hombre arrullaba al niño
el niño estaba ahí llorando
el niño estaba ahí.

De tierras lejanas *(Cucapá)*

De lejos
de muy lejos
de tierras muy lejanas
lejanas
de tierras muy lejanas
lejanas

The Mocking-Bird *(Cochimí)*

The mocking-bird up there
is singing above us
it's night and up there the mocking-bird
is singing
the mocking-bird is wrong
singing at night
far from the dawn

(repeat twice)

it's night
it's night and up there, far from the dawn
the mocking-bird is singing
up there, up above us
the mocking-bird is singing

The Man Who Would Sing a Lullaby to a Little Boy *(Cochimí)*

Every day the man would sing a lullaby to the little boy
the little boy was there
the man would take him in his arms and sing him a lullaby
the little boy was crying there
every day the man would sing a lullaby to the little boy
the little boy was there
the little boy was crying there
every day the man would sing a lullaby to the little boy
every day the man would sing a lullaby to the little boy
every day the man would sing a lullaby to the little boy
the little boy was crying there
the little boy was there.

From Distant Lands *(Cucapá)*

From far away
from very far
from very distant lands
distant
from very distant lands
distant

de lejos
de muy lejos
de tierras muy lejanas
lejanas
lejanas
de tierras muy lejanas
lejanas
de tierras muy lejanas
de lejos
de muy lejos
de tierras muy lejanas
de lejos
de lejos
de lejos
de muy lejos
de tierras muy lcjanas
de lejos
de muy lejos
de tierras muy lejanas, lejanas

La sonaja canta *(Cucapá)*

La sonaja canta,
canta,
canta.

En invierno y en verano;
canta,
canta.

Al coyote pegado a la luna;
canta,
canta.

La luz *(Kiliwa)*

Llegó el gran padre con cara
de coyote,
y le dijo a la negrura,
"¡No estás sola, yo soy la luz!"
Y así le dijo tres veces
Y así le dió la luz a la negrura.

from far away
from very far
from very distant lands
distant
distant
from very distant lands
distant
from very distant lands
from far away
from very far
from very distant lands
from far away
from far away
from far away
from very far
from very distant lands
from very far
from very far
from very distant lands, distant

The Rattle Sings *(Cucapá)*

The rattle sings
sings,
sings.

In winter and summer;
sings,
sings.

To the coyote stuck to the moon;
sings,
sings.

Light *(Kiliwa)*

The great father arrived with the face
of a coyote
and said to the darkness,
"You're not alone! I am the light!"
Thus he spoke three times
And light dispelled the darkness.

Cinco poemas *(Paipai)*

I. *La puesta del sol*

Lentamente, el sol se pone y deja de alumbrar.

(se repite 7 veces)

Pero el sol sale y se vuelve a poner, repitiéndose siempre.

(se repite 2 veces)

repitiéndose siempre

Lentamente, el sol se pone y deja de alumbrar.

(se repite 6 veces)

Pero el sol sale y se vuelve a poner, repitiéndose siempre,
pero el sol sale y se vuelve a poner, repitiéndose, lentamente,
el sol se pone y deja de alumbrar lentamente, el sol
se pone y deja de alumbrar, pero el sol sale y se vuelve a
poner repitiéndose siempre.

II. *La media noche*

La oscuridad nos cubrió y no hay luz

(se repite 24 veces)

Oscuridad.

III. *Primer cantido del gallo*

El primer lloro del primer gallo: el primer
lloriqueo, el primero.

(se repite 4 veces)

El primer gallo, el gallo, el primer gallo lloró, lloró
el primer cantido del gallo, el primer gallo cantó, cantó
el primer cantido del gallo, el primero el primero
el primer lloro del primer gallo: el primer lloriqueo,

Five Poems *(Paipai)*

I. *Sunset*

Slowly, the sun sets, dying out.

(repeat 7 times)

But the sun rises and then sets again, over and over.

(repeat twice)

over and over

Slowly, the sun sets, dying away.

(repeat 6 times)

But the sun rises and then sets again, over and over,
but the sun rises and sets again, repeating, slowly,
the sun sets, dying away slowly, the sun
sets, dying away, but the sun rises and then sets
again, over and over.

II. *Midnight*

Darkness has fallen and there's no light

(repeat 24 times)

Darkness.

III. *First Cock's Crow*

The first cry of the first cock: the first
whimper, the first.

(repeat 4 times)

The first cock, the cock, the first cock cried, wept
the first crowing of the cock, the first cock sang, sang
the first crowing of the cock, the first the first
the first cry of the first cock: the first whimper,

27

el primero
el primer lloro del primer gallo: el primer lloriqueo,
el primero
el primer gallo, el gallo, el primer gallo lloró, lloró
lloró el primer gallo,
el primero, el primero.

IV. *La madrugada*

La claridad llega y yo me voy.

(*se repite 2 veces*)

Me voy cargando la claridad
la claridad llega y yo me voy
la claridad llega y yo me voy

(*se repite 5 veces*)

la claridad llega y yo me voy

(*se repite 5 veces*)

me voy cargando la claridad
la claridad llega y yo me voy
la claridad llega y yo me voy
me voy cargando la claridad
la claridad llega y yo me voy.

(*se repite 5 veces*)

Me voy cargando la claridad
la claridad llega y yo me voy
la claridad llega y yo me voy.

V. *La salida del sol*

El sol sale y da la claridad a la tierra
el sol sale da claridad a la tierra
el tapacamino sale a la claridad.

(*se repite una vez*)

the first
the first cry of the first cock: the first whimper,
the first
the first cock, the cock, the first cock cried, cried
the first cock cried,
the first, the first.

IV. *Dawn*

Light arrives and I'm going.

(repeat twice)

I go carrying the light
light arrives and I'm going
light arrives and I'm going

(repeat 5 times)

light arrives and I'm going

(repeat 5 times)

I go carrying the light
light arrives and I'm going
light arrives and I'm going
I go carrying the light
light arrives and I'm going.

(repeat 5 times)

I'm going carrying the light
light arrives and I'm going
light arrives and I'm going.

V. *Sunrise*

The sun rises and sheds light on the earth
the sun rises sheds light on the earth
the road-runner rises to the light.

(repeat once)

El sol sale da claridad a la tierra
el tapacamino sale a la claridad
el sol sale da claridad a la tierra
el sol sale da claridad a la tierra
el tapacamino sale a la claridad.

(se repite 4 veces)

El tapacamino sale a la claridad
el sol sale da claridad a la tierra.

(se repite 3 veces)

El tapacamino sale a la claridad
el tapacamino sale a la claridad
el sol sale da claridad a la tierra.

(se repite una vez)

El tapacamino sale a la claridad.

El oscuro cielo *(Kumiai)*

El oscure cielo, el oscuro cielo,
en el oscuro cielo el tecolote se pone
a cantar.

(se repite 8 veces)

The sun rises sheds light on the earth
the road-runner rises to the light
the sun rises sheds light on the earth
the sun rises sheds light on the earth
the road runner rises to the light.

(repeat 4 times)

The road-runner rises to the light
the sun rises sheds light on the earth.

(repeat 3 times)

The road-runner rises to the light
the road-runner rises to the light
the sun rises sheds light on the earth.

(repeat once)

The road-runner rises to the light.

The Dark Sky *(Kumiai)*

The dark sky, the dark sky,
in the dark sky the owl lands
and sings.

(repeat 8 times)

Note: The Spanish versions of all of these poems were drawn from Yolanda Sánchez and Gabriel Trujillo Muñoz, editors, *De tierras muy lejanas. La cultura indigena de Baja California* (Mexicali: Secretaría de Educación Pública, 1987) . They were translated from the original languages by María Emes, Herminia Domínguez, and María Antonieta Fernández ("El Cenzontle"), María Emes ("El hombre que arrullaba a un niño"), Juan García Aldama ("De tierras lejanas" and "La sonaja canta"), Cruz Ochorte Espinosa ("La luz"), and Fernando Olmos Cañedo ("Cinco poemas [Paipai]" and "El oscuro cielo").

H.P.

Corrido del Gato Félix

Voy a cantar un corrido
de alguien que yo conocí
periodista distinguido
por su pluma era temido
desde Tijuana a Madrid.

Le decían el Gato Félix
porque se le oía decir,
era como un felino
que tenía siete destinos,
y los tenía que cumplir.

Era de Choix, Sinaloa,
era su tierra natal,
pero se quedó en Tijuana,
porque le pegó la gana,
porque quería ayudar.

Con lo que escribía en el diario,
al gobierno hizo temblar.
Se acabó el abecedario,
de amenaza hizo rosario
y a la *Zeta* hizo popular.

Con una pluma valiente,
señaló la corrupción,
ayudó siempre a la gente
y más de dos presidentes
le pusieron atención.

De una forma traicionera
le llegó al "Gato" el final,
en caballo de carreras
la muerte corrió a ganar.

Ya se murió el Gato Félix
ya lo llevan a enterrar,
era uno más en la lista
de valientes periodistas
que así han querido callar.

Felix the Cat Corrido

I'm going to sing a corrido
about a man I knew,
a famous reporter
feared for his pen
from Tijuana to Madrid.

They called him Felix the Cat
because as it was said,
he was like a cat
that had nine lives,
nine lives to complete.

He was from Choix, Sinaloa,
it was his birthplace,
but he stayed in Tijuana,
because he wanted to,
because he wished to help.

With what he wrote in the paper,
he made the governor tremble,
His abc is finished,
he collected a rosary of threats
and made *Zeta* popular.

With a courageous pen,
he pointed out corruption,
always helped people
and more than a couple of presidents
paid attention to him.

In a treacherous fashion
"The Cat" met his end,
Death on a race horse
raced to win.

Felix the Cat has died
they're carrying him to the grave
he was one more on the list
of brave reporters
they silenced this way.

A Héctor Félix Miranda,
le dedico mi cantar,
pero no tengas pendiente,
ya anda por ahí un valiente
que ocupará su lugar...

Corrido a Colosio

A quinientos de la línea,
en la ciudad de Tijuana
mataron al candidato.
Y dicen que fue complot;
que la orden venía de arriba.
Que el gallo que la dio
cra del partido oficial.
Y dice y dice mi gente del pueblo
que fue por cierto discurso
que el candidato habló.

Luis Donaldo Colosio Murrieta,
sonorense de mucho valor,
tu gente ignoraba que
en Lomas Taurinas
manos asesinas tu vida acabar.

No puedo negar señores
lo incapaz de aquella escolta.
Eran las cinco con diez
cuando perturbado demente
se abrió paso entre la gente
y a boca de jarro dos balazos
disparó.

Rodeado de mucha gente,
en el centro del poder,
cayó un valiente al atardecer.

Luis Donaldo Colosio Murrieta,
marcaste un guión en la historia.

En México el cambio ya empezó
Tijuana en primera plana
México en el mundo entero

To Héctor Félix Miranda,
I dedicate my song,
but you don't have to worry,
somewhere there's another
ready to take his place.

Corrido for Colosio

A quarter mile from the border
in the city of Tijuana
they killed the candidate.
And they say it was a conspiracy;
that the order came from above
that the rooster who gave the order
was a member of the ruling party.
And my townspeople all say
it was for a certain speech
that the candidate gave.

Luis Donaldo Colosio Murrieta,
valiant Sonoran,
your people didn't know
that in Lomas Taurinas
an assassin took your life.

I can't deny, gentlemen,
the faults of his bodyguards.
It was ten after five
when a crazy man
broke through the crowd
and shot two bullets
at point blank range.

Surrounded by many people,
in the center of power
a brave man fell at dusk.

Luis Donaldo Colosio Murrieta,
you marked a page in history.

In Mexico change had already begun
first in Tijuana
then in Mexico and the whole world

y el partido en el poder sigue
matando gente.
Después vino Ruiz Massieu,
el cochupo de Tabasco, Yucatán y
Puebla.
Y el ganón de este juego sucio de
barajas
fue Zedillo, el mentiroso y dientón.

México de mis amores, creo en ti
por tu templanza en la desgracia
inesperada
por tu solidaridad ante la crisis
porque eres mío y soy de ti.

but the ruling party
goes on killing.
Next came Ruiz Massieu,
the kingpin of Tabasco, Yucatán, and Puebla.
And the winner of this dirty card game
was Zedillo, that big-toothed liar.

Mexico, my beloved, I believe in you
for your composure in disgrace
for your solidarity in crisis
because you are mine and I am yours.

Note: "Corrido del Gato Félix" (lyrics: Enrique Franco) commemorates the assassination in
1988 of the crusading journalist and co-founder of *Zeta*, Tijuana's weekly news magazine. It was
recorded by the group "Los Tigres del Norte." "Corrido a Colosio" (lyrics: José Palma Herrera)
commemorates the 1994 assassination of Luis Donaldo Colosio Murrieta at a political rally in
Lomas Taurinas, an impoverished neighborhood adjoining the Tijuana border with the United
States. Colosio was the very popular reformist candidate of the then-ruling PRI (Partido
Revolucionario Institucional), considered an almost certain winner in the presidential election
that was about to take place. José Francisco Ruiz Massieu, Secretary-Treasurer of the PRI, was
assassinated later the same year. After Colosio's death Ernesto Zedillo, the Secretary of Education
in the sitting government, became the PRI's candidate and was president from 1994 to 2000.
Both corridos were published in *Zeta*, the first on June 9, 1989, the second on April 26, 1996.
They were included in José Manuel Valenzuela Arce, *Nuestros piensos. Culturas populares en la frontera
México-Estados Unidos* (San Ángel, D.F.: CONACULTA, 1998).

H.P.

Perdón por tener todavía mis ojos

I

He visto hoy con párpados roídos
en lo último de la ciudad, parias abandonados
–grises escupitajos–
latiendo innombrados entre faldas
arrugadas de los cerros.
Casucas de cartón rajadas a puñal de frío y agua nieve.

Niños, perros, gallinas,
revueltos entre tumor de lodos,
geranios tiesos, viejas dolientes de mirar decrépito,
pájaros ojerosos picoteando el enfado,
quinqués trizados de fastidio que alumbran zahurdas
pequeñas como cáscaras.

He visto hoy desechos escarchados de lámina a millares
fijos en los tejados contra el alud de viento
por piedras de promesas que pronunció el político,
o estáticas, en raros equilibrios
por hierros oxidados de desprecio.

Saqué fotos de tugurios de semi-vivir
en carros fantasmales pudriéndose de viejos
–sin motor y sin ruedas–
habitados por seres extravagantes de niebla y soledad
caídos en estadísticas;
cubierta la ausencia de cristales por tablas
tiradas al muladar o por cartón de empaque diciendo:
"Made in France", "Made in USA",
"Made in Japan", "Made in Hong Kong";
o anuncios impresos en el inglés de "England"
o en español de Barcelona.

Cuevas al viento sin amor de los otros
–ancladas en cielo que reflejan los charcos–
oliendo a sudor agrio
–textura de muñequitas rotas–;
desechos de muebles hurtados al "dompe" municipal
con música de silencio
en microbios del tercer mundo.

He oído la noche caer al son de mentadas de madre

Forgive Me for Not Being Blind

I
Today through reluctant eyes I saw
on the city's outskirts abandoned outcasts
–wads of gray phlegm–
the unnamed howling
in the crumpled folds of the hills.
Cardboard shacks with holes punched by fists of cold and sleet.

Children, dogs, hens,
mixed with a tumor of mud,
stiff geraniums, sick decrepit old women,
bleary-eyed birds pecking out their anger,
lanterns torn by boredom lighting pigsties
no bigger than a crust of bread.

Today I saw dumps crusted with thousands of sheets of tin roofing
weighted down against the avalanche of wind
by the stone promises of politicians
or steadied in odd equilibrium
by chains rusted with contempt.

I took pictures of hovels of the half-alive
in ghostly cars rotting with age
–wheelless, motorless–
homes to extravagant beings of fog and solitude
become statistics:
absent panes of glass replaced with boards
pulled out of dumps or cardboard crates declaring
"Made in France," "Made in USA,"
"Made in Japan," "Made in Hong Kong"
or covered with ads in British English
or the Spanish of Barcelona.

Cellar-holes open to the loveless wind
–anchored in a sky reflected in puddles–
the fetid stench of sweat
–texture of broken dolls–
wrecked furniture stolen from the city dump
set to the music of silence
and third world germs.

I heard night fall to the sound of cursing the name of the mother

–negra madre noche–
como la tierra entre las uñas de los pobres;
como fondo de pozo sin pozo
empolvando la negra negritud en el disperso caserío.

II
Estos hermanos de hambre coagulada, mis únicos hermanos,
viven como los cactos, del rocío,
mueven las herramientas de sus brazos
en quehaceres odiosos para el burgués;
los hay pedigüeños a las puertas de los templos
–borrachos con ojos de escapulario–;
sirvientes de rubios extranjeros
sin título en escuelas de servilismo;
vendedores de tacos de tifoidea o caldo de cahuamas
para revivir muertos;
chiquillos vagos pululando pandillas que talonean la droga
para sacar al padre preso;

cargadores de agua de la llave;
obreros de huesos machacados por la demencia;
rameras viejas, desahuciadas, sin vocación y sin zapatos;
viudas de soltería tenaz
–marimba de hijos,
cachorros de lobo-técnicos-del-sexo
que cobran en dólar su erotismo–;
expertos del dos de bastos
fichados con el nombre supuesto;
muchachas aletargadas que anónimas se entregan
por un carrujo de mariguana
o pingas
en el retrete obscuro de las gasolineras;
exemigrados que expulsó el Tío Sam Imperial
por enfermos mentales o agotados;
evangélicos de ojos de error que van golpeando puertas
a estruendos del "armagedón";
proclamadores de cambios de estructuras
con fósforo en los párpados
–materialismo histórico con pelambrera de años;
marxistas en la barba –odios mesiánicos–
lapidando relámpagos contra la clase ociosa;
cristianos socialistas de caridad violenta;
vendedores de biblias elegantes, a plazos,
que firman con huella digital;
chiquillos raquíticos

–black mother night–
like dirt under the fingernails of the poor,
like the bottom of a pit where there is no pit
powdering the black blackness of this scattered village.

II
These brothers curdled with hunger, my only brothers,
living on dew, like cactus,
wield the tools of their arms
in tasks abhorrent to the middle class;
nuisances at church doors
–sharp-eyed drunks–
servants of blond foreigners
unlicensed by schools of servility;
sellers of typhoid tacos or turtle-shell soup
to revive the dead;
swarming gangs of idle kids pushing drugs
to spring their fathers from jail;

bearers of water from the only spigot,
laborers whose bones are crushed by madness;
old hopeless whores with no work and no shoes
widows of tenacious spinsterhood
–a marimba of children,
sex-tech wolf cubs
who sell their eroticism for dollars;
experts in sleight of hand
known only by aliases
numbed girls who surrender themselves anonymously
for a joint of marijuana
or cocks
in the dark bathrooms of gas-stations;
ex-emigrants expelled by Imperial Uncle Sam
for being worn-out or crazy;
shifty-eyed evangelists who knock on doors
and thump out armageddon;
proclaimers of structural change
with glittering eyes
–historical materialism gone bald with age;
bearded Marxists
throwing thunderbolts of messianic hatred at the leisure class;
Christian socialists filled with violent lovingkindness;
sellers of elegant bibles on the installment plan
who sign their names with thumbprints;
kids with rickets

que vocean con arrullo el periódico
en el primer cuadro de la ciudad.

Ancianos que anduvieron con Villa
acribillando en la matanza,
escribiendo con Carranza la Constitución de papel,
héroes de la Revolución blancos de canas,
sin encías y sin habla, semi-paralizados,
evocando exterminio de los ricos.

III
No hay en el desvarío
progresismo fronterizo frívolo
ni alucinante pragmatismo que conquistó la luna.

No llega aquí la tecnología de exacta computadora,
no se habla de cueros de rana en inglés
ni de maquila turística
ni deshauciado ejido de ensueños.

Esta Tijuana sórdida de sombra y de locura
boquea invernal vestida de mendiga,
desamparada en los suburbios con tatuaje ignorado
brillando de ultraje y orfandad.

Ésta es mi verdadera casa depauperada
y estos moquientos ulcerados son mis hermanos
que mueren de cangrena
bajo la bóveda turística de luces.

Corre en este abandono sangre del tercer mundo
por cauces masacrados de odio entre las venas.
Urbe mínima que aplastó la codicia.

Perdón por mi oficio
de entretejer tortura en las palabras.
Perdón por tener todavía mis ojos,
la plenitud se pudre en mi garganta.

Mis pequeños hermanos,
pido perdón-amor por no saber hacer nada.

hawking papers at the tops of their lungs
on the fanciest street in town.

Old men who rode with Villa
demanding massacre
writing the paper Constitution with Carranza,
heroes of the Revolution white with age
toothless, speechless, half-paralyzed
calling for the extermination of the rich.

III
In this delirium
there's none of the border's inane cult of progress
nor the deluded pragmatism that conquered the moon.

The technology of exact computing doesn't reach here
no one speaks of c-notes in English
nor of tourist mills
nor the hopeless ejidos* of dreams.

This sordid Tijuana of shadow and madness,
the wintery gasp disguised as a beggarwoman
abandoned on the outskirts with an unknown tattoo,
resplendent with outrage and orphanhood.

This is my true impoverished home
and these my brothers and sisters,
ulcerated, snivelling, dying of gangrene
beneath the canopy of tourist lights.

In this foresakenness the blood of the third world flows
through hate-massacred courses among the veins.
Greed-crushed small-minded city.

Forgive me my craft
my weaving of torture into words.
Forgive me for not being blind,
I am filled with this, it rots in my throat.

My little brothers and sisters,
I beg your forgiveness for my helplessness.

*Ejido. Village in which land is held in common.

E.B.

Cuando muere septiembre

Las primeras luces del otoño,
padre mío
vistieron a la muerte
de púrpura estridente
en tu funeral

Todos la miramos pasar
sin darnos cuenta
(tal vez)
de su cruel impiedad,
inexorable

Fue entonces cuando supe
que ahí te quedarías para siempre
cubierto de flores, raíces tierra
y serías otra vez
dueño de los minutos postreros de la tarde,
yo, dueña de la agonía infinita del vivir

Ni tú ni yo sabremos ya
quién te llenó de flores, padre mío...
pues tus mañanas estarán cerradas,
como todo lo muerto, lo doliente...

Ni siquiera jugar podremos
a aquellos acertijos:
que el martes sigue al lunes
por ejemplo
o, a encontrar el fin del mundo
tras la próxima montaña

Ya nada alcanzo a decir
padre mío...
nada que dé sentido,
a este cúmulo de frases despojadas

Ahora otra tristeza nos acerca...
cuando desde el cuadro ahí colgado
me miras dubitativo, cierto...
o, tal vez
ahora eres quizá otro bosque

When September Dies

The first autumnal light
dressed death
in garish purple
at your funeral
father

We all saw it happen
without noticing
(perhaps)
its cruel, inexorable
impiety

That's when I realized
that you would stay there forever
covered with flowers, roots, earth
and become once again
master of the final minutes of afternoon,
and I, mistress of the infinite agony of living

Neither you nor I will know
who filled you with flowers, father...
your tomorrows will be finished now,
like everything dead or in sorrow...

We can no longer pretend
to simple certainties:
that Tuesday will follow Monday,
or that the end of the world
is behind the next mountain

I am left with nothing to say
father...
nothing that will make sense
of this accumulation of impoverished phrases

Now another sadness approaches us...
when, questioning, you watch me
from the painting on the wall...
or maybe now
you are another forest

con hojas renovadas,
en la pequeña isla de todo lo callado

Algunas veces
–padre–niño–
suelo imaginarte
como fruto centelleante
de alguna constelación secreta,
porque la muerte es eso:
universo distinto, misterio puro
donde en alguna tarde volveremos a vernos

Y, ese día,
tu camisa tendrá otro suave bordado,
(reminiscente oficio de ternura)
luciente, blanca tu camisa,
la misma que usabas
cuando me llevabas de la mano
a mirar la virgen azul del mayo cantarino
de mi infancia

Sabré entonces, padre mío
que tu modo de estar muerto
es como septiembre,
que da paso a la dulzura del otoño
cuando muere.

with renewed leaves,
on the tiny island of all that is hushed

Sometimes
—father—child—
I imagine you
like a resplendent fruit
in a secret constellation,
which is what death is:
a separate universe, the purest mystery,
where we will see each other again some evening

On that day
your shirt will bear a different soft embroidery
(memory's gentle task)
shining, your shirt white,
the shirt you wore
when you took me by the hand
to see the blue virgin of the singing May
of my childhood

I'll know then, father,
that your death
like the death of September
leads
to the sweetness of autumn.

A.P.

La ciudad que recorro *(fragmentos)*

I

Para echar los orines en tus postes
y contar tus esquinas, las paredes,
las cien cuadras de espejos flagelantes,
fuimos llegados.

Perros flacos, mestizos,
con encías y lengua schlupt schlipt
dimos fe de tu piel, zorra en neblina.

IV

Pienso a veces, ciudad, que voy buscando
sin linterna tu ruta:
soy el ave que devora los vientos del retorno
con hambre verdadera, hambre infinita.
Trato de armar tu voz, tus escondrijos,
salto puertas, sí, no: deshojo margaritas;
desmancho identidades, cataduras
que descubren tu máscara frontera;

navegante febril,
me desvelan tu esencia, tu apellido.

XVI

No es muy fácil burlar tus horas flacas
–polvo que nutre el polvo de nuestros huesos secos–,
pues estériles son, no anuncian partos bellos.
Lenta te desmadejas como siempre
en monótono *strip tease,* exangüe, circular;
tus martes descubrimos con arrugas de jueves,
los domingos enjutos anclados en la abulia
                                        de otro fin de semana
remedan del espejo la misma soledad.

Vamos siendo en tus charcos, ciudad, ballenas presas,
encalladas, posesas de un monstruo demencial.

from The City I Cross

I

It was to piss on your lampposts
to count your corners, your walls,
your hundred blocks of cruel reflections,
that we had come.

Skinny dogs, mutts,
with gums and tongue slurp-slurp
certify your skin, vixen in the fog.

IV

City, I sometimes think I'm searching through
your streets without a lantern:
I'm the bird that devours the returning winds
with infinite, insatiable hunger.
I arm your voice, your hideouts,
I trespass through doorways, or not; I strip daisies;
I clean up identities, glances
that reveal your border mask;

feverish navigator,
your name and your being keep me awake.

XVI

It's not easy to laugh at your feeble hours
–dust feeding the dust of our dry bones–
they're sterile, announce no beautiful births.
As always you slowly weaken
into a monotonous striptease, repetitious, bloodless;
your Tuesdays are covered with Thursdays' wrinkles,
lean Sundays anchored
to the listlessness
                    of another weekend
reflect an identical solitude.

We remain in your puddles, city, imprisoned whales,
beached, possessed by a crazed monster.

XXVIII

....Zorro nocturno acechando las palabras
sabiendo que sólo el tiempo nos dará el silencio

O. F. Contreras

¡Nos quedaron tan grandes las palabras, ciudad!
Si dijimos amor resultó flirt
cuando gritamos día nos bramaba la noche
clamábamos por vida y el genocida aullaba
cuando pensamos viaje los pies tejían raíces
dije: ¡Somos lo mismo!
                    y el eco sin cosquillas, reía alucinado

Nos quedaron muy grandes, ciudad,
las condenadas, las malditas palabras,
esas bestias sin amo.

Blues de la esquina

Quizás pueda usted enlistarme con los desencantados.
Entre los ilusos sin abolengo.
Esos personajes fáciles de encontrar en cualquier ciudad:
en las lavanderías por ejemplo
muy atentos a las relaciones del jabón con el agua y la ropa sucia
bebiendo ron o whisky en una cantina desaliñada
descifrando un diario ajado en un café mugriento.

Muchos de nosotros
                    usted acaso
jamás recobraremos la luna de los viejos sueños
el *happy end* de las películas americanas de mediados de siglo
la risa que no sabemos ya quién clausuró.

Entre ellos
            posiblemente
                        deberá anotarme...
para el juego inocente de las comparaciones.

Hombre en azul

a l.o.n.

Le ha dado en estos tiempos
por destapar botellas y husmear en derredor
lento distraído caviloso.

XXVIII

...Nocturnal fox spying on words
knowing that only time will bring us silence.

O. F. Contreras

We still had such big words, city!
If we said love flirt came out
when we cried day night brayed at us
we begged for life and genocide howled
when we thought to travel our feet took root
I said: "We're the same!"
                    "deluded," the sober echo laughed

They were too big for us, city,
these damned, cursed words,
these beasts without master.

H.P.

Streetcorner Blues

Perhaps you could list me among the disenchanted.
Among the deceived who lack inheritence.
People to be found in any city:
for example in laundromats
profoundly aware of the relationship of soap to water and dirty clothes
drinking rum or whisky in a scruffy dive
deciphering a faded diary in a greasy spoon.

Many
        you perhaps among us
will never recover the moon of old dreams
the happy endings of American films of the 50s
the laughter that we don't know who ended.

Among these
            possibly
                    you would have to inscribe me...
by playing the innocent game of comparisons.

Man in Blue

to l.o.n.

These days it occurs to him
to open bottles and lurk about,
slow distracted thoughtful.

51

Camina en despoblado y hurtadillas:
largas sombras dibuja
                    su cuerpo
                            en los crepúsculos.

Desolado musita salmos tan amarillos por el uso
incoherentes
                    secos
patas de araña al capricho del aire.

Pervierten sus pisadas
                    las ramas y veredas
el hostil arenal de nuestras costas frías.

Ha llegado al infierno de las noches eternas
se ha metido en la cueva de las propias heridas
se sumerge en los rumbos de donde no hay regreso
su pantano es el hambre de los ensueños idos.

Hormiga
            de tal frasco no encuentra la salida
su castigo es dormir con los ojos abiertos
quizás llegue al final con las manos vacías.

Oda al suicidio

Se fueron y ya.
Del manual de urbanidad
ni la envoltura rasguearon
y el adiós a la calle y su fauna hormigueante
pospusieron para mejor ocasión.

Con sonrisa helada se burlaban
                                seguro
de las corcholatas en el pavimiento
de las vidrieras sucias
de las colillas de cigarros
pisoteadas por los transeúntes.

¿Qué taza quedó esperándoles en un café
qué asiento en cuál cine
qué palabras a punto de salir...
besos o conciliábulos de abrazos y suspiros?

He walks stealthily in deserted places:
his body draws
                    long shadows
                                    at dusk and dawn.

Disconsolate he whispers psalms yellow with age
incoherent
                dry
spider legs at the whim of the breeze.

His steps transform
                            branches and pavements
the treacherous sands of our chilly coast.

He has arrived at the hell of eternal nights
he has entered the cave of his own wounds
he has immersed himself in paths from which there is no return
his swamp the hunger of lost dreams.

Ant
        he will find no exit from such a jar
his punishment is to sleep with open eyes
perhaps to arrive at the finish emptyhanded.

Ode to Suicide

They've gone, and that's it.
They haven't even scratched at the cover
of the manual of civility
and they've put off their farewell
to the street and its teeming fauna
to a more convenient time.

With a frozen smile they mock
the bottlecaps in the asphalt
the filthy shop windows
the cigarette butts trampled
by passers-by.

What cup awaits them at the café
what seat in what theater
what words at the point of utterance...
what kisses or trysts, embraces or sighs?

A la siguiente navegación
al otro recorrido
a la esquina de un nuevo ciclo
dirigieron los pasos
                        las frustraciones
la torrencial catástrofe de un pesimismo
difícil de tolerar y comprender.

Hacia nosotros vendrán

                        ahora
                        todos sus vientos encontrados
                        estrellas mal nacidas
                        alboradas con tormenta.

¿Quién esquivar podría
los malos augurios a ellos destinados
las oquedades que nunca pudieron llenar
los escalofríos ante el desamor
la desesperanza o la incertidumbre?

Nuestros son
                en cambio
pues hemos rechazado su modo de partir
la decisión que tomaron esos pobres
–nunca entendieron la risa de los rostros ajenos
la dicha de los humanos casi prójimos
esa alegría que se prodigan los venturosos
en días de aniversario
                        en las celebraciones permitidas–.

Se fueron y ya.
Se marcharon en sólo un parpadeo…

Los que nunca lo haremos
lamentamos su ausencia a cada paso
en cuanto abismo de silencio se presenta
en el sinfín de arrugas de la noche
en el sendero de los mismos sueños.

Arte poetica

Hecho a la voz
a la estúpida referencia de los acontecimientos interiores.

To the next crossing
the other voyage
the corner of the new cycle
they have directed their steps
                              their frustrations
the torrential catastrophe of a pessimism
difficult to tolerate or understand.

They will come to us
                    now
                    all winds against them
                    inauspicious stars
                    stormy dawns.

Who can stay clear
of the grip of misfortunes destined for them
the hollow places that can never be filled
the shudder in the face of indifference
hopelessness or uncertainty?

They are ours
              but we
have rejected their way of leaving
rejected the choice they made
–they never understood the laughter on other faces
the happiness of those almost close to them
the joy that the fortunate squander
on birthdays
              in acceptable celebration.

They have already gone.
They have left in the blink of an eye...

Those who have done what we never will
we lament their absence at every step
at the moment when the abyss of silence appears before us
in the numberless creases of the night
in the trace of the recurring dream.

The Art of Poetry

Made for the voice
by the stupid reference to internal events.

Testigo en la conversación del lápiz y el papel.

Metido en escarceos
                    esgrima
la floritura de los entreactos que permiten los días
las tristes noches cada vez más ingratas y delgadas.

Mago en el cabalgar:
                    de la estepa boreal
al centro mismo de las interpelaciones agobiantes.

Del higar al hijar.

Registrando la concupiscencia del tenedor y las botellas
las abstracciones de las locomotoras y los misiles.

En el páramo casi del ensueño y la risa.

Atento al hambre y los lucubraciones de la gula
            a la esclerosis de los besos
                        de las tibias tocándose ¡ay! a veces.

A las vueltas del año y el chabacano.
A las inhumaciones y sus ósmosis.
Al alarido huyendo de la vida.

Hecho a la voz.

Resistiendo.

Witness to the conversation between pencil and paper.

Entered prancing
                fencing
the flourishing of the intervals that the days allow
the sad nights each time bleaker and harsher.

Mounted magus
                of the boreal steppe
at the very center of overwhelming interpellations.

From figtree to family tree:

Examining the concupiscence of forks and bottles
the abstractions of locomotives and missiles.

In the near wilderness of dreaming and laughter.

Attentive to hunger and to the lucubrations of gluttony
                to the sclerosis of kisses
                                and of tibias–ah!–touching sometimes.

To the return of the season and the apricot.
To inhumations and their osmosis.
To the scream in flight from life.

Made for the voice.

Resisting.

M.W.

ESTELA ALICIA LÓPEZ LOMAS (ESALÍ)

Alicia en la cárcel de las maravillas *(fragmentos)*

a

¡ay! alicia fue la niña rara que encerraron desde antes de nacer
la que encerraron en una almendra amarga cuando nació de otra almendra amarga
   la misma que encerraron en una almendra amarga
por negada la mujer que sola se encerró por obediencia en otra almendra amarga
   por costumbre la crédula verbujer la mujerlabra

e

ella a quien dijeran no intentes regresar no es posible volver a la carne natal a la
semilla al soplo uteridor jamás nadie osa nadie vuelve a la casa que no tuvo a la
madre que no está a la tierra extraviada en el éxodo nadie vuelve sólo el aroma
dulce de la almendra vuelve sólo la almendra insiste mirar atrás

i

¿ir al hogar de nada? pero a la casa de la palabra que se teje a esa mujer que está
tejiendo su cuerpocasa su rostrocasa hecho de letras a esa mujer se le rompió el
candado del dolor la celda del encierro se rebeló a la cruz de la obediencia y alicia
aquí promete habitar el infinito de este número dúctil de amolabras

o

oh magialabra del soplo apetecido de dos soplos en uno las arenas
del mar todas sus aguas dios la medida del amor medida el canto desmedido que
reniega ser grito reniega alicia de la casa soledad de la tortuga del fardo del camello
el reloj acelerado del espejo la reina cimitarra la cárcel lacrimal aquí renuncia
alicia

u

ustorio país donde el canto curte el cántaro donde sigue cantando
la guitarra junto al cuento pesadilla de la abuela santiaga tan sintacta tan sin tacto
alfabeteando ¡infancia es destino! "y porque a mí me encerraban mis abuelos y
lo que fue bueno para mí es bueno para todas mis semillas" ¡encierren a alicia!

from Alice in Wonderjail

a

ay! alice was the strange little girl they locked away before she was born
the one they locked away in a bitter almond when she was born from another
        bitter almond in turn locked away in a bitter almond
because alone unnoticed the woman who out of obedience locked herself away
        in another bitter almond out of habit the gullible verboman the woman-
        word

e

she to whom they might have said don't try to come back it's impossible to re-
turn to the birth flesh to the seed to the uterine wind never again no one dares no
one returns to the home she didn't have to the mother who isn't there to the
earth lost in the exodus no one returns only the sweet smell of the almond returns
only the almond insists on looking back

i

to go to the hearth of nothing? but to the home of the word that is woven to this
woman who is weaving her bodyhome her facehome of letters this woman who
broke the lock of pain the cell of confinement rebelled against the cross of obe-
dience and alice here promises to live the infinite of this ductile number of
lovewords

o

oh magic word of the desired breath of the two breaths in one the sands
of the sea all its waters god the measure of love measured the measureless song
that denies being a cry denies home to alice solitude of the tortoise of the pack
of the camel the clock of the mirror sped forward the scimitar queen the lacrimose
jail relinquishes alice here

u

usurious country where song cuts the bassoon where the guitar continues singing
along with the story the nightmare of the grandmother from santiago so syntactic
so tactless alphabeting–infancy is destiny! "and why did my grandmother lock
me away and what was good for me is good for my seed"–lock alice away!

alphabetum

alphabetum de signos designios herencias diluvias sin alfa sin omega principio de la niña de nunca jamás la literata alicia en la cárcel de las maravillas del país de las letras purgatorio infierno y al fondo del túnel cuando la bruma cede y los ogros dormitan–los hados discurren–las letras despiertan:
　　　　　　　　¡ay! el cielo

a l e p h

amado aleph coito mayor volvamos a los juegos verborosos amorosos cogitando ergo aleph ergo beth ergo ghimel...de aquí a la eternidad con dios y flor y amor completos amo amor amo tus infinitas letras
para completarte estoy lun...a h h h　la eternidad del amor tuya es complétame aleph yo tau te completo a ti sol que me faltas a mí creada para ti no para luna sol-aaaaaa ni tú sol para estar sol-oooooooo

sol y luna girando los dos solunados los dos solecidos
que más que sean tres que sean cuatro las letras
　　　　　　si es amor quien concilia las lenguas
　　　　　a la hora del éxtasissssss
bajo el manzano tú aleph yo tau　ahhhhhhh
　　　　　¡amo ergo sum! hmmmmmmm

　　　　　　tú aleph yo tau

　　　　　　　a h h h h h h h

　　　　　¡amo ergo sum!

h m m m m m m m

alphabetum

alphabetum of signs designs heritages deluges without alpha without omega beginning of the girl of never again the author alice in the wonderjail of the country of letters purgatory hell and at the bottom of the tunnel when the fog yields and the ogres sleep–the fates infer–the letters awaken:

　　　　　　　oh! the sky

a l e p h

beloved aleph major coitus let's return to the verbaling loving games cogitating
　　　　　ergo aleph ergo beth ergo gimel...from here to eternity with god and
　　　　　flower and love complete I love love I love your infinite letters
to complete you I am moo o o o n　　the eternity of your love is complete me
aleph I tau complete you sun
　　　　　that I lack created for you not for the moon suuuuun nor you sun to be
in soooolitude
sun and moon turning the two sunmooned the two made solo
who the more they be three they be four letters
　　　　　if it's love that harmonizes tongues
　　　　　　at the moment of ecstacyyyyyy
beneath the apple tree you aleph I tau ahhhhhhhh
　　　　　amo ergo sum!*　hmmmmmmmm

　　　　　　　you aleph I tau

　　　　　　　　a h h h h h h h

　　　　　　　amo ergo sum!

h m m m m m m m

*amo ergo sum. I love therefore I am. A play on René Descartes, "Cogito ergo sum"–I think therefore I am.

　　　　　　　　　　　　　　　　　　　　　　H.P.

MARÍA EDMA GÓMEZ

Minutario

> ...Hice conmigo lo que no sabía hacer
> Y no hice lo que podía.
> El disfraz que me puse no era el mío...
>
> *Álvaro de Campos*

Ni leche ni miel fueron mi tierra prometida.
Crecí como la yerba en el canto del muro.
Mariposa de sol,
                 pájaro de nubes;
fui tortuga lentísima explorando el jardín.

Junio, lluvias de junio,
                   mis pies entre el barro
germinados renuevos.
Salutación de amor al sol de primavera.
Piel negra de los dátiles,
                   terciopelos de higos;
mieles en florecidos vientres.

Quise derribar barreras,
                 desabrigar secretos,
descender profundidades,
                   ascender cimas.
Sutil veneno fue corrompiendo mi alma.
Fui escarpa cruel, borde punzante.

Este es el minutario de mi vida,
piel arrancada a la existencia.
Pulpa del amor,
            cáscara,
                 huesos.

Así se cumple la diminuta permanencia
                   de seres instantáneos
que brotan en algún rincón del mundo.
¿Qué hará Dios con nosotros los que no fuimos nada?

Ni zumo ni licor abriga el deshumedecido tinte de la tarde
El púrpura, dosel de luz extremo
madura en frágiles frondas de laureles,
quejas de gorriones flotan en la inercia del ocaso.
Imprevista partícula soy de este páramo.

MARÍA EDMA GÓMEZ

Minutes

> ...I did with myself what I didn't know how to do
> And did not do what I was able to.
> The disguise I wore wasn't mine...
>
> *Álvaro de Campos*

Neither milk nor honey was my promised land.
I grew like a weed by the wall's canted ledge.
Sun's butterfly,
                    cloud bird,
I was a slow turtle exploring the garden.

June, rains of June,
                    my feet in mud
the shoots fledged.
Love's greeting to the spring sun.
Black skin of the date,
                    the velvet of figs;
honey in blossoming wombs.

I wanted to tear down barriers,
                    reveal secrets,
plumb depths,
          climb peaks.
A subtle poison corrupted my soul.
I was a cruel slope, a sharp ledge.

This is the record of my life,
skin torn from existence.
Pulp of love,
          husk,
                    bones.

Thus is fulfilled the miniature permanence
                              of momentary beings
that sprout in some corner of the world.
What will God do with those of us who have counted for nothing?

Neither juices nor spirits protect the desiccated color of afternoon.
Purple, final canopy of light
ripe in the laurel's fragile foliage,
plaints of sparrows floating on the sunset's inertia.
I am an unexpected fragment of this wilderness.

H.P.

Escena

El olor a café sube por la escalera
la mesa está dispuesta para otra tarde
la llave gotea

El olor de la abuela es de cedro
sostiene las paredes
nadie parece oír el ruido de sus pasos
la turbación de su mano
encuentra la puerta
abre la última ventana

La memoria **se** detiene en los labios

En la tibieza de la habitación
los ojos de la abuela
bulbos de tulipán
crecen bajo los párpados caídos

Se desvanece en la lengua
el pastel de ciruela
la ración de pan sin levadura

El salero cae
la abuela me ve a los ojos

Scene

The smell of coffee rises from the stairs
the table is set for another afternoon
the faucet drips

Grandmother's smell is like cedar
It holds up the walls
nobody seems to hear the sound of her steps
her trembling hand
finds the door
opens the last window

Memory hesitates on her lips

In the warmth of her room
Grandmother's eyes
tulip bulbs
grow beneath their lowered lids

The plum tart disappears on her tongue
the morsel of unleavened bread

The salt shaker falls
Grandmother looks into my eyes.

P.I.

Tijuana Border

La tarde golpea al suelo,
                 oscilan ilusiones
estoy en el bordo del río.

Un cauce de papeles estrujados
navegando a fuerzas de sudar
amaneceres que no nacen
                 Ahogados, bajo rayos lunares
por la magia de otro día
             (testigos: binoculares y
                 helicópteros suspendidos).

¡Mórbido desfile de las horas!

Esperaré la noche
y la luna muestre su propia versión
                 del próximo amanecer.

¿Qué pasó, "ése"?

Réquiem para Clark Kent

Sí, en los diarios la noticia
Adivino desbaratarse una estrella
Se tinta en el espacio una luz de sangre
La velocidad monótona del universo imaginariamente se quebranta en un
         instante.
Una nave de papel se abre del útero galáctico.

La xenofobia se oxida en la memoria y de la intolerancia capitalizamos fuego y
         muerte.
Compárteme tu sueño.
Algo debe protegernos más allá de la oscuridad
Mientras dormimos el sueño ancestral
La Tierra que absorba su vuelo:
La Esperanza.
Desde el pararrayos un búho prepara la mirada:
Parecía
alejar las pesadillas
De día,
De noche,

Tijuana Border

Afternoon beats at the ground,
                              illusions quiver
I'm at the river's edge.

A channel of crushed papers
navigating by dint of sweat
dawns never born
                    Drowned, beneath lunar lightning
by the magic of another day
                        (witnesses: binoculars and
                            hovering copters).

Morbid parade of hours!

I'll wait for night:
the moon displays its own version
                            of the coming dawn.

What's Happening, *Ése*?*

Requiem for Clark Kent

Yes, the news in the paper
I divine a star unbalanced
A bloody light colors space
The monotonous velocity of the universe bends for a moment in the
        imagination.
A paper boat is born from the galactic uterus.

Xenophobia rusts in memory and we fund fire and death with intolerance.
Share your dream with me.
Something should protect us beyond the darkness
While we sleep the ancestral sleep
Earth must absorb his flight:
The Hope.
From the lightning rod an owl prepares its gaze:
He arrives in his human disguise
to drive away the nightmares
Of day,
Of night,

En su traje de hombre.
Aparece cada semana y entonces soñamos y soñamos.
Nos envuelve, nos protege la magia de sus ojos
En las calles, entre las sombras, los rascacielos nos inventan enemigos:
Luthor (la fechoría) y aquél cuyo nombre al revés, le desaparece.

Pero no,
Él adivina el designio, cual lectura de gitana que en la mano refiere tus
          destinos.
¡Fuego tendido en la comodidad del aire!
Ave impasible de "S" privativa
A Luisa Lane y a Jaime, los consagra a la asexuada presencia.
Los mismos que anunciaron la llegada de "ese", entre telones, anuncian la
          agonía:
No la kriptonita. No;
Fueron el desgaste de los días y los actos aburridos de justicia.
El tipógrafo, (en nombre de la nueva generación que jamás te entenderá)
Pone el punto final.

He appears each week and we dream and dream.
He envelops us, the magic of his eyes protects us
In the streets, among shadows, skyscrapers inventing our enemies:
Luthor (villainy) and that other, whose name said backwards makes him
        disappear

But no,
He's figured out the plan, which gypsy reading revealed your fate in your hand.
Fire courses through the comforting air!
Impassive bird of the proprietary "S"
To Lois Lane and Jimmy he dedicates his asexual presence.
Those who had theatrically announced "the ess's"* arrival announce now his
        death throes:
Not kryptonite. No–
It was all those wasted days and tiresome acts of justice.
The typesetter (in the name of a new generation that will never understand
        you)
Sets the last period.

Ése. Slang for "dude," "man;" a pun on the letter "S" (*ese*) on Superman's shirt, it also suggests the
shape of the lightning bolt.

H.P.

La mujer de Caín

Pueblo de polvo
dijiste
soplándome en el rostro
      me esfumaste de tu vida
y yo
con el olor de tus entrañas
en mis sienes
          te llevé a enterrar
            al pueblo del olvido
en el cementerio
de las cruces rotas
          que mal sueño
              por las noches
                  pueblo en ruinas
te fuiste
siete soles a lo lejos
          siete veces comí de tu mano
          raíces profundas
              y amargas
setenta veces siete
maldita estoy
sobre la tierra
        al malograr tu descendencia

Luzbel

> Bástate mi gracia, porque mi poder se perfecciona en la debilidad.
> *2 Cor. 12/9*

Lo siento, te digo
no puedo atar tu amor
a mi cuello
ahogarme entre tu carne
costilla prisionera

Me doy a luz
en el dolor de tu herida
génesis del orden
hombre, Dios
imagen inconclusa

Cain's Wife

A village of dust,
you said,
blowing into my face
      your life fades away from me
and I
the smell of your entrails
in my nostrils
              I bring you for burial
                  to the village of forgetfulness
to the cemetery
with its broken crosses
              what a bad dream
                      these nights
                            a village in ruin
you left
seven suns into the distance
              seven times I ate from your hand
              deep bitter
                    roots
seventy times seven
I am cursed
upon the earth
        for spoiling your progeny.

Luzbel

> My grace is sufficient for thee: for my strength is made perfect in weakness.
> *2 Corinthians 12:9*

I'm sorry, I tell you
I can't tie your love
around my neck
stifle myself imprisoned rib
within your flesh

I bring myself forth
in the pain of your wound
genesis of the order
man / God
unfinished image

Despliego mis alas
de mujer, ave
murciélago
el fuego del aire
en mi pulmón
es el paraíso

I unfold my woman's
bird's
bat's
wings
the fiery air
in my lungs
is paradise

J.L.

Bajo la lluvia

I

Altos muros y vitrales,
con búcaros en llamas,
y adentro, con los puños
de silencios y sueños escombrados,
aparece la mitad del cuerpo.

En ese instante me refugio,
después de los senderos de pinos,
largas espinas de cristales,
con huellas y sombreros de copas,
y largas levitas de hastío,
y muestras de lluvia en los bolsillos.

Si las cortinas fueran de nubes,
no habría más que derribar las puertas de espejo
a fin de que mi rostro,
–el de todos–,
desapareciera en los nudos corredizos,
en el asfalto de los alienados.

II

Caracoles y peces se adormecen
en mis manos y en mis uñas,
en mi piel que sale con el sol,
esperando el agua;
la misma que ayer,
la de tu pelo,
caía perdida en tus labios,
en el siempre arrullo
de tejer y tejer sueños
para romper la soledad de los espejos
y la de muros reblandecidos;
con historias para abuelos,
como si cayendo el agua
rompiera diques de mentiras
y brazos en espasmo
y vasijas de libélulas.

Beneath the Rain

I
High walls stained-glass windows
flaming vases,
and inside, with fists
of silences and sanitized dreams,
half of the body.

Now I hide myself,
after paths among pines,
long spines of glass,
trails and top hats,
and long weary frock coats,
specimens of rain in their pockets.

If curtains were clouds
one would have to knock down the mirrored doors
so that my face,
–everyone's–
could disappear into slipknots
in the asphalt of the insane.

II
Snails and fish sleep
in my hands and fingernails,
in my skin that emerges with the sun,
awaiting water;
the water that yesterday
would fall from your hair
to be lost on your lips,
in the endless cooing
of dreams woven and woven again
to break the solitude of mirrors
and softened walls;
with stories for grandfathers,
as though in falling the water
could break dikes of lies
and arms in spasm
and bowls of dragonflies.

Sobresalto de los que esperan
a que escampe,
o a que la gaviota encuentre nido
en una tierra rota por melancolía.

III
Rompo relojes con el grito del recién nacido,
el osario florece en mi conciencia
y una muchacha se apresta a romper las nubes,
tomada de mis huesos,
llenos de luciérnagas.

Navegando entre polvo y sal,
en la conciencia del paraje antes oculto,
como briznas de cristal entre las hojas,
en cascadas derrumbándose sobre los párpados,
de manos quietas.

Y los peces duermen en las arenas
con sus ojos de sol y un viejo,
sentado a la vera del camino
–con capa de caracoles
escudriñando huellas de gaviotas.

IV
Compartimos el pan, sudor, sueños y piel,
en las migajas del futuro
con vasijas llenas de peces con sahumerio;
en una memoria sin pesadillas,
como caída de bruces
de los niños
en la arena.

Volver a casa

Se apilan los duraznos
las peras las manzanas
su vaho asume al hombre
un fruto cae al agua
otro le sigue
el frío agita a los transeúntes
les habla entre la radio
y lo inútil del gesto
del taxista

The fright of those who wait
for the rain to stop,
or for the seagull to find its nest
in a land broken by melancholy.

III
I break watches with a newborn's cry,
the catacomb blooms in my awareness
and a girl prepares to break the clouds,
drawn from my bones,
full of glowworms.

Navigating between dust and salt,
aware of the place once hidden,
like bits of glass among leaves,
in cascades tumbling upon eyelids,
hands at rest.

And the fish sleep in the sand
with their eyes of sun and an old man,
seated at roadside
–in a cloak of snails
examining the tracks of gulls.

IV
We share bread, sweat, dreams and skin,
in the crumbs of the future
bowls full of fish with aromatic smoke;
in a memory without nightmares,
like children
fallen flat
in the sand.

H.P.

Returning Home

Peaches
pears apples
in piles, the man overwhelmed by the smell
a fruit falls in the water
another follows
cold shakes the passersby
between the radio and the cabdriver's
useless gesture it
talks to them

Los niños en silencio desayunan
se ponen su uniforme
¿Quién sube primero?
¿Quién dice? ¡Buenos días!

Nocturno

Son pocas las gentes en el delirio de la noche
dos tres fumadores
vasos limpios sobre la mesa
la noche oculta el reconocimiento
de las hojas que disuelven
el hambre por la vida

Los frutos de la naturaleza guardan
la distancia
se mueven hacia la playa
de donde los niños son

Nuestras manos mueven
temporalmente
los retratos de familia.

El pensamiento de la zorra

Lentamente la mano acaricia
la hoja
navega el margen que le corresponde

Inútil la húmeda palabra
en un corazón cenizoso

Los ojos de la zorra
estallan la bombilla y
la tinta sale de donde las cosas son

Sumamos nuestro peso
a la sal y los cambios
ellos no preguntan sueñan
sus gargantas van al grano

Los niños esperan quietos en esta dimensión
saben que el mar se recupera siempre
y dicen:

The children breakfast in silence
they wear their uniforms
Who stands up first?
Who says: "Good Morning!"

Nocturne

There are only a few in night's delirium
two or three smokers
a table with clean glasses
night hiding from sight
the dissolving leaves
the hunger for life

The fruits of nature maintain
their distance
proceeding towards the beach
where the children come from

Our hands for the moment
stir
the family pictures.

The Vixen's Thought

Slowly the hand caresses
the page
running along the appropriate edge

The damp word useless
to a heart full of ashes

The vixen's eyes
burst the lightbulb and ink flows
from the source of things

We add our weight
to the salt and the changes
they ask no questions they dream
their throats get down to business

In this dimension children wait patiently
they know that the sea always returns
and they say

más vale un espejeante mar
que un corazón en mano.

Casa vacía

a Germán Gilbert

La zorra se acerca hacia la mesa
sus ojos fríos acerados
vuelcan el piso
mientras la abuela acaricia al niño
que jala violento del mantel

la leche derramada y sucia
contempla la agonía de la mosca

la luz del otro cuarto
se desvanece y golpea
la orilla del tenedor de plata
que timbra estalla en el otoño

las hojas vuelan en la sangre
de la zorra untándose a su sombra

los niños contemplan la noche oscura
las estrellas destacadas
sonríen se agazapan son llamados.

El hueso del mundo

1
Se esponja el trazo y
el barranco se derrama
hila el cielo el papalote

2
El niño descifra
la cifra del cielo
y caen los vuelos
de este frágil papel del mundo

that a sparkling sea is worth more
than a heart in the hand.

Empty House

The vixen approaches the table
her cold eyes
tip the floor
while the grandmother caresses the boy
who tugs violently at the tablecloth

spilled filthy milk
contemplates the fly's last agony

the light from the other room
dissipating strikes
the edge of the silver fork
that rings exploding in autumn

leaves fly in the vixen's blood
smearing themselves in her shadow

children contemplate the dark night
the insistent stars
they smile they hide they are summoned.

The Bone of the World

1
The outline billows
and the gorge overflows
the sky spins the kite

2
The boy decodes
the sky's code
and flights fall
from the fragile paper of this world

3

El niño que sueña la cifra del cielo
sujeta los hilos
breves las bocas
agua en el ojo

4

Los hombres que cruzan
son muñecos pequeños
pero los niños sujetan el cielo

5

En la ventana fijo el mundo
pero hombres y niños escapan
por un sendero infinito

6

Los rojos de las mujeres
no alcanzan el cielo
sus hilos están en la tierra
¡Qué oscura la llama!

7

Mujeres hombres y niños
levantan el vuelo
en mi ventana queda fijo
el papalote.

3

The boy who dreams the sky's code
controls the strings
the mouths
water in the eye

4

The men who pass
are tiny puppets but the boys
control the sky

5

The world stays fixed within the window
but men and boys
escape down an endless path

6

The reds of the women
don't reach the sky
their strings are in the earth
How dark the flame!

7

Women men and boys
raise the flight the kite
fixed
within my window.

M.W.

Puertas oscuras

Voy entre hojas y raíces. No veo tus huellas en el patio.
No tienes lugar en la mesa.
En las puertas oscuras de otras casas, en otras voces
te pierdo.
Hundo la mano para sacar tu rostro del estanque,
eres el silencio del agua en mis oídos.
En el ruido de los molinos, en las piedras molidas
tu voz en otra boca me ordena avanzar. Veo tu cuerpo
entre hilos de agua, miro el bosque al fondo del abismo
y me quedo como un pino, girando.
Sobresalta el corazón con pájaros
que renuevan la luz, con ramas
secas que caen.
Desde la puerta vi las nubes amarillas y pensé en ti,
en tu olvido. Eres la noche de mi memoria;
despierto en la sangre y no te reconozco en el espejo, en el
polvo vivo
que los hombres apartan de sus ojos.
Las puertas se cierran sin saber en qué momento descendiste,
en qué momento llegaste hasta aquí.

Mujeres en la puerta de la tortillería

Una mujer desnuda ha entrado en la tienda.
Mientras espero el taxi la veo salir
arrastrando un pedazo de franela roja.
Pasa indiferente junto al lote de autos, cubiertos de tierra
sus senos y su vientre que ha tenido hijos. Alguien le silba
y una muchacha sonríe nerviosa
al dar la vuelta en su carro. Sólo alcanzo a ver las caras desconsoladas
de otras mujeres en la puerta de la tortillería.

Dark Doorways

I walk among leaves and branches. I don't see your footsteps in the yard.
There is no place for you at table. I lose you
in the dark doorways of other houses,
in the sounds of other voices.
I plunge my hand beneath the water to pull your face from the pond,
you are the silence of water in my ears.
Your voice, in the noise of mills, in the milled stones,
from another's mouth commands me to come forth. I see your body
among streams of water, I see the woods at the bottom of the abyss
and I stand like a pine tree, turning.
One's heart is startled by birds
that transform the light, by the falling
of dry branches.
From the door I saw yellow clouds and thought of you,
of your loss. You are my memory's night;
I awaken, I don't recognize you in the mirror,
in the blowing dust
that men push away from their eyes.
The doors lock themselves not knowing when you descended,
when you arrived here.

M.W.

Women in the Doorway of the Tortilla Shop

A naked woman has entered the shop.
While I wait for the taxi I see her leave
dragging a piece of red flannel behind her.
Indifferent, she passes a used car lot, her breasts,
her womb that has borne children, covered with dirt.
Someone whistles at her and a girl smiles nervously,
turning around in her car. I catch a glimpse of other women's
unhappy faces, watching from the doorway of the tortilla shop.

S.B.

A la orilla de la montaña

A la orilla de la montaña
ya no recuerdas
ya no necesitas

otro trago.
Ya no tienes

que visitar a nadie
ni que construir una casa.

La luna y el aullido de los perros
deja en tu cara el frío,
el llanto que te precipita.

Voces de tierra

Gota oscura, respiro
del filo en el cuchillo.
Aleja a los caballos
olor de sangre
que las tinieblas vierten.

Arden los harapos,
se enciende la semilla.

De la arboleda el llanto
me lleva al fruto

por la calle olvidada;
entre raíces
                    pasos,
voces de tierra
en el jardín.

At the Foot of the Mountain

At the foot of the mountain
you have forgotten
you don't need

another drink.
Nor need

to visit anyone
nor build a house now.

The moon and the howling of dogs
leave on your face the chill
and tears
that rush you along.

Voices from the Earth

Dark drop, I breathe
from the knife's edge.
The horses avoid
the smell of blood
spilled by the dark.

Rags burn,
seeds ignite.

The sound of weeping from the grove
leads me to the fruit

through the forgotten street;
among roots
                steps,
voices from the earth
in the garden.

La muchacha de risa resplandeciente

La niebla cubre al sauce, entra
en tablas encaladas.
                              Un perro blanco me guía.
No quiero que me lleven sus ladridos.

Desde la ventana
                    los niños ven llegar a la ambulancia.
Se abre un círculo al dolor verdadero.

Por la calle
              viene la muchacha
                          de risa resplandeciente.

Los niños crecen,
                  cantan
abrazan a esa mujer que en la cocina
prodiga la luz de sus manos.

El policía y el último cliente esperan

Tazas prestadas a mis labios
borran las palabras; mi cara y mi mano se alejan
otra tarde en que pienso
                        recobrar lo perdido.
Desde el fondo de un vaso
                        a la luz de la barra
tiran sus dados los apostadores.
No hay lugar para mí
sólo la franja oscura de los pasos.

Las manos de una mujer se evaporan
y nadie vuelve la mirada, nadie parece oír
el mar.
Cierro la llave del agua que se derrama.
No puedo más que ansiar el cuerpo de la envidia,
vigilar el deseo de la mujer ebria, de su amante y del testigo
de los abrazos.
El policía y el último cliente esperan el silbato del tren.
Llegados del dolor los viajeros se niegan a seguir al reloj de la estación.

The Girl with the Dazzling Smile

Fog covers the willow, it enters
in whitewashed boards.
                                      A white dog leads me.
I don't want to follow the path of its barking.

From the window
                        the boys see the ambulance arrive.
A circle opens to true pain.

Through the street
                        comes the girl
                                      with the dazzling smile.

The boys grow,
                        they sing
they embrace the woman who in the kitchen
spills cascades of light from her hands.

                                                                    M.W.

The Policeman and the Last Customer Wait

Borrowed drinks at my lips
erase the words; my face and hand drift off
another afternoon in which I think
to recover my losses.
By the bar's light
                        gamblers shake the dice
in the bottom of a glass.
There's no place for me,
only the dark edge of my steps.

A woman's hands evaporate
and no one looks back, no one seems to hear
the sea.
Where the water overflows I close the tap.
All I can do is long for the body of envy,
observing the desires of a drunk woman, her lover and the witness
to their embraces.
The policeman and the last customer wait for the train's whistle.
Driven by sorrow the travelers refuse to obey the station clock.

El testigo sueña mi sombra y el canto de los gallos.
Oigo mi prisa en la arena, su alrededor cercado.
La calle sigue al taxi, la carretera al autobús.
A ciegas la doble fila, el estacionamiento que se mueve
como el descenso de las gaviotas
por la piel de un pez.

El amante

Oscuro amante frente al espejo bebe
un trago más.
         La ciudad llama al milagro
de la calle vacía.
         En los charcos cambian
sus distancias las estrellas
            y el amante
contempla la flama de su encendedor...

(La mujer que hablaba sola en el bar, quiebra
una botella a media calle).

         La fiesta
sigue en luminosas ventanas.

         Canta
la noche; su voz

         mis labios reconocen.

The witness dreams of my shadow and the rooster's song.
I hear my haste in the sand, its fenced surroundings.
The street follows the taxi, the road follows the bus.
Blindly both lanes, the parking lot, move
like the descent of gulls
onto the skin of a fish.

S.B.

The Lover

The dark lover facing the mirror drinks
another drink.
                The city calls upon the miracle
of the empty street.
                  In its puddles
stars change their distances
                      and the lover
contemplates the flame of his lighter...

(The woman who talked to herself in the bar
breaks a bottle in the middle of the street)

                          The party
continues in luminous windows.

                    The night
sings; my lips

          recognize its voice.

M.W.

Inventario del mundo

El mar se escapa hacia el desierto
y las dunas se ocultan
bajo su eterna imprecisión de brillos

Todos los signos del mundo verbales
y corpóreos
van al mar

Una tarde cobriza sobre el rostro
concede figuración de ave a las cabezas
Bajamos agitando los brazos
por la senda huidiza
con los tobillos clavados a la arena
o corriendo sin pies

Vasto mar
sepultura de todo
inventario del mundo

Las palabras son remos
que el desierto reclama

¿Dónde la señal del poder?

En el desierto de California,
cuya erosión se extiende a Santa Rosalía
a Mulegé,
fue encontrado el esqueleto desafiante
de una ballena gris,
con la mirada clavada hacia la llaga del mar
y con la sombra crecida,
carcomiendo la piedra y el salitre

De la submarina consistencia de sus huesos
nacieron el mezquite y las vetas del cobre,
la lágrima y el grito mineral
bajo los tiros

Y del ondulante lecho de arena,
bajo su peso enorme,

RAÚL ANTONIO COTA

The World's Inventory

The sea escapes toward the desert
and the dunes hide
beneath the blinding light's eternal vagueness

All the world's signs, verbal
and bodily,
flow to the sea

Late afternoon colors our faces copper
bestowing upon our heads the look of birds
Waving our arms we descend
the unsteady path
ankles nailed to the sand
or running footless

Vast ocean
sepulchre of the whole
inventory of the world

Words are oars
that the desert reclaims

Where Is the Mark of Power?

In the California desert
whose erosion extends to Santa Rosalía
to Mulegé
they found the puzzling skeleton
of a gray whale,
its gaze fixed on the wound of the sea
its shadow swollen,
gnawing away at stone and salt

From the submarine solidity of its bones
were born mesquite and veins of copper,
tears and the mineral scream
beneath the mine shafts

And from that undulating bed of sand
from beneath its enormous weight

se sugirió a los vientos y a las hojas
la locura de los montes,
los nidos más fugaces de los pájaros
y ese vacío que llevamos en el alma

El esqueleto permanece

Sólo el mar o el desierto
parecen contener un ser de huesos cristalinos
¿Dónde está la California que me prometiste?
¿Dónde la soberana de los cielos marinos?
¿Dónde la hija del aire y de los siglos?
¿Dónde aquella a quien delate su condición terrena
y en su piel encontremos la señal imprecisa del poder?

El mito posible

Creo en la California que convino soñar
al europeo del siglo XVI;
en aquella que va de las "Sergas de Esplandián"
a la imaginación colectiva: valientes guerreras
en la lucha a favor del turco
y contra el cristiano;

en la California que Baegert celebró
con su desprecio;
en la California que perdieron guaycuras,
pericúes, cochimíes con la tala del contacto;

Creo en la California de los enigmas:
las pinturas que el sol tiñó de ocre,
torsos y manitas en la huella
en su vigilancia desde los acantilados,
las montañas de sal que vencen a la luz,
la ballena y su puntual arribo
a los refugios de la playa,
el ignorante nomadismo de la arena;

en el tibio y silencioso fluir de las mareas
en el estuario del Golfo de Cortés;
en nuestros cuerpos, manos, ojos que ruedan
revueltos en el gran chorro de arena

                              que cae
                    a los abismos
                    del mar;

the madness of mountains came forth
into wind and leaves
and the most fleeting of birds' nests
and this emptiness we carry within us

The skeleton remains

Only the sea or the desert
can contain a being of crystalline bones
Where is the California you promised me?
Where is the queen of marine skies?
Where is the daughter of wind and centuries?
Where is she who denounces her earthly state
and on whose skin we find the vague mark of power?

The Possible Myth

I believe in the California that 17th century Europe
agreed to dream
which began with *The Labors of Esplandián* and became
the collective imagination: woman warriors
in the struggle
between Christian and Turk;

in the California the Jesuit Baegert* celebrated
with his contempt;
the California that the Guayacuras, Pericús
and Cochimís lost in the catastrophe of contact.

I believe in the California of the enigmas:
paintings that the sun tints ocher,
bodies and hands on the path,
in lookouts along the cliffs,
mountains of salt that defeat the light,
the whale and its punctual arrival
at the protective shores,
the sand's ignorant wanderings;

in the warm and silent flow of its tides
into the estuary of the Gulf of Cortes;
in our bodies, hands, and eyes which roll
topsy-turvy in the great river of sand

                                        which falls
                          into the sea's
                          depths;

en el atónito ajetreo de cardúmenes
y la altivez espinosa de los cactus
desde su verde amargura silenciosa;

creo en la California,
invención obstinada de jesuitas
que hicieron florecer en el desierto
los imperios de piedra de la fe;

creo en la California
donde el sordo laborío se ejercía en las misiones
y toda voz era una orden
no por la ciega obediencia al mando,
sino por el repetido reflejo de una serie de actos
dispuestos ya desde tiempo inmemorial
por algo más poderoso que la cruz o la espada;

en la California que construyó templos
y horadó con voces
misioneras o indígenas, claustros, oratorios, capillas,
pasadizos, gruesos muros agotados por
los irregulares destellos
de los cirios;
creo en la California
que ejerce su poder en los signos del terrible mar
y del desierto desnudo;

creo en la California despreciada
por solemnes que esperan explicaciones exhaustivas
de su origen y su historia;

Creo en la California de aquel indígena
que murió de asombro ante el primer tañido de campana;

Creo en el Paso de Anián
que une al Atlántico con el Pacífico
y que aún no es encontrado;

creo en la insalubridad de California
y en las islas Rica de Oro y Rica de Plata
que nunca fueron encontradas
pero que Vancouver y Cook las señalaron
en sus atlas de viajes;

in the astonished agitation of shoals of fish
the spiny haughtiness of the cacti
wrapped in their green and bitter silence;

I believe in California,
obstinate invention of Jesuits
who made empires of the stone of faith
flower in the desert

I believe in the California
where deaf labor spent itself in the missions
and any voice became a command
not out of blind obedience
but as reflex, repetition of a series of acts
waiting since the beginning of time
for something more powerful than cross or sword;

in the California that built temples
echoing
with Indian or missionary voices, cloisters, oratories, chapels,
passageways, thick walls worn down
by flickering tapers;
I believe in the California
which exercises its power by the signs
of the terrible sea and the naked desert;

I believe in the California despised
by the solemn ones awaiting exhaustive
explanations of her origin and history.

I believe in the California of the Indian
who died of fright at the first toll of a bell.

I believe in the Strait of Anián
which joins the Atlantic to the Pacific
and has yet to be discovered;

I believe in the uninhabitable California
and in the never-discovered Islands-Rich-with-Gold and
Rich-with-Silver
that Vancouver and Cook
marked on their charts;

creo en la California que los franceses saquearon
llevándose el oro escondido en la aparente
explotación del cobre
y en la no asimilada lección

de los extensos cementerios del desierto;

en la California de perplejos esqueletos
de mineros que yacen en el fondo de los tiros
entre el limo metálico del cobre;

creo en la retórica que ejerce el silencio del ranchero
californio,
en su lenguaje anafórico:
                    ironía entre pausas y repeticiones;
en la California de rancheros y pescadores
que lucharon con rifles y con piedras
e hicieron la marcha de protesta sobre el mar:
                    en filas sus canoas
                    con cantos y pancartas al aire
                    alternando con los pájaros marinos;

creo en California,
la del mito,
la única posible.

I believe in the California the French sacked
carrying off gold hidden
in make-believe copper mines,
and in the unlearned lesson

of the vast desert cemeteries;

in the California of mysterious skeletons
of miners who lie in the depths of gunshots
in the copper's metallic slime;

I believe in the silent rhetoric
of the California rancher,
in his anaphoric language–
                    irony between pauses and repetitions;
in the California of farmer and fisherman
whose weapons were rifles and stones
who made their protest at sea–
                    canoes in a row
                    songs and placards aloft
                    among sea birds;

I believe in the California
of myth–
the only one possible.

Note: The name California is first used in Garcia Ordoñez de Montalvo's 1510 romance novel *Las Sergas de Esplandián*, translated by William Thomas Little as *The Labors of the Very Brave Knight Esplandian* (Tempe: Medieval & Renaissance Texts & Studies, 1992): "Know that on the right hand of the Indies there is an island called California very close to the side of the Terrestrial Paradise; and it is peopled by black women, without any man among them, for they live in the manner of Amazons. They were of strong and hardy bodies, of ardent courage, and great force. Their island was the strongest in the world, with its steep cliffs and rock shores. Their arms were of gold, and so was the harness of the wild beasts they tamed to ride, for in the whole island there was no metal but gold."

The Jesuit Baegert. Johann Jakob Baegert (1717-1777), Jesuit missionary and founder of San Ignacio, Baja Califonia Sur. In 1773 he published *Nachrichten von die amerikanisher Halbinsel Californien (Observations of Lower California)*, which contains the best early ethnographic data we have for the indigenous peoples of Baja California. His comments were nonetheless largely disparaging.

J.L.

La última función del mago de los espejos

> No más embustes:
> Que el Poeta se quite el antifaz
> y muestre su pico afilado.
>
> *Manuel Scorza (in memoriam)*

Si usted vive en el valle de la felicidad
y hace ejercicio diariamente con su traje azul de ieicipenis
mientras su esposa se acuesta con su mejor amigo,
pásele, pásele.

si su esposo es un inútil
y usted es dama benefactora y ofrece dulces
y juguetes rotos a los niños pobres de la obrera
cada seis de enero
y se siente feliz por su acción del año,
pásele, pásele.

si usted es una señorita de nombres extraños
y paga al periódico por salir en las sociales
en busca de un junior o un apuesto ejecutivo
que la rescate del palacio de sus padres,
pásele, pásele.

si usted es un ejecutivo
un maniquí de oficina sonrisa de fluoruro
y traje impecable de la sirs
y cree que la realidad es ser patrón de una empresa
y al llegar a casa golpea a su mujer e hijos,
pásele, pásele.

si usted es una secretaria frustrada
y lee diariamente su horóscopo y las novelistas inéditas
de vanidades y cosmopolitan
o el cómo atrapar a su patrón en tres pasos
y una posición horizontal,
pásele, pásele.

si frecuenta los bares
repletos de gente sola
donde un trío canta las mismas canciones
desde hace veinticinco años
o va a las cafeterías

The Magician of Mirrors' Last Show

> No more tricks:
> Let the poet shake off his disguise
> To reveal his sharpened beak.
> *Manuel Scorza (in memoriam)*

If you live in the valley of happiness
and exercise daily in your blue jayceepenny outfit
while your wife is in bed with your best friend,
step right up.

if your husband is a good-for-nothing
and you're a philanthropist
giving candy and broken toys to poor kids in the slums
for the Day of the Three Wisemen*
and that's what keeps you happy all year
step right up.

if you're a girl with foreign names
and you pay to to be mentioned on the society page
to scare up a rich kid or a well-dressed executive
to rescue you from your parents' palace,
step right up.

if you're an executive
an office puppet with a fluoride smile
and an impeccable sears suit
and you believe that real life is being the boss
and at home you beat your wife and kids,
step right up.

if you're a frustrated secretary
and every day you read your horoscope and the latest
novelists in vanidades* and cosmopolitan,
or how to snare your boss in three easy steps
and one horizontal position,
step right up.

if you hang out
at singles bars
where a trio's been singing the same songs
for twenty-five years
or if you go to coffee shops

a platicar sobre el destino de la nación
mientras ve pasar a las jóvenes empleadas
acariciadas por pantalones de mezclilla sergio caliente,
pásele, pásele.

si usted es un hombre solo
o una mujer quedada
perdida entre la multitud silenciosa
y vive en un cuarto de hotel o un apartamento sin nada,
pásele, pásele.

si usted hace cola para comprar tortillas o leche
para entrar al cine, tomar el taxi o el camión,
y se empuja para ganar asiento
o se pelea en silencio,
pásele, pásele.

si usted lee en el periódico
que una niña fue violada por un anciano
que una anciana fue asaltada por un joven
que la guerra estalló en todas partes
que el precio del azúcar sigue subiendo
y no está conforme,
pásele, pásele.

si eres un estudiante de futuro incierto
con los libros bajo el brazo
y un cuaderno de notas innecesarias,
pásele, pásele.

si eres un profesor
que ve en cada alumna una posibilidad latente,
que impartes clases incomprensibles
para cubrir cincuenta minutos
y cobrar un sueldo insuficiente,
pásele, pásele.

si eres un escritorcillo
que sueña que sus obras serán publicadas
en letras de oro,
pásele, pásele.

si usted es un policía nocturno
resentido violador de cholitas,
pásele, pásele.

to talk about the future of the nation
while leering at working girls
embraced by their cheap tweed pants,
step right up.

if you're a single man
or an abandoned woman
lost in the silent crowd
and you live in a hotel room or an empty apartment
step right up.

if you stand on line to buy tortillas or milk,
to get into the movies, to take a taxi or bus
and push your way to a seat
or fight your way through in silence,
step right up.

if you read in the paper
that a little girl's been raped by an old man
or an old woman by a young man
or that war has broken out everywhere
and the price of sugar's still going up
and you don't agree,
step right up.

if you're a student with an uncertain future
books under your arm
and a notebook full of unnecessary notes
step right up.

if you're a teacher
who sees every girl in class as a latent possibility
and you teach incomprehensible classes
to fill the fifty minutes
for lousy pay,
step right up.

if you're a budding writer
dreaming of your work being published
in letters of gold,
step right up.

if you're a night-beat cop
raping the girls who hang out in the street
step right up.

si eres un cholo
y la policía te persigue
por el sólo hecho de ser cholo
y apareces diariamente en la nota roja
y tus pantalones tu paliacate y tu virgencita tatuada,
se desvanecen rápidamente,
pásele, pásele.

si usted es un albañil
que desayuna gansitos con soda
y espera con ansiedad el día de pago
para comprar su alarma y su kalimán
y tomarse unas tequilas en la zona norte,
pásele, pásele.

si usted es una prostituta de la zona norte
donde las fuerzas vivas no se alcoholizan
y desde los quince años ha envejecido
y bebe con obreros y gringos
y homosexuales vestidos de mujer,
pásele, pásele.

si usted es un vende-ramos-de-rosas
limpia-ventanillas periodiquero
traga-fuego
pordiosero que pide por dios
afuera de los bancos los bancos los bancos,
pásele, pásele.

si usted es un sureño en busca de trabajo
y camina cabizbajo por calles de anuncios y ofertas
con un morral de colores chillantes y bolsillos rotos
perseguido por ser ilegal,
encarcelado por ser ilegal,
condenado por ser ilegal,
pásele, pásele.

si usted es un pepenador
que arrastra su mugre por las calles de la ciudad
o un borrachito o un loco urbano,
pásele, pásele.

si usted lee lo que está aquí escrito
y se pregunta a dónde voy,

if you're a cholo*
and the cops are after you
because you're a cholo
and you show up daily in the local news
and your pants, your bandanna and your tattoo of the virgin
are wearing out,
step right up.

if you're a bricklayer
and you breakfast on candy and soda
waiting anxiously for payday
to buy a tabloid and a hero comic
and a few tequilas in the *zona norte*,*
step right up.

if you're a prostitute from the zona norte
where the high and mighty never get drunk
and you've been getting old since you turned fifteen
drinking with workmen and gringos
and homosexuals in drag,
step right up.

if you're selling flowers on the street
cleaning windshields or hawking papers
a fire-eater
a beggar who begs in god's name
outside the banks the banks the banks
step right up.

if you've come from the South looking for work
and you walk with lowered gaze through streets full of ads
with your backpack of screaming colors and your broken pockets
pursued as an illegal
jailed as an illegal
condemned as an illegal,
step right up.

if you're a trash-heap scavenger
dragging your garbage through the city
or a pitiful drunk or a street crazy
step right up.

if you read what's written here
and ask yourself where I'm going with this,

qué trato de hacer o decir,
pásele, pásele,
dentro de unos instantes comenzará
la última función del mago de los espejos.

what I'm trying to do, what I'm trying to say,
step right up.
it's a few minutes to the start
of the magician of mirrors' last show.

*Day of the Three Wisemen. January 6th, on which children are traditionally given presents.

*vanidades. A Mexican woman's magazine.

*cholo. A street tough, a delinquent; also, any young man dressed in the style of a cholo.

*zona norte. Tijuana's red light district.

J.L.

Dream song

Costillas de arena blanca,
huellas de la estación erguida
sobre el cuerpo femenino del desierto,
caricias del viento seco
deshaciendo senos, muslos,
mentones recios, cabelleras de aluvión.

> Junto a la carretera y el rumor de los camiones
> un jacalón con piso de tierra,
> mesas de metal, sopa de fideos y cerveza.

Velámenes del polvo,
foques gualdrapeando en los estrechos del viento,
lago de viento, vientre seco.
Cuánta espera, mujer de arena, ¡cuánta espera!
Hay un tambor que suena por dentro,
Pájaro-Trueno del paciente deseo.

> Junto a la carretera, la oscuridad de la fonda
> sólo intensifica el paisaje marino, deslumbrante,
> más allá de las ventanas rotas.

Ahí donde brota la hierba:
una lengua de verdosos rumores
se aclara,
como el agua en tus entrañas
la savia sube por la fronda de mis venas.
Pájaro-Trueno en el corazón de una nube lejana.

> Lejos de la carretera, los chorros cristalinos,
> los hilos, urdimbre de mar en los vientos mentales.
> Canciones que mojan la piedra en el abrazo.

Una gota basta
y vuelta brasa la piel crepita.
Una gota
y con la fuerza de una tromba
te viertes cantando:
miles de ranas despiertan a la vida.

Dream Song

Ribs of white sand,
tailings of the upraised season
on the desert's feminine body,
the dry wind's caresses
unmaking breasts, thighs,
strong chins, tresses of sediment.

> *Next to the road the hum of trucks*
> *a dirt-floor hangar,*
> *tin tables, noodle soup, beer.*

Sails of dust,
jibs flapping in the wind's narrow passages,
a lake full of wind, dry belly.
Woman of sand, such patience, such expectancy!
A drum beats within
Thunder Bird of patient desire.

> *Next to the road, the diner's darkness*
> *intensifies the dazzling landscape of the sea*
> *beyond the broken windows.*

There where the grass breaks through:
whispered green language
becomes clear,
like the water in your deepest self,
sap rises through the foliage of my veins.
Thunder Bird in the heart of a far cloud.

> *Far from the road, crystal streams,*
> *threads, warp of the sea in the mind's winds.*
> *Songs that drench the rock in an embrace.*

A single drop
and the skin crackles like burning coal
A drop
and with the force of a waterspout
you gush forth singing:
thousands of frogs awaken to life.

Quien está soñando que sueña
huele la cercanía de un océano
próximo a despertar.

Prenda de amor

Soñé una mujer dorada
y cabellera de lumbre:
los ojos volátiles indescifrables.
Desperté en medio de la noche
con un tambor africano en el pecho.
Recordé un viejo poema:
"deja rastros en tu camino
para no perderme cuando partas",
mas la deseada prenda de amor
era innecesaria,
la tenía ahora
aquí en mi propio cuerpo:
mi verga, potente, dura,
palpitaba hacia las alturas.
Me puse las manos en la nuca
y me quedé así,
respirando una pasión sin objeto.
Aquella mujer del sueño
era como la Vía Láctea,
no había manera de agregar o quitar nada.

Tijuana moods/Ch. Mingus

Más que una ciudad
un recorrido:
discurrir en la niebla/islas prismáticas
difracción de acentos.
Un jardín con árboles de oro
y polvo de oro en los jardines:
y polvo polvo
como de cinescopio, ruido blanco.

Calles enlodadas/motivos al claroscuro,
serpientes eléctricas,
volutas de neón radiante.
Ulular que aclara la cercanía
de una embocadura tensa,

Dreaming that he dreams
the dreamer smells
the nearness of a waking ocean.

Love Token

I dreamed a golden woman
and tresses of flame:
volatile, indecipherable eyes.
I awoke in the center of the night
with an African drum in my chest.
I remembered an old poem:
"leave a scent on your trail
so as not to lose me when you go."
But the love token
was unneeded,
I kept it a part
of my own body:
my cock, hard, potent,
pulsing upward.
I laced my hands behind my neck
and stayed there,
inhaling objectless desire.
That woman in my dream
was like the Milky Way
there was nothing to add or take away.

Tijuana Moods/Ch. Mingus

Not just a city
a trajectory:
a ramble in the fog/prismatic islands
the diffraction of accents.
A garden filled with trees of gold
golden dust in the gardens
dust dust
like a T.V. screen, white noise.

Muddied streets/motifs in chiaroscuro
electric snakes
glowing undulant neon.
The howl through pursed lips
that clears the area,

contrabajos, acordeones y redovas.
Coloraturas frías
que se suben a la cabeza.
Chirriar de gaviotas y lechuzas
en la frontera del día.

Más que una ciudad,
un arrebato/asonada lúbrica
botón encarnado y desprovista
desnudez a toda prueba/y desnudez
a secas...
Harapos o camisas bien planchadas,
todos madrugan
con un clamor en el vientre:
moneda de cambio/cifra cambiante,
paridad cotidiana.

(Entre tambos, láminas y cajones,
los músicos encuentran su cobija
en la seguridad de un rincón mudable:
para desayunar en el humo jugoso
para tomar una cerveza bajo la luz del día.)

Más que una ciudad,
el rostro y la máscara que se despegan:
la fachada y el traspatio;
el cádilac y la zahurda;
las dulces intenciones de la burguesía
y el sueño ácido de los demás.

"Al margen indomable" *(fragmentos)*

1

Lo siento cerca. Islotes bajo las nubes, leopardo de cobre. Los mechones negros escurren del cielo y surcan. La piel, de cristal y hielo amarillo.

Inmóvil como una bestia al acecho, como un pozo de basalto ardiendo.

Por dentro invisibilidad, trama ciclónica; ropa, lienzos de luz, corpusculares sardinas mordidas al cable de la superficie. También el patio trasero a medianoche: las camisas volando y heladas en la cellisca, los árboles grises, rogatoria del mástil, ballestas cargadas, entenas zumbantes en la oscuridad que vacía los contornos.

basses, accordions, polkas.
Cold coloraturas
mounting to the brain.
Screech of gulls and owls
at the edge of day.

Not just a city
a rapture/a lubricious mob
bud of flesh uncared-for
nakedness tested/and nakedness
alone...
In rags or well-ironed shirts
all wake at dawn
belly clamoring:
money-changer/changing sum
the daily rate.

(Among flophouses, tin sheets or packing crates,
the musicians bed down
in the safety of whatever corner:
breakfast in greasy smoke
and a beer in daylight.)

Not just a city
a face and the mask peeling off it:
the façade and the backyard;
the cadillac and the hovel;
the sweet caprices of the bourgeoisie
the sour dream of everybody else.

E.B.

from "Towards the Untameable Shore"

1

      I feel it close. Small islands beneath the clouds, a copper leopard. Black tufts drip from the sky. Skin of glass and yellow ice.

      Motionless as a beast poised for the kill, as a pit of burning basalt.

      Inside invisibility, cyclonic weft; clothing, linen of light, corpuscular sardines bitten from the rope of the surface. Also the backyard at midnight: shirts flying, frozen in the sleet, gray trees, the mast's prayer, crossbows loaded, yardarms humming in the darkness that empties shapes.

La fosa común del conchero y sus hedores negros. Las balizas esquiladas. La espiga tuberosa y entumida del erizo. Un abrir y cerrar de ojos en la luna tangencial del faro.

En la enramada las trampas rotas y la langosta fugitiva que levanta las antorchas contra el viento (dicen que no tiene boca, ¿de dónde venían pues, tantos suspiros?).

Arrecia. Todo arrecia. Las luces se asfixian por la velocidad del viento, renacen a pelo sobre el lomo rayado de la lluvia.

El sueño es un mar negro y vapores, la salgruesa hundiéndose en la carne blanca. Un solo ramaje impersonal: Hiere y llora el viento, tensa troza las vocales, quiere llegar más lejos. Rechina, estira: nudo marino.

La noche se disuelve como la greda en los arroyos.

Es invierno: es la luna que saca chispas en la escarcha.

19

Los pequeños cuerpos de los bañistas, copos de ceniza, ventanas.

Aquel hombre corpulento con el mentón y la cabeza afeitados, el pelo del pecho entrecano, regresa a la orilla escurriendo como un oso y se recuesta, dócil, en las piernas de su madre sentada al borde del agua. Trato de pensar en esa relación. El rostro de la mujer es casi cuadrado, los pómulos anchos como la mandíbula; su boca es una ranura con las comisuras correctas y serenas, bajo los labios muy delgados crecen, como la raíz de un lirio, delicadas arrugas que rodean la barbilla y descienden por el cuello hasta las clavículas cubiertas por el tirante de la ropa interior mojada. Las cejas y el pelo blancos son la flor del lirio que oscurece la piel aceitunada. Tiene las manos metidas en la arena y los brazos delgados y nudosos como el tronco de una vid. No es muy firme de espalda y empuja los hombros hacia enfrente. Entre los párpados hinchados salen destellos grises. Trato de pensar en esa relación ahora que empiezo a ver sus ojos, pero el conjunto se deshace: el hijo se achispa, retira la cabeza del regazo, toma de las manos a su madre y levanta de un envión el cuerpo frágil. Se tambalean por la orilla, se alejan en la playa como un copo de ceniza. Ventanas.

El cuerpo de mi mujer que sale del mar, su rostro de luna llena que tantas veces he besado, lunas de México, "lugar del ombligo de la luna"; luna de trigo en Kensington Gardens; lunas españolas en el Albaicín, rojas como el agua suspirante de Granada; luna de nieve y vellón salvaje sobre San Pedro Mártir y La Rumorosa.

Se ve tan hermosa con sus lóbulos mojados como perlas nativas. Y pensar que nos encontramos en la orilla, nos abrazamos en nuestras soledades, nos perdemos tristes a lo lejos como un copo de ceniza. Ventanas, luminosas ventanas.

The common grave of the shell midden and its black stench. The shorn buoys. The sea urchin's numb, tuberous spike. Tangential moon of the lighthouse blinking.

In the bower broken traps and the fugitive lobster that raises torches against the wind (they say that it has no mouth; where could so many sighs have come from?).

It gains strength. Everything does. The lights asphyxiated by the wind's velocity reappear riding bareback on the striped back of the rain.

The dream is a black ocean and mists, the thick salt sunk to the white flesh. A single impersonal branch: the wind strikes and shrieks, tense trunk of vowels, it wants to reach still further. It screeches, stretches: a sailor's knot.

Night dissolves like clay in a stream.

Winter, and the moon discovers sparks in the the frost.

19
The little bodies of the bathers, flakes of ash, windows.

That stout man, chin and head clean-shaven, grayish chest hair, returns to shore dripping like a bear and rests, docile, against his mother's thighs at the water's edge. I try to imagine their relationship. The woman's face is almost square, her jaw and cheekbones wide, her mouth a groove with calm, correct corners. Beneath thin lips grow delicate wrinkles like lily roots encircling her chin and descending her neck to collar bones covered by damp underwear. Her white hair and eyebrows are lilies shading her olive skin. Her hands are in the sand, her slender naked arms like the trunk of a vine. Her back is not very straight, her shoulders pushed forward. Gray glints emerge from between her squinting lids. Now that I begin to see her eyes I try to imagine this relationship, but they separate: the son sways, pulls his boyish head back, takes his mother's hands, and with one pull raises her fragile body. They wobble by the water's edge, into the distance down the beach like a flake of ash. Windows.

From the ocean my wife's body, her full-moon face that I've kissed so often, moons of Mexico, "place of the moon's navel"; moon of wheat in Kensington Gardens; Spanish moons in the Albaicín,* red like the sighing waters of Granada; moon of snow and savage fleece over San Pedro Martir* and La Rumorosa.*

So lovely, her damp earlobes like native pearls. And to think that we met on the shore, embraced in our solitudes, lost ourselves sadly in distance like a flake of ash. Windows, luminous windows.

20

Marianne Moore: "…O tumultuous / ocean lashed till small things go / as they will, the mountainous / wave makes us who look, know / depth."

(la línea en llamas y telón de carne rosada reverberantes en el cuerpo sin cuerpo de una ola sombras incoloras que se desgajan desde otras vidas y la mía y el miedo el alma la trampa sueños máscaras sucesión de ropajes de agua que se hinchan como bocas de anémona se vierten como relámpagos de jibia en la férrea profundidad anudada trabazón y palanca de una lengua perdida *in illo tempore* como la línea blanca en el fondo la estela de una espadilla el flagelo volátil de la anguila en la cerviz del antílope en las remeras del cormorán y el collar del jabalí la línea la marca el ombligo el entrecejo la llama pálida que inflama incolora la coronilla la mancha de plancton sus dcdos dc tinta roja extendiéndose por la negrura elevados en las burbujas blancas del sitio donde emergen los esquifes de nuestra partida la ceniza que flota en la superficie de tensiones puras que ya son con su brillo martillado
…el fin de la pertenencia…)

Pero no basta el tumulto ni la transparencia de las viejas sombras. Sumergido en el paisaje de la mente hay un paisaje todo él hecho de dolor y desconsuelo, piedras quebradas, brechas de fuego, zanjas, huesa de ciudades perdidas, pavesas en el humo que se quedan, vibran como una mancha de sol en la retina.

20

Marianne Moore: "...O tumultuous / ocean lashed till small things go / as they will, the mountainous / wave makes us who look, know / depth."

      (the line aflame and a curtain of pink flesh reverberating in the bodiless body of a wave colorless shadows broken from other lives and my life fear the soul the trap dreams masks succession of water–clothes swelling like the mouths of anemone mouths spilling like cuttlefish lightning in the iron knotted depth link and lever of a lost tongue *in illo tempore* like the white line at the bottom wake of an insignia the volatile eel whipping the antelope's womb in the cormorant's flight feathers and the boar's collar the line the mark the navel the space between brows the pale flame that colorlessly inflames the crown of the head the plankton stain their fingers of red ink extending through the blackness elevated in the white bubbles of the place where skiffs of our departure emerge ash floating on the surface of pure tensions that now with their hammered glitter are
...the end of belonging...)

      But neither tumult nor the transparency of old shadows suffices. Submerged in the mind's landscape there is its own landscape made of pain and sorrow, broken stones, fire holes, ditches, the bones of lost cities, embers enveloped in smoke, vibrate like a stain of the sun on the retina.

San Pedro Mártir. The highest peak in Baja California.
La Rumorosa. A pass through the mountains west of Mexicali.
Albaicín. A hillside district of Granada, Spain.

H.P.

Cuaderno de San Antonio

A mis padres

Y yo entraré con pies advenedizos...

Ramón López Velarde

I
El aire.
La brevedad de los gorriones.
Esa tierra ocre y rojiza por las tardes.
Las miradas.
Los rumores,
el agua que nos falta.
La procesión de días. El otoño
que nunca más veré
caer
      de los ciruelos.

II
Casa grande,
ventanas con barrotes de hierro
que daban a la luz,
al campo abierto,
a la desnudez del palo Adán.
Casa húmeda, a ratos:
brasa,
      isla de ceniza lenta
que iba
atada en sus ladrillos
más allá del polvo.

Allí viví mi claridad,
el grito,
la fundación de espacios
bajo el sol de junio.

Van los años de paso,
dejan su geometría calcinada
por los rincones
que acumulan sombra,
pero arde la imagen,
la transparencia dura
se derrama.

The San Antonio* Notebook

for my parents

> And I will enter on newly-arrived feet...
> *Ramón López Velarde*

I
The breeze.
The brevity of sparrows.
This earth ochre and red at evening.
The glances.
The noises,
the missing water.
The procession of days. Autumn
that I will never see again
falls
        from the plum trees.

II
A big house,
iron-barred windows
that open out
to the countryside,
the naked ocotillos.
At times the house is damp:
coal,
        an island of slow ash
bound beyond the dust
to its bricks.

There I lived my clarity,
the scream,
the origin of spaces
beneath the June sun.

Years go by unheeded,
leave their stony geometry
in the corners
where shadows
accumulate,
but the image burns,
transparency endures
and overflows.

Aparecen mis nombres,
mis fantasmas
–tus fantasmas

que nada envejecieron
y ya me recuerdan–;
aprendizajes que se anclaron
en la marea blanca
del papel:

todo habla
en la noche
de la casa amarilla
que visitaba el aire:
el dibujo de olores
en la tarde,
cuando el sol de las cinco
me borraba los ojos:
caligrafía de canela
y madreselvas
en la cena puntual.

Sí.
Habrá que despertar
el agua
que por las noches
se escurría
al lado.
Habrá que despertarlo todo,
cuando la mano acerque la memoria
que me espía
en la tinta.

Mis hermanos jugaban
en el patio.
            Con ellos,
subía las escamas
del mezquite,
su plantel ondulado.
Por la maraña
ciega
de los árboles
me deslicé cantando,
vine al vacío
de los días secos.

My names appear,
my ghosts
–your ghosts

that haven't aged
that remember me now–
lessons anchored
in the white tide
of the paper:

everything speaks
in the night of
the yellow house
that the breeze once visited:
a sketch of smells
in the afternoon,
when the five o'clock sun
would rub my eyes out:
calligraphy of cinnamon
and honeysuckle
at the punctual dinner.

Yes.
One must awaken
the water
that at night
drips off
to the side.
One must awaken everything,
the hand bringing close the recollection
that spies on me
from within the ink.

My brothers would play
in the yard.
          With them
I climbed the scales
of the mesquite,
its undulant garden.
I slipped singing
through the blind
thicket
of trees
and arrived at the emptiness
of arid days.

Vine.
      Me hallé.
–¿Aquí apareces tú?

Llegas de otro lugar,
de sitios vacilantes;
parques adormecidos sin ninguna respuesta
que la presencia verde,
cautelosa,
ramas impronunciables,
desfiladeros fríos
donde las perlas casi descubrieron
la enfermedad curvada
de su sombra.

Llegas,
sí,
pero nadie te siente
pliegue,
ala,
      Alja.
Ninguno me despierta
tus dedos,
              las fichas
de mi cuerpo,
tu piel.

Y ese ruido salobre,
silencioso,
la marea que pule con su aliento
la ciudad habitual,
que moja los rincones olvidados,
que desemboca siempre en nuestro polvo
para ganar miserias
o la cáscara seca del murmullo.

Todos se han ido.

Yo me aparté del agua,
de la escritura
que por las noches
crece,
sube los peldaños,
gira en las facciones
y adivina.

I arrived.

        I found myself.

"Is this where you appear?"

You arrive from somewhere else,
from unsteady places;
sleepy plazas with no answer
but the cautious green
presence,
unpronounceable branches,
cold canyons
where pearls almost found
the bent infirmity
of their shadow.

You arrive,
yes,
but nobody feels you
fold
your wing,
        Alja.
No one awakens me
your fingers
        the tokens of
my body,
your skin.

And this silent, briny
noise,
the tide that with its breath polishes
the usual city,
that moistens forgotten corners,
that always flows into our dust
so as to earn misery
or the dry husk of a murmur.

Everyone has left.

I have withdrawn from water,
from its writing
that grows
at night,
climbs the stairs,
visits one's features
and makes a guess.

–Esos días, Alja,
por la ventana de barrotes negros
miraba el cielo claro,
la enredadera
–llamarada inocente.
Quemaban los lenguajes.
Una calandria frágil
cruzaba
el mediodía.

III
Tú quedas,
tejido a la deriva,
polvo,
ceniza
en la estación borrosa,
trazo estéril
                    quedas
pájaro de sal,
                    aquí,
donde crecimos.

Las hojas se amarillan.
¿No ves las ramas?

Esta tierra nos pudre.

IV
Desde la arena
miré las estrellas
de la madrugada.

Eran pocas,

y el viento
andaba
entre los árboles.

Una sombra de frío.
Una sombra me tocaba los labios.

El sabor de la noche
entraba por mi cuerpo.

     –In those days, Alja,
through the black bars of the window
I'd watch the clear sky,
the vines
–the innocent flame.
Languages would burn.
A delicate lark
would fly
through noontime.

III
You remain
woven aimlessly,
dust,
ashes
in this blurry season,
this sterile outline
                    you remain
bird of salt,
         here,
where we grew up.

The leaves turn yellow.
Don't you see the branches?

This land makes us rot.

IV
From the sand
I watched the stars
of dawn.

They were few,

and the wind
would walk
among the trees.

A cold shadow.
A shadow would touch my lips.

The flavor of night
would enter my body.

V

(Porque la luz sólo
ara
en esas piedras
que desata
la ceniza).

VI

Había que caminar poco en el monte para mirar las piedras, piedras rodadas, inútiles. A cada paso se asomaban en las faldas de los cerros los pedazos de piedra, piedras sueltas, puestas unas sobre otras, de tamaño mediano, grandes, sin un matorral, una hierba, algo que las acompañara. –Malpaís llamaron a esos lugares donde las piedras se encienden con el sol, se queman y duran en el color del fierro como piedras secas.

Yo anduve los arroyos para verlas. Seguí con los ojos las pequeñas piedras que las corrientes de julio y agosto habían dejado de trecho en trecho. Las piedras rajadas, rotas, repartidas en la arena.

Estas piedras atraviesan de lado a lado la tierra donde nací. Forman sus cimientos. Piedras inmensas, jaspeadas, negras, rocas azules, que dan o niegan el agua escondida debajo de ellas.

Quién sabe si todo ese sur esté cortado en la piedra, si la vida haya crecido de las piedras, en lo más agrio de la sierra. Quién sabe si un viento pesado nos dejó allí, piedras, cuando alguna escasa lluvia mojó aquel suelo apagado.

VII

Bajo este cielo
infiel
a fuerza de mirarlo,
en la hora
tensa
del calor,
la dureza
del aire
quiere ser
sólo
una paloma.

VIII

Mis mayores
han entrado a la tierra
como peces,
como salmones

V

(Because only the light
ploughs
among these rocks
that the ash releases

          from its grip).

VI

I didn't have to walk very far into the brush to find rocks, scattered, useless rocks. At each step at the foot of the hills were shards of rock, loose rocks, piled on top of each other, small ones, large ones, and not a single plant, nothing. We called these places badlands, where rocks catch fire from the sun, burn and become dry rusty stones.

I walked through the arroyos to see them. With my eyes I followed the small stones that the currents of July and August had left in the hollows. Split, broken stones, scattered in the sand.

Those stones stretched across the land where I was born. They were its foundation. Immense, mottled, black stones, blue boulders, that offer or refuse the water hidden beneath them.

Who knows, maybe the entire south is cut in stone, maybe life has sprung from these rocks, in the harshest of mountains. Maybe a heavy wind left us there, rocks, when sparse rain dampened the lifeless ground.

VII

Beneath
this
faithless sky
to see it
in the taut
hour
of heat,
the harsh
        breeze,
one could wish
to be
     a dove.

VIII

My forebears
entered the earth
like fish,
like salmon

que regresan un día
sin cuidar la piel
por vetas de apagado tepetate,
bajo los hongos simples
que amontonan el ocre,
muy abajo del cielo,
a los metales,
donde dejaron sueños
y espinazo.

IX

Decían la verdad:
en los sueños
se enreda una esperanza,
algo como la fruta
regalada
         del aire,
eso decían,
    y yo miraba
las palmeras
y la luz que tejían
y, en la noche,
vacía
la exactitud
de las estrellas.

X

Llueve
con un sonido blanco.
Una lluvia muy lenta
se desliza
por los techos de zinc,
lava los emparrados,
las acacias,
disuelve
los naranjos.

Y el agua
baila
agujas,
las oxida en el suelo,
en el bramido
ocroso
del arroyo.

unconcerned for their bodies
returning
through veins of played-out ore,
under primitive fungus
they heaped up ochre
far beneath the sky
among the metal,
and they left their dreams
and their bones.

IX
They would tell the truth:
a hope
is entwined in dreams,
a sort of fruit
that the air
                offers,
they would say that,
                and I'd watch
the palms
and the light they wove
and in the empty night
the stars'
precision.

X
It's raining
with a white sound.
A slow rain
slides down
the zinc roofs,
washes the vines,
the acacias,
dissolves
the orange trees.

And the water
is needles dancing
that rust in the soil
in the howling
ochre
of the arroyo.

–Es el verano, Alja.

Afuera hay unos niños con lluvia
moviendo cada sorpresa de la tarde.

Desde acá los veo.

Aquí no llueve.

XI
Me arranqué los ojos.
Me corté la lengua.
No hice lo que pude
con las manos.

Dormí como una piedra
la certeza de mi ausencia.

Trabajé la nada.

FINAL
Es difícil
ahora
ganar la noche,
apoderarme de la hierba
–perdí hace tiempo
las estrellas.
Regreso de lugares
empañados
por un aire lento
                de palomas
        que se desprenden
grises.

¿Entraré al patio
donde tomé la sal,
veré la luna,
jugaré con la sombra
entre mis dedos
mientras
no desmorono?

–It's summer, Alja.

Outside there are children in the rain
inciting each surprise of the afternoon.

I see them from here.

Here where it doesn't rain.

XI
I pulled out my eyes.
I cut out my tongue.
I didn't do what I could have
with my hands.

I slept like a stone
the certainty of my absence.

I worked at nothingness.

LAST
Now it's
difficult
to win the night
to control the grass
–a long time ago
I lost the stars
I return from places
wrapped
in a slow breeze
               of gray doves
falling away.

Will I enter the yard
where I tasted salt,
will I see the moon,
will I play with the shadow
between my fingers
and not
disintegrate?

*San Antonio. A small mining town in the arid mountains of Baja California Sur.

M.W.

MARCO MORALES

A padre

Los cerros que tanto quieres,
me dijo, allá te están esperando.

A. Yupanqui

I

no encontramos a padre
y le buscamos hasta el final
de las cervezas

el recorrido por la infancia es interminable
y tampoco le econtramos

los rincones de tecate no tienen
los tangos de gardel que padre tanto repite

mamá explica el problema
y dándose vueltas se quita lágrimas

y parece que padre no regresa más
¡ah qué viejo!
le salieron los sesentaitantos años
por el orgullo

nosotros
para celebrarlo,
nos echamos otro trago
y es que padre
no vino a dormir ayer

II

padre no habla
nada demuestra
pero él así es
vive un concubinato estrecho
con el silencio
se refugian en su cuarto
y se aman con locura
puede ser que alguno de nosotros
abra la puerta sin llamar
para sorprenderlos,

To Father

> The hills that you love so much,
>   he told me, await you.
>
> *A. Yupanqui*

I
we didn't find father
and we searched for him
until the last beer

the journey through childhood is unending
and we didn't find him

in tecate there are none of the tangos
of gardel that father plays endlessly

mom explains the problem
and always in motion she wipes away tears

and apparently father's not coming back
oh, that old man!
he has reached some sixty years of age
out of pure pride

To celebrate
we have another drink
and yesterday
he didn't come home
to sleep

II
father doesn't speak
he shows nothing
but that's his way
he lives in an intimate relationship
with silence
the two of them hide in his room
and make love like crazy people
if one of us without knocking
opens the door
to surprise them,

ellos impasibles
ignoran todo
nos invitan a salir
sin siquiera un pestañeo

padre es terco

III
padre no avejenta
a ratos camina como doliéndose
(de lado y no avejenta)
la frente ancha pelo negro
muestran su lozanía
sus brazos fuertes y manos callosas
contrastan con nuestro endeble cuerpo

nos derrumbamos
cuando su fortaleza se pierde
tras una máscara de rudeza
que esconde no sabemos qué

IV
recuerdo
a la edad de 6 años o menos
ver llegar a padre con amigos
en un taxi (un "de soto")
después hablarme
para medir mi pie
(con su cinta stanley)
un rato de risas e irse
a embriagar, con el quico, el chicle y los demás
seguramente yo no salía a vagar en todo el día
esperando a padre y el paquete
y él me despertaba por la mañana
para ponerme los zapatos
(inevitablemente negros y altos)
que deberían durarme el año

V
nosotros ya no somos los mismos que empezamos
aquello quedó como una forma de mirar el
entendimiento que
supuestamente conocíamos
lo obvio no era tal y desconocíamos gran parte del juego

they, impassive
ignore the intrusion
and without a moment's hesitation
ask us to leave

father is stubborn

III
father doesn't age
he walks a little as though in pain
(sideways, and he doesn't age)
wide forehead dark hair
are evidence of his vitality
his strong arms and callused hands
in contrast with our feeble bodies

we fall down
when his strength wanes
behind the crude mask
that hides whatever

IV
I remember
I must have been six at most
father arriving with friends
in a taxi (a De Soto)
to measure my foot
(with his Stanley tape measure)
a few laughs, and off again
to get drunk, with *el quico*, *el chicle*,* and the others
All day I would stay at home
waiting for father and the package
and he would wake me in the morning
to put my shoes on
(inevitably black and high-laced)
that would have to last
the whole year

V
We aren't as we began
that which remained as a way of looking the
understanding that
we were supposed to know
that the obvious wasn't what it seemed
and we didn't know a lot about the game

al final seríamos padre e hijo
que olvidamos el significado de la palabra
y sólo un gruñido bastaba para entender todo
no se eludían respuestas
a preguntas a boca de jarro
simplemente ignorar todo
y quedar relegados a lo imprevisto
a las respuestas obligadas
como el obligado reflejo del espejo

In the end we would be father and son
for whom, the meaning of words forgotten,
a grunt would be enough for understanding
no answers
no questions avoided
rather ignored
everything relegated to the unforeseen
to the obligatory answers
to the obligatory image in the mirror.

el quico, el chicle. Common nicknames.

S.B.

Baja Times

I
Fumarse un porro de "chocolate" marroquí
–obsequio de un viejo capitán recién desembarcado–
en el 110 del Hotel Plaza de la Calle Mayor
(Cuatro Crujiente, mi hogar aquí y ahora, ¡ampárame!)

Ofrenda del Magreb
Para la Antigua California
                    la del Mito
Y el narcomitote de las Playas de Coca

Oh Baja!
Magnificent Peninsula!

Gran Ballena varada a orillas de América

De Tijuana a San Lucas
              un Arco Iris
Una enervada brisa
De la *Revolución* al *Boulevard Marina*
Del *Mike's* al *Cabo Wabo*
Del *Bordo* a la *Playita del Amor*

El pueblo de cardones
con los brazos al cielo
            –Jesus Christ!–
                       reverdece
La espina muere
Cuando la flor dilata
Sus pétalos de sal
              iridiscente
Oh Baja rumorosa:
Rumor baja
        la Baja
            deleitoso:

"Los dátiles de San Ignacio
Regresaron cargados
De una suave embriaguez
               esta temporada...
Su pulpa agridulce

Baja Times

I

To smoke a stick of Moroccan "chocolate"
–gift of an old captain just washed ashore–
in room 110 of the Plaza Hotel on the Main Drag
(Creaking room, my home for the moment, god help me!)

The Maghreb's offering
To Old California
                        the California of Myth
And the narco-gossip of coke beaches

Oh Baja!
Magnificent Peninsula!

Huge Whale stranded on the American shore

From Tijuana to San Lucas
                        a Rain Bow
A limp breeze
From *Revolution* to *Marina Boulevard*
From *Mike's* to *Cabo Wabo*
From *El Bordo* to the *Playita del Amor**

Cactus town
its arms to the sky
                    –Jesus *Christ!*–
                                    it blooms
When the flower blossoms
The thorn dies
Its salt petals
                iridescent
Oh noisy Baja:
low murmur
                dclightful
                                Baja:

"The date groves of San Ignacio*
This season
Came back loaded
                        with a soft intoxication...
Their bittersweet meat

Es la carne de Dios
Es el sabor del Sueño"

Corrió el rumor
Y se dejaron ir
                    se dejaron venir
Mariposas de *Frisco*
Comediantes de *Elei*
Cholitos de *Tiyei*
Pirates de Ensenada

¡La horda fronteriza!
Límite de sí misma
Como el Agua Cero
                    que cae
Y disuelve las brechas
Las vertientes del tiempo
Los estanques posibles
                    los espejos
"Te ponen hasta atrás, hasta la madre"

¿Y?

Que doblan las campanas de Loreto
                              y el cristal
De las Torres de Aguacaliente
                              cruje y se apaga

La urbe se adentra
En otra noche
De cuchillos largos
Y cuernos de chivo

Giran
Entre el azul y el rojo
                    las sirenas
Gimen y cantan
De espaldas al Océano

La Madre Perla se abre

Salta una lágrima de plata
Sobre el fondo del Golfo
                    entre ardientes corales

Is the flesh of God
The taste of Dreams"

The rumor made the rounds
And they set out
                    they came
Gays from *Frisco*
Comedians from *L.A.*
Cholitos from *T.J.*
Pirates from Ensenada

Horde of the border!
Limited only by itself
Like the Down Pour
                    that falls
And dissolves the dirt roads
Slopes of time
Possible ponds
                mirrors
"They got you smashed, wasted"

And?

May the bells of Loreto★ ring
                            –and the light
Of the Towers of Aguacaliente★
                            wavers and goes out

The metropolis withdraws
Into one more night
Of long knives
And AK-47s

From blue to red
                the sirens turn
Wailing and singing
From stars to sea

The pearl shell opens

A silver tear
Spills onto the floor of the gulf
                            among flaming coral.

Allá abajo
Las proas del naufragio
La sombra de una cabellera
Enredada en el Puente de Mando

Los ojos del vigía
A la deriva

Allá arriba
Los fantasmas del Yonke
alebrestados:
De las ruinas del *Cadillac*
Saltan a la defensa del *Pick Up*
O a la portezuela del *Toyota*

Danzan entre los fierros retorcidos

                    y los espejos rotos

En la radio la música se apaga
y se enciende la voz del locutor
con la noticia de Último Minuto:

En el hipódromo
Galgos y caballos
Han sido dopados
La pista es de cristal

                resbaladiza y transparente

Devoradora

En los *books* se han cerrado las apuestas:
Ni *Trifecta,* ni *Exacta,* ni *Cinco y Diez*

                          Baja Uno

                                Baja Cien

                                        Baja Mil

Bajamania
I'd rather be in Baja!
Baja Taco
Baja Fish
Baja Curios
Baja Dream
Baja Beach
Baja Flash
Baja Bug
Baja Telos...

Down below
The prows of shipwrecks
The shadow of tresses
Entangled in the bridge

The watchman's eyes
Wandering

Ashore
Manic phantoms
Of the junkyard:
From the ruins of Cadillacs
They leap to the bumpers of pick-ups
Or the doors of Toyotas

Dancing among twisted chassies
                        and broken mirrors

On the radio the announcer's voice
interrupts the music
for breaking news:

At the race track
Greyhounds and horses
Have been doped
The track is glass
                    slippery and transparent
Devourer

The betting windows have closed:
Neither *Trifecta* nor *Exacta,* nor *Five and Ten*
                        Baja One
                                    Baja Hundred
                                            Baja Thousand

Bajamania
I'd rather be in Baja!
Baja Taco
Baja Fish
Baja Curios
Baja Dream
Baja Beach
Baja Flash
Baja Bug
Baja Telos...

Salta, oh marlyn, de pico coralino
Sobre los *Baja Rainbows*

Sobre la cabellera del *Viet-Vet*
Que ante una postal de Sausalito

                    sonríe:

El *Golden Gate* cubierto por los humos
De la yerba quemada en el altar

                del *Filmore West*
La noche de antenoche

La noche de *The Cream*
La noche de la *Janis* y *Big Brother*
La noche de *Santana* y *Grateful Dead*

Y luego la larga marcha al sur

Seis de la madrugada
Kerry, el guía, prepara la excursión

                    a la Cueva Pintada
En los cristales de su vieja Carroza
(una Van 70)
Se diluye la escarcha

Cargada su mochila de campaña
De dátiles maduros
Para la resolana y la subida
Pasa lista:

La pareja de Seattle (Second Marriage)
Los cibernautas de Berlín
Las ancianas de Eureka
Las chicas de Quebec
Las mexiquillos cantarines

Let's get it on, oh Kerry!

(*He left his heart in San Francisco*
Y enterrará su culito rosado en Mulegé)

Es hora de partir, oh desvelados!
Que allá arriba, en la sierra
Los monos de la *Cueva de los Monos*

                    también se desperezan

Oh coral-mouthed marlin, leap
Over the Baja Rainbows

Over the long hair of the Viet-Vet
Who smiles at a postcard
                              from Sausalito:

The Golden Gate cloaked in the smoke
Of weed burned on the altar
                              of the Filmore West
The night before last

The night of Cream
The night of Janis and Big Brother
The night of Santana and The Grateful Dead

And then the long march south

Six in the morning
Kerry, the guide, prepares for the trip
                              to Cueva Pintada*

The hoarfrost melts
Off the windows of his old heap
(a van from the 70s)

His backpack loaded
With ripe dates
For the sun's glare and the climb
He calls the roll:

The couple from Seattle (Second Marriage)
The cybernauts from Berlin
The old ladies from Eureka
The girls from Quebec
The melodious Mexiquillos*

Oh Kerry, let's get it on!

(*He left his heart in San Francisco*
And he'll bury his pink ass in Mulegé*)

It's time to go, oh sleepless ones!
Up there, in the mountains
The monkeys at Cueva de los Monos*
                              are also stretching

145

Y es hora de volver

Volver al puerto
Que te llenó de luz
Y cultivó tu lengua

Volver:

De Fez para la Bella Cenicienta
Previa gira europea

¡Oh, Iberia, la Infiel!
La de la Eterna Reconquista
Cultivadora del instante
Y sus mercados con los nervios de punta

De Algeciras a Atocha
De Atocha a Sants
De Sants al Casco Viejo
Un fragmento de eternidad:
                              Allahu Akbar!

Incienso que recorre las cúpulas
                              de la Ciudad Condal

Y su vigilia al rojo vivo:
Resplandor del Rioja
En labios de una barcelonina
De ojos profundamente negros
Y cuello blanco de cine modernista

Esencias memoriosas que emergen del Mons Taber
Penetran el laberinto del Barrio Gótico
Se arremolinan en los portales de Plaza Real
                              con cenicientas alas de paloma
Y se posan sobre los hombros
Del Colón de bronce salitroso
Que vela sus memorias
Frente al abismo del Mediterráneo
En los linderos de la Zona Franca
                              y el Barrio Chino

"Toda la noche oímos cantar pájaros"

Deletrea la hija de San Jordi

And it's time to return

To return to the port
That filled you with light
And taught your tongue

To return:

From Fez* for that earlier
Beautiful Cinderella Tour
of Europe

Oh faithless Iberia
Of the Eternal Reconquest
Cultivator of the instant
And its nervous markets!

From Algeciras to Atocha
From Atocha to Sants
From Sants to Casco Viejo*
A piece of eternity:
                              Allahu Akbar

Incense encircling the domes
                              of the Ducal City:*
And the red hot sleepless night
The sheen of Rioja
On the lips of a girl from Barcelona
With the deep black eyes
And pale neck of an actress in a surrealist film

Fragrances fondly remembered emerge out of Mons Taber
Penetrate the labyrinth of the Gothic Quarter
Twist around the doorways of the Plaza Real
                              with the ashen wings of doves
And alight on the shoulders
Of the salt-stained bronze of Columbus
Shrouding his memories
His face to the Mediterranean's depths
At the edge of the Zona Franca
                              and the Barrio Chino

"All night we hear birds singing"

San Jordi's daughter lisps

Con la sangre del Rioja entre los labios

What's up
Mister Melancolía?

¡A sacudir la jerga!

El camino a casa
                    es un beso
                                con sabor a damiana
La yerba de la vida
La yerba del amor
La ycrba dc la sangrc calicntc
                        amotinada

Eco dc caracol
Oh Baja!
The Magnificent Tale!

Give me my turtle eggs
La Caguama bien fría
El Trópico de Cáncer
Los dátiles del sueño
The San Pedrito's waves
Las uvas de Santo Tomás
En el umbral de la noche fronteriza

Oh Baja!
Baja Blues
Baja Rainbow
Baja Sun
Baja Times

¡Baja Té!

II
Después de un desayuno de huevos con machaca
Tortillas de harina y café negro
Sales a dar un rol por las calles del puerto
Henchidas de luz mediterránea
Y perfumada brisa del Pacífico

Escala en la Ramírez
Para comprar el periódico de ayer
(El de hoy nunca llega)

On her lips the blood of Rioja

What's up
Mister Melancholy?

Get a move on!

The road home
                  is a kiss
                                    tasting of damiana*
Herb of life
Herb of love
Herb of hot blood
                        pulsating

The echo in the snailshell
Oh Baja!
The Magnificent Tale!

Give me my turtle eggs
A tall cold beer
The Tropic of Cancer
Dates of dreams
San Pedrito's waves*
The grapes of Santo Tomás*
On the threshold of the border night

Oh Baja!
Baja Blues
Baja Rainbow
Baja Sun
Baja Times

Baja Tea!

II
After a breakfast of machaca and eggs
Flour tortillas and black coffee
You sally forth for a stroll through the streets of the port
Brimming with Mediterranean light
And the fragrant Pacific breeze

You climb Ramirez Street
For yesterday's paper
(Today's never comes)

Febrero del 94:

Marcos en todas las portadas:
"Soy un mito genial"

Grita el subcomandante desde algún lugar
                                    de la selva Lacandona
Y México se cimbra de Ocosingo a Ensenada

Boom de la literatura de emergencia:
¡Qué intenso fulgor trágico el de esta novísima
                                    novedad de la patria!

¿Héroes a la altura del arte de la palabra flecha
de la palabra flor, de la palabra olvido
de la palabra fuego, de la palabra muerte?

¿Quién perdona a quién?

El evangelio según San Marcos
El profeta, el poeta rebelde que a los cuarenta años
–*Zarathustra revisited*–
bajó de la montaña hacia la catedral de San Cristóbal
a negociar la paz y la guerra, la vida y la muerte
con su pasamontañas negro y su mirada clara

Y en pleno protocolo saludó al mundo
envuelto en la bandera nacional:
El águila devoraba a la serpiente
mientras que Super C alcanzaba un pedazo de verde
en el último instante
"Para nosotros nada; para todos todo"

III
Chiapas, tan lejos y tan cerca

En cada mexicano más o menos jodido
                                    se esconde un *zapaneco*
En cada india mixteca que desde San Quintín
                              Valle de Oaxacalifornia

llega con sus críos panzones y chorreados
a vender "chingaderita y media" en la Calle Primera

Pero ahora volvamos al trajín
                        de la verbena fronteriza

February '94:

Marcos* on the covers of all the magazines:
"I am an inspired myth!"

Cries the subcomandante from some spot
                                        in the Lacandón jungle*
And from Ocosingo to Ensenada* Mexico trembles

And suddenly it's the golden age of the literature of urgency:
The intense tragic glow of this latest
                                        national news!

Heroes as great as the art of the word arrow
the word flower, the word oblivion
the word fire, the word death?

Who forgives and who is forgiven?

The gospel according to Saint Mark
The prophet, the rebel poet who at 40
–Zarathustra revisited–
descended the mountain to the cathedral of San Cristóbal*
to negotiate peace and war, life and death–
his black ski mask, his clear gaze

And wrapped in the nation's flag he addressed the world
with perfect protocol:
(The eagle devouring the snake
while Super C* grabbed a piece of green
at the last minute)
"Nothing for ourselves; for everyone everything"

III
Chiapas, so far but yet so near

A zapaneco* hides in every half-fucked Mexican

In every Mixtec woman who from San Quintín
                                        Valley of Oaxacalifornia*

arrives with her swollen-bellied snot-nosed kids
to sell "any godforsaken crap" on First Street*

But now we return to the bustle
                                        of the border fair

donde todos jugamos a ganar un buen día
una batalla más en la guerra de los cinco sentidos

–¿Cuál de ellos domina cuando se hace el amor?
–Ninguno, todos ganan

Qué lejos y qué cerca está Chiapas, don Benito
Y demás héroes del hemiciclo del bulevar costero

Ruge una escuadra de motociclistas
                          vestidos de *Hells Angels*
De muy cosmopolitas los muy putos
Los batos con sus trajes de piel negra
                          y sus morras en ancas
Largas y rubias cabelleras en busca de un poco
                          de sur crepuscular

Generación sin flores, duros, *heavy metals*
tránsfugas del futuro
Pasan frente al Riviera que se les queda viendo
con su mirada en blanco y ocre de joya colonial
                          californiana
¡Pinchis gringos mamones!

Mira que no pararse a contemplar nuestra reliquia
ex santuario del juego y capilla del drama cultural
                          de este puerto feliz

Time for a break
Volver al mar
Volver amar

Hora de refinarse una cerveza en un acto ritual
                          frente a la rada
en íntimo homenaje al océano y su embriaguez de leviatán
                          que canta y danza

–Hola compita, cómo te pareces a un hermano mío
el de la voz de trueno, trovador de estos rumbos
Invítame las ostras, hazle una seña al trío
cántame *Un mundo raro* si quieres que me quede
                          a seguirte la huella
Comprar un *six* de botes colorados y enfilar
                          rumbo a La Bufadora
como la tarde que enterramos a la nana Juanita

where we all play to win one more day
one more battle in the war of the five senses

"During lovemaking which one wins?"
"None–everyone"

How far but yet how near Chiapas is, Don Benito
And the other heroes of the half circle of the coastal boulevard*

A squad of motorcyclists roars by
                              dressed as Hells Angels
Very sophisticated, very chichi
The dudes in black leathers
                         their bitches
big-assed blonds come
                    for a bit of the dusky south

Generation without flowers, hard-hearted, heavy metal
deserters from the future
They drive past the Riviera* that looks at them
with the white and ochre gaze of a gem of California
                                        Colonial
Stupid fucking gringos!

They don't even stop to check out our sacred relic
once the sanctuary of gamblers, now chapel to the cultural drama
                                            of this happy port

Time for a break
To return to the sea
To return to loving

Time to partake of a ritual beer
                         by the bay
in intimate homage to the ocean and its whale-sized singing dancing
                                            intoxication

"Hey, man, you look like my brother
our troubadour, the one with the voice of thunder"
Invite me for oysters, tell the trio
to sing "A Special World"* if you want me to stay
                                    to follow you
To buy a six pack of dark bottles and stagger
                              towards La Bufadora*
like the afternoon we buried Granny Juanita

Nana Juanita duerme bajo la tierra colorada
Nana Juanita debe tener frío
Nana Juanita, suéñame mientras te canto una canción

                                    al filo de tu lápida

"Di que vienes de allá, de un mundo raro..."

Háblame del abuelo y sus manos de pianista
de su inconmensurable sed de ave nocturna
de su temple de yaqui en el exilio
de sus habilidades de plomero

Cuéntanos de aquel tiempo de Los Angeles
y de la muerte de tu único amor a la edad de Cristo
su tocayo Jesús: recuérdanos desde tu muerte

                                    profundamente muerta

Enséñanos de nuevo a no llorar cuando parten los barcos
y se pierden tras la ceniza de la tarde
con la tripulación diciendo adiós desde cubierta

Nana Juanita, concubina de Dios (te plagian, Jaime)

                                    ruega por nosotros
que ya mi hermano menor y yo vamos rumbo a La Bufadora

                                    a ofrecerte una lágrima

IV
Esta mañana de febrero, en el Mercado Negro
el mar vuelve a ser esa metáfora olfativa
que cala hasta la médula del ser peninsular

Bendito seas aroma de pescado
de vísceras crujientes,
almeja viva como el culito retozón
de las niñas del puerto

–Deme otro, doñita, de patemula, con un mucho de todo
para sentir el cuerpo en tierra firme y cargar la batería
porque esta noche el señor dice que irá a cumplir

                                    con sus deberes de hombre

(Alguna meserita de uno de esos bares del Bajío
con la que soñó anoche)

–¡Qué no dice el señor!, tan mentiroso, tan borracho

Granny Juanita sleeps beneath the red earth
Granny Juanita must be cold
Granny Juanita, dream of me while I sing a song
                                        beside your headstone

"Say that you come from afar, from a special world..."

Tell me of Grandfather and his pianist's hands
his insatiable night owl's thirst
his exiled Yaqui temper
his skills as a plumber

Tell us about that time in Los Angeles
and the death of your only love at the age of his namesake Jesus:
Granny Juanita, profoundly dead, remember us
                                        from your death

Teach us again not to weep when the boats sail off
and are lost behind the ashes of afternoon
the crew calling out farewell from the deck

Granny Juanita, concubine of God (they plagiarized you, Jaime*)
                                                    pray for us
now, as me and my baby brother head for La Bufadora
                                        to shed a tear for you

IV
This February morning, at the Mercado Negro*
the sea once more becomes the olfactory metaphor
that soaks into the peninsular resident's very bones

Blessed be the smell of fish
of rumbling guts
the live clam quivering like the little asses
of the girls of the port

"Miss, give me another big black clam, with lots of everything
to let me know that my body's on terra firma, to let me charge my batteries"
because tonight the gentleman says he'll be going out to fulfill
                                        his manly duties

(Some little waitress he's dreamed of at night
from one of those bars of the Bajío)

"What won't the gentleman say! such a liar, such a drunk

155

tan agridulce, tan mariguano, tan no sé cómo
Dice que hubo una noche en Las Playitas
(¿O fue en Playa Hermosa?)
alrededor del genio embotellado de don Santo Tomás
el fuego de una hoguera y una guitarra querendona
en que una chicanita de lengua quebradiza y salivita dulce
de coñito apretado como calzón de luchador
–con perritos y toda la *costura*–
tendida sobre un lecho pedregoso

                                   le llamó y le dijo:
"Te chuparé tu sangre de uva suave

                           tu savia peyotera

Nuestro hijo se llamará Euforión
¿Por qué tiemblas?"

Y dice el señor–¡*Oh mister Moonlight!*
que ahora, *tonight*, irán al carnaval
a bailar en alguna bocacalle

                           a pistear al *Hussongs*

donde una gringa vieja pide *Cielito lindo*

                              por enésima vez

otra tequila y otro beso al galán

Y mi carnal Lombillo cante y cante

Los poetas–dice el compa Carlitos Baudelaire–
se dan hasta en las mejores familias

¡Viva la diferencia!
Entre los hijos del usurero

                       del político

                                del profesor
y los hijos del poeta
se abre el abismo de la noche
poblado de cardones parlantes

El canto de la ballena jorobada
que cruza la bahía de Todos Santos

                               rumbo al sur
Hacia los puertos donde esperan

                          las viudas de siempre
con un crío en los brazos

                      en la playa de siempre

so bittersweet, such a pot-head, such an I-don't-know-what"
He says there was a night at Las Playitas
(Or maybe Playa Hermosa)
around the bottled genie of Sir Santo Tomás
an open fire and a moaning guitar
when a little Chicana with broken Spanish and sweet saliva
her pussy as taut as a wrestler's tights
–the kind with little dogs and all that other froufrou–
called to him from her lumpy bed:
"I'll suck out your blood like a smooth grape

                                          I'll suck your peyote sap

Our son will be called Euphorion
Why do you tremble?"

And the gentleman says, "Oh Mister Moonlight!"
now, tonight, they'll go to the carnival
to dance in the middle of some crossroad

                                  to drink at Hussong's*

where an old gringa asks the band to play "Cielito Lindo"

                                         for the nth time

another tequila and another kiss for her stud

and my homie Lombillo sings and sings

"Poets," says our friend Chuck Baudelaire,
"happen even in the best of families"

Vive la différence!
Between the sons of usurers

                            politicians

                                 professors
and the sons of poets
yawns the abyss of night
full of talking cactus

The song of the hump-backed whale
that swims southward

                            through Todos Santos Bay
Toward ports where the usual widow

                                   a babe in her arms
waits
            on the usual beach

el regreso del viejo capitán

¡Canta ballena jorobada, fantasma gris!
Los herederos del patriarca Jordán

                              saludamos tu canto

Tu paso de ola viva
la estela de tu navegación

Raya en el agua de la memoria del viajero

¡Loor a los herederos del Dios-Diablo!
Ojos de neón de la noche de Tijuana
Corazón de guijarro de El Sauzal
Sombra de San Luciano
Duende de los tiros del Boleo
Pirata náufrago de la bahía de La Paz

Los hijos del poeta piden otra tanda

                              de música y de vino

¡Viva la diferencia!
(Nana Juanita, ruega por nosotros)

V

Tres arlequines *fellinescos* tiran sus redes sobre un grupo de marineros coreanos
        que no saben que hacer ante tanta puteza occidental.
Crece la multitud frente a la barra del Hussongs; se concentra en sí misma, enerva-
        da por el olor a brea, a orines de borracho, a víscera de mar.

Y la ruca gabacha terca, terca, pide otra *margarita* y otra tanda de *Cielito Lindo*.
Abrazada al galán, nativo y con arraigo, recién engatuzado, la escucha como si
        fuera la primera vez.
Nuestros rostros de ahogados flotan en el espejo de la contrabarra
y el Hussongs es un barco que se hunde con las luces prendidas.

VI

Volver al carnaval
al desfile de las últimas máscaras
–¿A que no me conoces mascarita?–
listos para el acto final
en el puro corazón de la noche

"Vine a Ensenada porque me dijeron
que aquí vivía mi padre...Un tal..."

for the old captain's return

Sing, hump-backed whale, gray phantom!
Heirs of the patriarch of the Jordan
                              we salute your song

Your footstep on the living wave
the wake of your navigation

A ray of light in the water of the traveler's memory

All praise to the heirs of the God-Devil!
Neon eyes of the Tijuana night
Heart of the cobbles of El Sauzal★
Shade of San Luciano
Imp of the mineshafts of Boleo★
Shipwrecked pirate in the Bay of La Paz

The poet's sons order another round
                              of music and wine

Vive la différence!
(Granny Juanita, pray for us)

V
Three clowns out of a Fellini film throw their nets over a group of Korean
          sailors who don't know what to make of so much occidental stupidity.
The crowd grows in front of Hussong's, collapsing inward, weakened by the
          smell of tar, the piss of drunks, the sea's guts.

And the stubborn old gringa orders another margarita and another round of
          "Cielito Lindo."
In the arms of her native sweetie, her property, fresh from sweet-talk, he listens
          to her as if for the first time.
Our drowned faces float in the mirror behind the bar
and Hussong's is a ship going down with its lights on.

VI
To return to the carnival
the parade of last masks
"Little darling behind your mask, don't you know me?"
ready for the last act
in the deepest heart of night

"I came to Ensenada because they told me
that my father lived here...Some guy..."

En un lugar de Ensenada
que se llama Punta Banda
                    hay una ola
que canta, que ríe y que llora
le dicen La Bufadora

Gimes, eres una mujer de agua doliente
mariposas de sal danzan en rito subceleste
la noche grávida bebe la lejanía

Así quería verte
sola y a solas
ascendiendo y bajando
estallando y muriendo
como la vida misma

Aquí se puede creer en Dios

Gira ya el mundo
–el verdadero hijo de Jesús–
sobre su propio eje
                    ¡Éjele!

In a part of Ensenada
called Punta Banda
              there is a wave
that sings, that laughs and cries
that's called La Bufadora

You howl, you're a woman of sorrowful water
salt butterflies dance in an earthly rite
the pregnant night drinks distance

I wanted to see you
alone and single
ascending and descending
erupting and dying
like life itself

Here one could believe in God

The World
–true son of Jesus–
still spins on its axis
                    Let it spin!

*The sense is, "from one end of Baja California to the other." *Revolution:* the center of the tourist area in Tijuana. *Marina Boulevard*: the seaside boulevard in Cabo San Lucás. *Mike's:* a bar in Tijuana. *Cabo Wabo:* a disco in Cabo San Lucás. *El Bordo:* a rundown neighborhood near the border fence in Tijuana. *Playita del Amor:* the beach at the southern tip of the peninsula.

San Ignacio. A mission town and date oasis in the desert of Baja California Sur.

Loreto. Oldest European settlement in Baja California (founded in 1697) and its first capital, now in Baja California Sur. The bells are those of the mission.

Towers of Aguacaliente. The towers of Tijuana's 1920s casino, now a high school.

Cueva Pintada. A cave decorated with prehistoric paintings in the Sierra de San Francisco of Baja California Sur.

Mexiquillos. A derogatory term for residents of Mexico City.

Mulegé. A mission town near the shore of the Gulf of California in Baja California Sur.

Cueva de los Monos. Another painting-filled cave in the Sierra de San Francisco.

Fez. A city in Morocco.

Algeciras, Atocha, Sants, Casco Viejo. Various places in Spain.

Ducal City. Barcelona, site of all the places named in the next fifteen lines. *San Jordi* is its patron saint.

damiana. A medicinal plant, said to be an aphrodisiac, native to Baja California.

San Pedrito. A beach near Todos Santos, in the south of Baja California Sur.

Santo Tomás. A winery in Ensenada. Its vineyards are in the valley of the same name on the outskirts of the city.

Marcos. Subcomandante Marcos, spokesman of the Zapatista revolutionary movement in the state of Chiapas.

Lacandón jungle. On the border between Chiapas and Guatemala.

Ocosingo to Ensenada. One end of Mexico to the other.

San Cristóbal. San Cristóbal de las Casas, a city in Chiapas.

Super C. Manuel Camacho, federal official responsible for negotiations in Chiapas.

Zapaneco. A neologism, combining the words zapatista and chiapaneco (native of Chiapas).

San Quintín / Valley of Oaxacalifornia. San Quintín is an agricultural town on the coast south of Ensenada. Many of the field hands are Mixtec Indians from Oaxaca, hence Oaxacalifornia.

*First Street. Like the rest of the place names that follow in Part III, a place in Ensenada.

*Don Benito and the other heroes. A monument consisting of twelve foot tall heads of Mexican presidents Benito Juárez and Venustiano Carranza and Father Miguel Hidalgo, hero of Mexico's rebellion against Spain.

*Riviera. A former casino and hotel, built in 1929 in Mission style, since 1977 the Centro Social, Cívico y Cultural of Ensenada. Perhaps the most beautiful building in Baja California.

*A Special World. "Un Mundo Raro," by singer/composer José Alfredo Jiménez. Source of the quotation eight lines below.

*La Bufadora. A blow hole on the coast south of Ensenada, popular with tourists and residents.

*Jaime. Jaime Sabines (born 1926). Popular Mexican poet given to sentimental themes.

*Mercado Negro. Literally, "black market." The fish market of Ensenada, a major tourist attraction.

*Bajío. An entertainment district of Ensenada.

*Las Playitas, Playa Hermosa. Beaches near Ensenada.

*Hussong's. The oldest and most popular bar in Ensenada.

*El Sauzal. A coastal town just north of Ensenada. The beach is covered with cobbles.

*Boleo. The copper-mining district surrounding Santa Rosalía, Baja California Sur. San Luciano was one of the mines.

H.P. & M.W.

Preceptos de la antigua y verdadera religión

Póstumo homenaje a Jorge Luis Borges

Honra al sol y al mar
como Galamata la piedra dura,
muchos años el hombre no vive.

No matarás león alguno,
porque aún después de muerto se vengará de ti.

No robarás el fruto de otra mente.

No jures en el nombre de tus dioses.
El monoteísmo se hace servir
por espíritus inferiores y sufrirás represalias.

Festeja las lunas nuevas,
las ofrendas de la carne se liberan sin la luz del día.

No sigas a la mayoría,
eres semejante por la herencia divina: busca tu canto,
siempre será mejor.

Desconfía de los sueños del poder,
pero no se te permite tener un sueño a medias.

Busca un reflejo de la luz eterna,
el verdadero conocimiento
todo lo atraviesa y cuando se vislumbran sus atisbos,
todo esplende.

ERNESTO ADAMS

Precepts of the Ancient and True Religion

Posthumous homage to Jorge Luis Borges

Honor the sun and the sea
as Galamata* honors the stone,
man does not live many years.

Kill no lion;
even in death it will seek revenge.

Steal not the fruit of another's mind.

Swear not in the name of thy gods.
Monotheism exists to serve
inferior minds, and thou shalt suffer reprisals

Celebrate the new moon,
In the dark the meat sacrifices will free themselves.

Follow not the majority,
Thou art equal by divine inheritence; search for thy song,
it will always be better.

Distrust the dreams of power,
but thou may not dream a half dream.

Search for reflections of the eternal light,
the true knowledge
it penetrates all things and when its merest hint is glimpsed
everything shines.

*Galamata. An indigenous diety.

A.P.

165

En secreto

a Ruth Vargas

Dicen, mujer,
que no cantamos a la rosa y su fragancia,
que nuestras palabras son obscenas.
Y es que olvidan, mujer,
que para orinar
tenemos que bajarnos los calzones y sentarnos,
somos el colchón del coito
que a fuerza de golpes se magulla.
Pero no les digas, mujer,
que en nuestros pechos pequeños y redondos
y sobre la piel de nuestro vientre,
lloran estrías luminosas
porque se olvidarían de nosotras.

Mary Key

I

Mary Key se volvió *hippie* en los sesenta,
se fue a la India y no volví a saber más de ella;
entonces yo era demasiado idiota como para volverme *hippie*,
con trabajos me enteraba de Viet Nam
y de la Plaza de las Tres Culturas
(en Tijuana, difícilmente se oía hablar de los Black Panthers o del Movimiento
        Chicano).

II

Mi novio me chantajeaba con su leucemia;
dos años le quedaban, dijeron hace veinte,
y ahora lo veo con su mujer y sus cinco hijos.
Me narraba su entierro por teléfono para oírme llorar,
haciéndome prometer que lo recordaría para siempre.
Yo no entendía a los Beatles y era demasiado ingenua como para volverme
        hippie:
Me entretenía con *Chucho el Roto* en la radio o leyendo a *Memím Pingüin*.
María Isabel fue mi tormento mientras mi madre me enseñaba a cocinar con
        enlatados.

ROSINA CONDE

In Secret

for Ruth Vargas

Woman, they say
that we don't sing of the rose and its fragrance,
that our words are obscene.
They forget, woman,
that to piss
we have to drop our pants and sit.
We are the mattress for coitus
bruised by their pounding.
Woman, let them forget us
don't remind them
that within our small round breasts
and under the skin of our bellies
luminous grooves weep.

Mary Kay

I

Mary Kay became a hippie in the sixties
went to India and I heard no more about her;
back then I was too stupid to become a hippie,
barely found out about Vietnam
or the Plaza de las Tres Culturas*
in Tijuana it wasn't easy to learn about the Black Panthers or the Chicano Move-
        ment

II

My boyfriend was blackmailing me with his leukemia,
they gave him two years twenty years ago
and today I see him with his wife and five kids.
On the phone he would describe his funeral to hear me cry,
making me promise I'd always remember.
I hadn't heard the Beatles, I was too naive to become a hippie:
Chucho el Roto and Memím Pingüín were enough for me.
I wept over María Isabel* while my mother taught me to cook out of cans.

III

Mi padre se negó a que compitiera para Reina de la Primavera;
sus hijas, aseguró, valían por ellas mismas sin tener que demostrar que eran las
        más bonitas.
Hoy tengo un marido que piensa que voy a apoderarme de él y de su cartera.
Me reta con el abandono
y competimos para ver cuál de los dos es capaz de despreciar más al otro.
Mi único error, dice, fue haber nacido mujer.

IV

Cuando conocí a Mary Key conocí el sabor de la cebada y el arroz integral;
supe también de la guerra sin entenderla.
Pero a mí me preocupaban la leucemia y su curación;
yo juraba estudiar medicina para atacarla.
Mi padre se negó.
Mi novio no murió a los dos años como le pronosticaran.
Me había mentido para oírme llorar, pensé después,
cuando terminó conmigo para irse con alguien que no conociera a una Mary
        Key.
Entonces supe de unas ruinas del Templo Mayor y pensé estudiar antropología;
pero mi padre se negó también:
me buscó una carrera apropiada y me envió a u.s.a. a estudiar decoración de
        interiores.
Ahora visto casas con cortinas de terciopelo y muebles *art deco*.

V

Gracias a Mary Key escuché a Dylan y a los Rolling.
Yo, a cambio, le mostré Tijuana.
Entonces no entendí por qué lloró con Cartolandia,
la de debajo del Puente,
con su lepra y disentería.
Fue cuando me dijo que se iría a la India.
Usaba pelo largo y huaraches mexicanos.
Era muy gringa.
Cocinaba en ollas de barro y había tirado la licuadora a la basura cuando mi
        madre descubriera el abrelatas eléctrico.
Mi padre se negaba a que la visitara;
pero, decía, él era el culpable por haberme enviado a estudiar a u.s.a.
Luego se preguntaba qué sería peor:
si mi amiga *hippie* o la Plaza de las Tres Culturas;
porque, decía, de los males, el menor,
y lo comprendo ahora al ver a mis hijos imitar a Capulina o al Chavo del Ocho.
Bueno, Mary Key usaba pelo largo y huaraches mexicanos;
compraba aretes de chaquira y pulseritas elaboradas por los pieles rojas;

III

My father wouldn't let me compete for Queen of the May;
His daughters, he said, should know their own worth; they didn't need to
         prove themselves in a beauty pageant.
Now I have a husband who thinks I want to control him and his wallet also.
He threatens to leave me and we compete
to see who can put the other down.
My mistake, he says, was being born a woman.

IV

When I met Mary Kay I discovered the taste of barley and brown rice;
I learned about the war, too, without understanding it.
But all I thought about was leukemia and its cure;
I swore I'd go to medical school to combat it.
My father refused.
My boyfriend didn't die in two years as predicted.
He had lied to hear me cry, I later thought, and then he dropped me
to go out with someone who didn't know any Mary Kays.
Then I heard about the ruins of the Templo Mayor and thought I'd study
         anthropology.
But my father said no again:
he found me a proper career and sent me off to the States
to study interior design.
Now I deck out houses with velvet curtains and art deco furniture.

V

Thanks to Mary Kay I listened to Dylan and the Stones.
In return I showed her Tijuana.
I couldn't understand why she wept over Cardboard City,
the one beneath the bridge,
with its lepers and dysentery.
That's when she told me she was going to India.
She had long hair and *huaraches*.
She was very *gringa*.
She cooked in clay pots and tossed out the blender while my mother was
         learning about electric can openers.
My father wouldn't let me see her and said
it was his fault for sending me to the States.
He asked himself which was worse:
my hippie friend or the Plaza de las Tres Culturas;
because, he'd say, you have to choose the lesser evil,
which I understand now, watching my kids imitate Capulina or Chavo del
         Ocho.*
O.K., Mary Kay's hair was long and she wore *huaraches*,
bought bead earrings and Navajo bracelets,

169

gustaba de las blusas bordadas de la India y largas faldas con estrellitas o flores
de colores.
Igual que Lucy.
Ella sí vio *I Love You Alice B. Toklas*
y fue violada a los quince por su novio que partía para Viet Nam.
Él murió allá.
Entonces yo no sabía del hambre, ni del frío, ni de la falta de un hogar,
y oía de los biafranitos como quien escucha sobre las Cataratas del Niágara:
¡asombrosos!
No sé si mi amiga Mary Key sabría mucho de eso;
pero se volvió vegetariana y se fue a la India.

VI
Eugenia se enamoró de su maestro de matemáticas;
rompió todos los poemas que había escrito y leído, así como sus cartas de
Mary Key
porque su maestro la obligó a hacerlo;
tuvo una hija a escondidas, ya que él, divorciado y con mujer, no podía
comprometerse,
por eso se enclaustró mientras encontró la manera de emigrarse.
Ahora él la visita cada mes o se van de vacaciones
y se jacta de cuidar muy bien sus tres casas.

VII
Mi amiga Alicia fue más lista, dice ella;
se mantuvo virgen y consiguió abogado de renombre.
Lo veía poco, para su suerte,
y de vez en cuando lo acompañaba a Acapulco y Europa.
Ha enviudado.
Ahora sabe que no tiene que esperarlo toda la noche,
con la cena enfriándose y las piernas abiertas;
ahora puede estirarse en su *chaise longue* y dormirse si quiere
sin tener que vestir su *négligé* que de cualquier forma no lucía.

VIII
Cuando decidí volverme *hippie* ya habían pasado de moda;
luego me enteré de que María Sabina había muerto
y que Woodstock y Avándaro habían ocurrido viente años atrás,
mientras mi novio me atormentaba con su leucemia y yo le juraba que me
haría monja.
Entonces comprendí que ya no estaba para Reina de la Primavera y que los
négligés son demasiado largos para mí.
Fue cuando recordé a Mary Key y deseé volver a verla para saber de sus
andanzas en la India.

and liked embroidered Indian blouses and full skirts covered with stars or
	flowers.
Just like Lucy.
She had seen *I Love You Alice B. Toklas*
and was raped at fifteen by her boyfriend who left for Vietnam
and died there.
And me, what did I know about hunger, cold, or homelessness,
when I heard about the Biafran children the sound could have drowned out
	Niagara Falls. I was overwhelmed!
I don't know if my friend Mary Kay knew much about that;
she turned vegetarian and left for India.

VI

Eugenia fell in love with her math teacher;
she tore up all the poems she had read or written, and her letters from Mary Kay,
because he told her to;
she gave birth to a baby girl in hiding, since he, already divorced and with a
	new wife, couldn't endanger his position,
and she shut herself away until she found a way to emigrate.
Now he visits her once a month or they go on vacation
and he boasts that he satisfies three households.

VII

My friend Alicia was smarter, she says;
she kept her virginity and found a famous lawyer.
She rarely saw him, luckily,
and now and then went with him to Acapulco or Europe.
She was left a widow.
Now she doesn't have to wait up all night,
her legs spread and dinner getting cold;
now she can stretch out on the chaise longue and sleep if she likes
without having to wear the negligée that never did the trick anyway.

VIII

When I decided to become a hippie it had already gone out of style;
I found out that Maria Sabina had died
and that Woodstock and Avándaro* had happened twenty years before
while my boyfriend was tormenting me with his leukemia and I was promising
	to become a nun.
Then I understood that I would never be Queen of the May and that negligées
	were too stylish for me.
That was when I remembered Mary Kay; I wanted to hear about her Indian
	adventures.

¡Quizás y hasta tuviera un hijo que le enseñaría a los míos el compromiso con
        la existencia!
Éstos piensan, igual que su padre y su abuelo, que aún existe el feudalismo,
que la mujer ideal es aquella que no habla
y que heredarán la tierra junto con los vasallos.

Maybe she'd had a child who could teach my kids about life!
Like their father and grandfather they think that feudalism still exists,
that an ideal woman says nothing
and that they're going to inherit the land and the vassals too.

Plaza de las Tres Culturas. Plaza de Tlatelolco, site of an anti-government demonstration (October 2, 1968), at which several hundred peaceful demonstrators were killed when units of the army fired on the crowd. One of the pivotal events of recent Mexican history.

Chucho el Roto. Nom de guerre of Jesús Arriaga (died 1885), a bankrobber who has become in the popular imagination a Robin Hood figure. The hero of many films and, beginning in 1968, a long-running television show. *Memím Pingüín.* The eponymous hero of an enormously popular comic book (1963-1977; reissued in the 1980s). A young black boy who is a sort of universal innocent. *María Isabel.* A literary, film and soap opera heroine.

Capulina. A childlike comic character, hero of numerous films and comic books of the 1980s and 1990s. *Chavo del Ocho.* Eponymous hero of the long-running (1973-1994) comedy show, played by the adult Roberto Gómez Bolaños as a child, and dressed in children's clothing. For the entire duration of its run the most popular show on Latin American television.

Avándaro. An outdoor rock concert (September 11-12, 1971) attended by hundreds of thousands, many of whom indulged in public consumption of recreational drugs and public nudity. The Mexican Woodstock. A seminal moment in the history of the Mexican counterculture.

J.L.

Aliteral poema elástico para linotipistas

Sentémonos frente a las brasas, compa
y tómate otra cerveza
hay que callar lo que la noche hace con sus estrellas
este sol ha chamuscado las ideas de la sombra
nos lleva adormilados a la frontera del día
ha hecho trizas nuestros alimentos: huevos, espíritu,
tortillas, poca cosa.

Escucha cómo dicen por la radio
que vayas y te mueras
mientras gente hace cola por trozos de nada
y amaneces con la punta de una bomba en la garganta
jugo matutino en que estallan tus ojos en todos los países;

Andamos descalzos sobre picudas piedras (ama y calla, oh dolor)
con esta mudez tan llena de palabras
con ganas de patear los asilos del silencio.

El río corre, inmundo el cabrón, viene del norte
pobre de tu alma
ropas colgadas y amorosas presencias en dientes de la muerte
calaca que te toca, carne que hace fila, trenes sin amor
deportes de la prensa en la mañana la patada
en medio de una guerra
que a todos nos retuerce el hígado, las tripas
y el triste corazón.

Échale leña, compa, se nos apaga
se nos va como pendejos la historia de mi abuela
de carabinas, naranjas, leche y pólvora
tejida por hermanas, madres, hijas amorosas
en lo oscuro de este siglo que agoniza.

Entonces el recuerdo,
las manos de mi abuelo apretando el hambre en los trenes de la leva
sacando pan, ladrillos, hijos y estallidos de amor de un solo horno
rojo, colérico, sanguíneo
sin ayes de cobardía o pizca de congoja
gritando de locura
¡libertad, ponte a bailar desnuda esta noche
acércame tus nalgas que las quiero coger!

TOMÁS DI BELLA

Aliteral Elastic Poem for Linotypists

Let's sit by the embers, buddy,
and drink another beer
We've got to keep what the night does with its stars under wraps
this sun has scorched every notion of shade
and left us slumbering at the day's border
it's shredded our nourishment: eggs, spirit, guts,
tortillas, little enough.

Listen to what they say on the radio
that you go off and die
while people line up for scraps of nothing
and you wake up with the tip of a bomb in your throat
the morning juice that blows your eyes out in every country

We walk barefoot over sharp stones (love and keep still, oh sorrow)
this muteness teeming with words
eager to trample the sanctuaries of silence.

Filthy old goat, the river runs
from your soul's impoverished north
clothes hanging loose and amorous presences in death's teeth
the grinning skull that clatters against you, flesh in rows, loveless trains
sports in the morning paper the kickoff
in the midst of a war
that twists our liver, intestines,
and saddened heart.

Throw another log on the fire, it's going out
my grandmother's story is passing us by as if we were useless, her story
of carbines, oranges, milk and gunpowder
woven by sisters, mothers, loving daughters
in the darkness of this dying century.

Then memory, hunger squeezing my grandfather's hands
in the troop trains
pulling bread, bricks, sons and lovelorn explosions
from a single angry, bloody, red hot oven
without groans of cowardice or the least anguish
shrieking in madness
liberty! dance naked tonight!
bring your sweet ass closer so I can fuck you!

Ábrete las piernas, memoria
atízale al fogón, mi compadre
la selva se la tragan los voraces
que rompen la tenue y delicada piel que cubre el sueño de tus hijos
nuestros hijos, los herederos de las chanclas viejas, y sin embargo
únicos dueños eternos de la plata de la Kodak
de la pulpa de papel del billete verde
de la planta de hule de la llanta que rechina idiota
estos nuestros hijos, únicos dueños de lo verde que nos roban
del barro que saquean, del café que se aglutinan
del tabaco que se chupan
del maíz que nos robaron.

Ábreme los ojos memoria, ponle tinta, compadrito, que se pierde
enjúgate la sal de esa mirada que lenta corre bajo tus pupilas,
que no te acojone el desconcierto
está aquí, a la vuelta de la esquina este holocáustico desmadre
aunque el sol reparta aún sus trapos amarillos
sobre las azoteas de esta parte tan jodida del mundo

Pero me gana la nostalgia,
¿Quiénes son estos hijos de puta?
¿Quiénes son los que se chupan la sangre de mi gente?
¿Quiénes nos quitan este poema eterno de amor?

Desarruga ese papel, compita
hoy yo hablo de esta metáfora de piedras lanzadas al vacío
mientras negras aves graznan impúdicas nuestra muerte;

Oh queridos rostros hechos de barro
yo quisiera y no puedo traerlos a mi mesa
y que hablen solitarios del camino al ventarrón
del olor a cuero viejo del taller del enemigo
de los juegos de pelota sin acróbatas ni cuentas
de las luchas con gandules en horarios de agonía;

Yo quisiera, pero es la conciencia
redonda, vieja desguanzada
que carga la fruta que nos alimenta
y pone en claro, concreta y amorosa
la punzante bala que llega rápida al vientre del trabajador
el que cae sin remedio en eternas alegatas
barriendo sin descanso lo roto del edén mortificado.

Spread your legs, memory
stir up the hearth, compadre
the greedy devour the jungle
breaking the delicate skin that covers your children's dreams
our children, heirs of tattered slippers, yet
the sole owners of Kodak's silver
of the paper greenback's pulp
of the rubber tree of stupidly squealing tires
these our children, sole owners of the green they steal from us
of the clay they extract, the caked coffee
the tobacco they suck at
the corn they rob from us.

Open your eyes for me, memory, ink it in, friend, it fades
wipe away the salt of this gaze that flows slowly beneath your pupils,
or this chaos will make you wet your pants
it's here, just around the corner, this holocaust of confusion
though the sun still spreads its yellow rags
over the roofs of this fucked-up part of the world

But nostalgia overcomes me
who are these sons-of-bitches?
who are these guys who suck my people's blood?
who steals from us the eternal poem of love?

Uncrumple that paper, buddy
today I'm talking about this metaphor of stones hurled into the void
while black birds shamelessly croak out our death;

O beloved clay faces
I would invite them to my table, if I could,
that they might speak, lonely ones of the road, to the gusting wind
about the smell of old leather from the enemy's workshop
the ballgames without acrobats and scores
the battles with vagrants in the timetables of agony;

I would like to, but there's always consciousness,
that spent old woman who
carries the fruit that feeds us
and makes clear, concrete, and loving
the bullet that suddenly rips the worker's belly
and he falls helplessly into eternal happiness
tirelessly sweeping the walls of a mortified Eden.

Hoy leo en la tarde de vencidos
con las ácidas lluvias y un sol enmarcado de misiles
como una paradoja llevo
los pantalones desgarrados de mi abuelo, árbol solo,
y la mano desecha con las plantas trituradas
por siglos de empuñar los instrumentos
de acariciar los surcos regados de sudor, la neta
para hacer germinar generaciones
que ahora caen enteras.

La historia ya no es nada
es una eterna noche en desvelo, un cuerpo sin césped
una sequía de ideas
una voz que desaparece entre el polvo del camino
palabras que palpitan poco tiempo y luego mueren
son manos hundidas en tierra requemada
es cabello que deforme abre puerta a la locura
alimento que rechaza un estómago perdido.

Entonces llegará otro tiempo,
el de hombre sin ataduras, sin límites ni glotonería
el del hombre asidero del intento, el de antes
del agandalle y arrebate y ojetería, el del
que compartía, el hombre del día.

Hoy es de noche.

This afternoon I'm reading of those vanquished
by acid rains and a sun disfigured by missiles
like a paradox I wear
my grandfather's torn-up trousers, that solitary tree,
and the hand thrown out with the pulp of plants
after centuries of holding in its grip tools
for caressing the furrows he watered with sweat, all of this
that generations now free-falling
might bloom.

The story is nothing now
it's a night of eternal insomnia, a body without sod
a drought of ideas
a voice that disappears in the dust of the road
words that briefly quiver and die
hands sunk in parched earth
hair that deformed opens the door to madness
food that the lost stomach rejects.

Another time will come,
the time of unbound men without limits or gluttony
of the man equal to the task, innocent
of selfishness, blind impulse and deception
the one who shares, the man of day.

Now it is night.

M.K.

Carta

```
S      f      p      p      q      ansias     s      Y              s
o      l      a      a      u                 u                     e
b      o      r      r      e        y        S              g
e      r      a      e                        S              U      u
r      e      t      c      s      poderes    t      D              r
a      s      i      e      i                 o      O              o
n             i             ocultos           r      R
a      m             q      v                 p      O              e
       u      m      u      a        c        e      S              r
t      e      i      e      l        a        z      O              e
r      r             e      d        a        a      S              s
i      t      l             e        a
s      a      u      t      l               en silencio             o
t      s      j      e      a                 i                     t
e             o      v               u        n                     r
       y      s      e      p        n        t      a              a
y             o      o      e        o        e      ll
       a             n                        l      á
t      l      y      o      a                 i
o      f             t      d                 g                     yo
d      o      v      r      e                 e      t
o      m      a      a      s                 n      e              a
p      b      c      s                        t                     q
o      r      í      v      c                 e                     u
d      a      o      e      u                 ..     q              í
e      s             z      b                        u
r             r      p      r                 E      e              n
o      p      e      r      i                 M      d              o
s      e      c      e      r                 P      a              m
a      r      u      g      n                 A      s              á
       f      e      u      o                 T      t              s
       u      r      n      s                 A      e              .
       m      d      t                        D                     .
       a      o      a                        O                     .
       d             n                        S
       a             d
       s             o
```

Letter

```
S   d   f   s   1   longings   i   &          s
o   e   o   e   f              t   S          u
v   a   r   e   i      &       s   W          r
e   d       m   t              i   E          e
r       y   s   i   hidden     n   A          y
e   f   o       '              t   T          o
i   l   u   I   s   powers     e   Y          u
g   o                          l
n   w   m   s   w      e       l   silently   w
    e   y   e   o      a       i              e
s   r       e   r      c       g   t          r
a   s   l   e   t      h       e   h          e
d       a       h              n   e
    &   v   y          o       t   r          d
&       i   o   t      f           e          i
    s   s   u   h              s   r          f
a   c   h   t          u       l              f
l   e       h   e      s       o   y          e
l   n   &   a   t              w   o          r
-   t       g   r              n   u          e
p   e   e   a   o              e              n
o   d   m   i   u              s   r          t
w       p   n   b              s   e
e   c   t   o   l              ..  m          m
r   a   y   o   e                  a          e
f   r       u                  B   i
u   p   m   b   t              O   n          o
l   e   e   a   o              U   e          n
    t   m   s                  N   d          l
    s   o   k   s              D              y
        r   i   p
        y   n   o                             h
            g   t                             e
                                              r
                                              e
                                              .
                                              .
                                              .
```

Amata

Si azul es el polvo de siempre
veo los días de agua pasar
por mis manos intocables, cercanas
a los dedos que resbalan
al valle de agua del cuerpo de la luna
Hasta más no saber

Y si abriera más tu puerta
si me abandonara
a este tinte brusco de palabras
que tomo y se disparan, por decir algo:

                        pájaros azules
                        que tú
                        encendiste
en la bruma que me arroja al rosal de tu blusa

(Hay voces que arañan a la voz desnuda
la retuercen en el taburete de los días
desolados dioses).

Metido en el callejón de los renglones
me muerden las espinas de agua

tocan mi vida
porque de esta noche está más cerca
la llamada que recoge tus susurros
un ave que desciende con todo y jaula
el horizonte que levanta infinidad
de soluciones dispersas conjugadas
en un verso
hongo reptil pez labios que se alzan.

25 de diciembre

El destello de luz en mi ventana
y una voz que me levanta entre las sombras de cobalto

Me veo en el espejo, me voy por el espejo...

Afuera llueve sobre todas las cosas

Amata

If the everyday dust is blue
through my hands
the days of water pass untouchable,
close to those fingers that slide
from the moon's body to the valley of water
Until nothing more is known

And if your door were to open farther
if you were to abandon me
to the harsh color of exploding words
that I grasp at, as if to say:
                    blue birds
                    ignited
                    by your hand
in the fog that propels me to the rosebush of your blouse

(There are voices that scratch at the naked voice
twirling it on the stool of days
those despairing gods).

Trapped within the lines of a notebook
bitten by spines of water

they touch my life
because since then the call
that collects your whispers approaches
a bird complete with cage descending
the horizon lifting an infinity
of dispersed conjugated solutions
in a line of verse
mushroom reptile fish lips rising

December 25th

The gleam of light in my window
and a voice that lifts me from among cobalt shadows

I see myself in the mirror, I pass through the mirror...

Outside it's raining on everything

los cuerpos vacíos brillan
los pinos tambaleantes se acurrucan en la tierra

La lluvia limpia nuestros techos de hule y de mercurio

En el viento los pájaros son eternos.

Nightfields

Desde esas estaciones
donde habitan las sombras
la loca se jala los cabellos
salta el beso rosa junto a la telaraña del diván

Esa oscuridad tocará mañana
este mismo paso lento sobre el concreto

Somos nosotros los que olvidamos
aquella fuente donde sueña la noche
amiga muerta que camina por la calle.

La bailarina del balcón

I
Sé que la gaviota que me ve, sabe dónde estás
tocando con tus manos largas otro viento

Ya la amapola extingue poco a poco tu aroma
pero sé que te quedarás por siempre en estas playas
en este espacio de mundo vivo derruido

Nunca supe que ya era tiempo para ese adiós
detrás de las bardas no hay tiempo que perder
nosotros nos quedaremos un rato más
con los ojos fijos en las olas que se forman
mirando con miedo a todas partes

II
El mar se compadece
un cigarro apagado
el café frío
un debo ir a comer,
la gaviota parada en su sombra
al tocar las arenas espejeantes.

empty bodies shine
trembling pines huddle against the earth

The rain washes the rubber and mercury from our roofs

the birds eternally suspended on the wind.

Nightfields

From these stations
where shadows live
a mad woman pulls out her hair
the pink kiss jumps next to the spider web of the couch.

Tomorrow this darkness will touch
the same footfalls on the concrete pavement

We are those we forget
the fountain where night sleeps
the dead friend walking the streets.

The Ballerina of the Balcony

I
I know that the seagull watching me knows your whereabouts
touching another wind with your long hands

Already the poppy has begun to extinguish your scent
but you will always remain on these beaches
in this living wreck of a world

I didn't know it was time for that goodbye
behind the garden wall there is no time to spare
let us stay a while longer
staring out at the the oncoming waves
our anxious eyes flitting nervously

II
The sea is understanding
an extinguished cigar
the cold coffee
an I-have-to-eat
the seagull in its own shadow
the sand sparkling to the touch.

La mesera de los ojos vizcos
regresa al Kena

"abdómenes flojos y protuberantes ¡detestables!"

Nos encontraremos cuando los geranios se bañen en la brisa

"Que súbele que bájale..."
Los muertos están con los muertos
y los vivos con los vivos
yo no sé dónde estás

III
La nostalgia del mar es diferente
el aire de las cuatro
mueve los manteles de las mesas del balcón
el radio se pelea solo

caen las hojas de la palapa destruida en el invierno
el sol se va diciendo tantas cosas...

Junto a la hora

A la hora de tu muerte, disminuidos
los minutos se extinguen,
poseyéndote en la cama un ser maligno
de encendidos ojos
y allá fuera dos jóvenes de blanco que te llevan.

En esa soledad has triunfado:
solos nos dejas, con el dolor del que gana.
Perdidos, abandonamos la ciudad decapitada
al arbitrio de los que jinetean sobre el tiempo.
Como si fuera un animal de carga,
cae el cemento sobre nuestro pecho.

No vayas, padre, a dejar tu respiración exhuberante
por aquella pálida cuesta del silencio.

Frente al ventanal; una cascada de casas,
el polvo cae de los cerros,

The cross-eyed waitress
returns to her *Kena**

"flabby and protruding bellies, disgusting!"

We will meet when geraniums bathe in the breeze

*"It goes up, it goes down"**
The dead are with the dead
and the living with the living
I don't know where you are

III
Nostalgia for the sea is different
the four o'clock breeze
rustles the tablecloths on the balcony tables
alone the radio fights on

Winter-battered the leaves of the palapa fall
the sun departs saying so many things...

*Kena. A Mexican women's magazine
*It goes up, it goes down. A line from a popular dance tune.

Close to the Hour

At the hour of your death the minutes, diminished,
extinguish themselves,
in your bed you are possessed by a malignant being
with eyes of fire
and two young men in white carry you off

You have triumphed in this solitude:
with a winner's sorrow you leave us behind.
Lost, we abandon the headless city
at the whim of those who trample time,
our chests weighted by cement
like beasts of burden.

Don't trade your exuberant breath
for that pale hill of silence, father.

Outside the window a cascade of houses,
dust falling from the hills,

y una bicicleta al encuentro de la mañana plena
arremete a la muerte,
con los ángeles sobre nuestra ignorancia,
contra nuestra deslealtad de no ser
lo que de todo hombre
se espera.

Vence la fatiga
contra los que te dieron la espalda
por su pequeñez; luego perdónanos,

y regresa al lugar de donde siempre fuiste.

Alabar el circulo

1
Padre
cubre tu cuerpo
has mudado
llévate mi suéter, mi almohada
has mudado
vecino al cementerio

2
Alabar el círculo
no el punto que se va
en la memoria
una flecha que se eleva
con su punta ardiendo

3
Padre,
te acuesto
cubro tu cuerpo
luego no sé
mi hermano César vendrá
a atestiguar tu cara

4
Alabar la caída y la tierra a donde vuelves
alabar los círculos concéntricos
de los muertos de cáncer
acostados en el corazón
el punto negro de la crucifixión

and a bicycle greeting the morning
challenges death,
angels hovering above our ignorance
in spite of our failure to be
what every man
is expected to be.

Fatigue defeats
those who turned their backs on you
out of pettiness; forgive us then

and return to the place you were always from.

Praising the Circle

1
Cover your body
father
you have moved
take my sweater, my pillow,
you have moved
close to the cemetery

2
Praising the circle
not the dot
that's lost in memory
an arrow ascending
its tip in flame

3
I put you to rest,
father
I cover your body
later, perhaps,
César my brother will attest
to your face

4
Praising your fall and the earth you return to
praising the concentric circles
of those at rest in our hearts
who die of cancer
the black dot of the crucifixion

K.A.E.

Hora cautiva

Alguna vez alguien se irá
y dejará la puerta abierta
y tú te preguntarás: ¿quién?
pero será muy noche
para esperar que alguien conteste.
El olvido caerá como la última lluvia
y ya no habrá nadie a quien le guste
ese olor a tierra mojada
y tampoco, ni al menos, una cena con velas
Se oye la marcha sorda de los autos
como niebla sonora.
Los minutos caen tan lentamente como la lluvia
en el cristal de la ventana.
Yo hace un momento desperté
y me sentí un intruso,
un habitante de otro sueño
entre los naipes del acaso.
Quiero luz; tengo sed de algo.
Soy un náufrago de luz.
Veo la luna y quiero pensar
que la luna es el cerrojo de una puerta
que está cerrada,
que hay incendios provocados por la ira
y que la soledad termina
en un fastuoso amanecer con música de orquesta.
Tener insomnio, qué problema,
es mirar la desnudez de la noche
pero con la legalidad de una playa privada.
Así es, todos nos iremos de este pueblo
pero vendrán otras personas, no sé cuándo,
con los mismos problemas emocionales,
para escuchar en bares a media luz
las canciones color de humo
que hoy escriben nuestros amigos.
Procedimiento ciego de la historia
que sin embargo no remedia
ni la sed ni los derrumbes,
las quimeras, los falsos profetas, la herejía...
en cambio abre la puerta al melodrama,
al poeta,
al enervante condimento de la fiesta.

Captive Hour

From time to time someone will exit
leaving the door ajar
and you ask yourself, who could that be?
but it's too late at night
to expect an answer.
Forgetfulness will fall like the last rain
there will be no one left with a taste
for the smell of damp earth
or even a candlelit dinner.
You hear the deaf progression of cars,
like a noisy fog.
The minutes fall as slowly
as rain on the windowpane.
A moment ago I awoke
feeling myself an intruder,
the inhabitant of another dream
among cards dealt by chance.
I am thirsty for anything; I wish for light,
I am a man drowned for lack of it.
I see the moon and I want to believe
that the moon is the bolt of a locked door
that there are arsons provoked by anger
and that solitude ends
in a kitsch sunrise
complete with orchestra.
What a misery! to be insomniac
is to see the night's nakedness
but legally, on a private beach.
So it is that we'll all leave town
but others will come, I don't know when,
with the same neuroses
to listen in dimly-lit bars to the smoky songs
that our friends compose now.
History's blind process
which doubtless cures neither thirst nor landslides,
chæmeras, false prophets, heresy...
Instead it opens the door to melodrama, the poet,
the nasty taste of the fiesta.

M.W.

Tormenta

Luz destellante por el viento,
valle blanco, árboles blancos.

Nuestra casa protegida
en el calor de la chimenea,
mi madre prepara ponches dulces
para mi boca amarga.

El viento agita mi cabello,
los vientos de Santa Ana ya cruzan la frontera,
el frío, después, reseca mi piel, soy
una corteza a la que sólo
sus raíces sostienen.

Despedida

Veo una mujer que sale del mar.
Enciende un cigarrillo.
Donde pudo encontrar un reino
disipa las cenizas.

Sobre la arena las huellas
van hasta un vestido de jade,
la cabellera se abre como medusa.

Me dice: "Para vivir en el mar
hay que flotar como los muertos."

La radio avisa:
"Mañana también
estará despejado."

Niños y pajaros y niños...

1
Niños que flotan como pájaros,
sus alas iluminan el charco.

Corren con el pensamiento

Storm

Light sparkling in the wind,
white valley, white trees.

Our house protected
by the warmth of the hearth,
my mother prepares sweet drinks
for my bitter tongue.

The wind ruffles my hair,
the Santa Anas now cross the border,
later the cold parches my skin: I am
the bark sustained
by the roots alone.

Farewell

I see a woman emerge from the sea.
She lights a cigarette.
Where she could have found a kingdom
she scatters ashes.

On the sand the footprints
end at a jade dress,
hair undulant as a jellyfish.

She tells me: "To live in the sea
one must float like the dead."

The radio announces:
"Tomorrow will be clear
again."

Boys and Birds and Boys...

1
Boys floating like birds,
the puddle lit by their wings.

As fast as thought they run

a las chimeneas, mientras tiemblan
en el azul del cielo.

El mundo es una línea curva
sobre la mesa.
En el mantel,
reflejos de una tarde con nubes;
tus ojos grises una mancha
que se extiende por la ventana.

2
Pájaros que flotan como niños,
sus alas en el charco,
alegría sin fondo.

Ellos corren con el pensamiento,
tiemblan en el azul del cielo.

El mundo como línea
curva sobre la mesa el mantel,
la tarde nublada.
Tus ojos de triste gris
se extienden por la ventana.

Canastos y dátiles

La tierra se parte en la sed de mis labios,
páramo ondulante
en el escozor de los ojos.
La mujer que amaba
me despidió
cerrando los ojos.
Su rostro se llena de arena
en el fresco de las montañas
como un reloj
que avisa el tiempo cumplido.

Una mujer de avanzada edad
teje canastos
y recoge dátiles,
cuenta la historia de dos en las montañas:
"Ella se fue evaporando en el mundo,
él busca apagar la melancolía
en el desierto."

to the hearth, trembling
against the sky's blue.

The world is a curved line
across the table.
On the cloth
reflections of a cloudy evening,
your gray eyes a stain
flowing through the window.

2
Birds floating like boys,
their wings in the puddle,
joy without end.

As fast as thought they run
trembling against the sky's blue.

The world like a line
curves across the table the cloth
the clouded evening.
Your sad gray eyes
flow through the window.

Baskets and Dates

The earth brings itself forth in my lips' thirst,
undulating prairie
in the stinging of my eyes.
The woman I loved
closing her eyes
has bid me farewell.
Her face is covered with sand
in the cool air of the mountains
like an hourglass
that warns of time passed.

An elderly woman
weaves baskets
gathers dates,
recounts the story of the couple in the mountains:
"She evaporated into the world,
he seeks to extinguish melancholy
in the desert."

Al desierto baja el invierno fresco,
así bajo la mirada a la página,
buscando un punto
que me revele tu rostro.

Restaurante judío

Sabrás del dolor,
llaga que recorre el cuerpo;
amor mío, un recuerdo,
felicidad del llanto.

Sabrás que sólo son extraños los silencios;
verás tus ojos como pozos,
la sangre del corazón;
temblor de los labios
entonando poemas gastados en los ojos.

Y eso qué importa
si en los cafés
se consumen los hombres de mi edad.

En los ceniceros un hombre busca
algo que florezca,
un olvido tejido en negro.

En un restaurante judío
olvidarnos es fácil;
parto una semita, sorbo café.

Jugando dominó

Mi padre,
llega al pasado atravesando palabras
tiene las cicatrices
de un árbol, a su paso caen las hojas
con cada movimiento del viento cae su sombra.

Ayer se reunió la familia
el sol trastocaba techos y paredes,
había luz con sabor dulce
en el comedor, y al movimiento de las manos
las fichas del dominó giraban,

Cool winter descends on the desert.
Glancing down at the page,
I look for the dot
that will show me your face.

Jewish Restaurant

You will know sorrow,
the wound invading the body:
my love a souvenir,
joy of lamentation.

You will know that only silences are strange;
you will see your eyes like wells,
heart's-blood,
a trembling of the lips
intoning exhausted poems for the eyes.

And what does it matter
if in the cafés
men my age are devoured.

In the ashtray a man seeks
whatever flowers,
forgetfulness woven in black.

To forget oneself is easy
in a Jewish restaurant:
I break bread, I sip coffee.

Playing Dominoes

My father
returns to the past by way of words.
Scarred
like a tree, at his step
leaves fall, his shadow falls with each gust of wind.

Once the family would gather,
sun transforming roofs and walls,
the light in the dining room
sweet to taste, and in a dance of hands
the dominoes revolved,

mi padre
como nosotros en espera de nuestro destino.

Hoy se ha reunido la familia
faltan mi tía Alicia y los abuelos,
hay una gran comida sobre la mesa
los colores brotan en todas direcciones;
mi padre
en el centro elige el pan,
los recuerdos lo callan
mueve los ojos y chasquea la lengua
pensando en su orgullo como el valor de una moneda

veo en sus ojos un corazón que sabe de despedidas
veo sus manos que han tocado las cosas
que sólo han sido tocadas por el tiempo,
me veo a mí mismo venir de él
y voy a él con este corazón.

Hoy no habrá discusión
porque las mil noches encerrado bajo su techo
y mil días bajo su sombra
impetu y furia fueron abatidos tiernamente

en este circulo él atravesará hasta su infancia
yo callaré mis culpas, seré paciente
pondré las fichas de dominó sobre la mesa
mientras esperamos nuestro destino.

my father
like the rest of us
awaiting his destiny.

Today the family gathers again,
Aunt Alicia and my grandparents gone,
a festive meal on the table
colors spilling in all directions;
my father
in the midst of the celebration chooses
which bread to take,
memories silence him,
rolling his eyes and moving his tongue he tests
his pride as if testing a coin.

I see in his eyes a heart that knows farewells,
I see his hands that have touched
only what time has touched,
I see myself come forth from him
and return, carrying this heart.

Today we won't argue,
because the thousand nights imprisoned beneath his roof
the thousand days beneath his shadow
the violence the rage
are suffocated by the weight of love.

In this place, with these people, he will return to his childhood.
I will silence my accusations and patiently
place the dominoes on the table
while we await our destiny.

M.W.

Gozo

Con la boca húmeda
Atravesó las líneas de su cuerpo
Lo cubrió de hojas ennegrecidas
Que nadie recogió aquel atoño
Se comió la historia
Se comió la piel amarilla de la tierra
Bebió las formas de sus pies

Quiero comerte aunque me duela
Esta lengua amoratada
Quiero el olor de tu cabello
De tus muslos tibios
Tocar aunque no sientas
Tu sexo
Unir tus células dispersas

No has muerto
No pesas como los muertos
Tus piernas
Tu carne acariciada ansiosa coronada
No pesa como los muertos

Cierto

I
Todo lo había inventado
La imagen de su rostro pegado a la ventana
La despedida, su abrazo, sus hombros
El sepulcro de su madre

El mar que no conoció
El caballo que en sueños relinchaba
Para silenciar la noche
Cuando la montaron

Que nada sea cierto   duele
Que ya no pueda escuchar el viento también duele
Que su cuerpo sea un objeto inerte
Duele

Bliss

With moist mouth
It pierced his body's lines
Covered it with blackened leaves
That went ungathered that autumn
History skipped over
Ate the earth's yellow skin
Drank down the traces of his feet

I want to consume you
Although it hurts me
This bruised tongue
I want the scent of your hair
Of your warm muscles
To touch your sex
Although you feel nothing
I want to collect your scattered cells

You haven't died
Your legs
Your caressed flesh greedy crowned
Is not as heavy as the dead

Certain

I
He'd invented everything
The image of her face against the window
The parting, her embrace, her shoulders
Her mother's grave

The sea she never saw
The horse neighing in her dreams
To silence the night
When they mounted her

That nothing is certain   hurts
No longer to hear the wind also hurts
That her body is an inert object
Hurts

II
Así eras
Queja ardiente en todas partes
Bajo el sol que ya no quema
En el rojo, triste clamor del llanto

Sobrevivir siempre es lo más difícil
Pero no lo sabes
No existes
Ni siquiera tienes nombre
Pero yo sobreviví

Aunque ya no miro hacia ningún lado

Omnipresencia *(fragmento)*

EL DÍA se pone verde
Apenas tu sueño se levanta
Entra la memoria y lo cobija todo

El poeta quiere ser oído
Pero su canto es lento
Espeso como el aceite

Dicen que por ahí corre un río de sangre
Y que llora cuando hace viento

Mi hermano murió
Porque no pudo atravesar el canal Todo Americano
Iba hacia el norte   al otro lado

Un día mi madre esperaba su llegada
En su lugar trajeron un cuerpo
Lleno de moretes

Desde entonces
Las vecinas se quejan porque el agua viene sucia
¿Cómo puede ser el lodo transparente?
Les pregunto

CIERRA tus ojos
Para que el olvido
No tiemble en tu pecho

II
That's how you were
Always ardently complaining
Under the sun that no longer burns
In the red, sad clamor of weeping

Surviving is always hardest
But you don't know that
You don't exist
Don't even have a name
But I have survived

Although I no longer look for anything

from **Omnipresence**

THE DAY becomes green
Your dream barely appears
Memory enters and covers everything

The poet wants to be heard
But his song is slow
And thick as oil

They say that a river of blood runs there
And that it sobs when the wind blows

My brother died
Because he couldn't cross
the All American Canal
He was going north   to the other side

One day my mother awaited his arrival
In his place they brought a body
Covered with bruises

Since then
The neighbors have complained
because the water's dirty
How can mud run clear
I ask them

CLOSE your eyes
So that forgetfulness
Won't tremble in your breast

Y ahí estará él
El emigrante ausente
Abrazando su recuerdo
Pensando en volver

¡VOLVER!
Palabra que retiene en sus labios
Y la muerde hasta convertirla en sangre
Y pinta con ella su recuerdo
Un cuerpo estremecido
Devorando la despedida
Deteniéndola   amándola

Y se quiere ir al cielo con ella
Con su rostro y su pelo enamorado
Y se pega a su cuerpo
A su boca
A sus pechos que son su casa
Cuarteados por el abandono
Luego
Con su húmeda compañía
Se amamanta

Ayer no quise dejarte
Y recordé que para tenerte
No hacían falta pretextos
Y aquí vine
Y puedo sentir tus manos
Pendientes de las mías
Invadiendo mi cuerpo
Que no quiere que lo entierren sin tu aliento

LLEVARTE así conmigo
No ha sido fácil
Ojalá pudiera confundirme en tu poema
Libre y malgastado
Manchando la tierra con tu puño
Oyéndote de cerca

Pero esta casa no es la misma
El viento se llevó tus pisadas
Y luego trajo otras
Desde entonces
Llenar la noche se volvió cotidiano

And there he will be
The absent emigrant
Embracing his memory
Thinking to return

TO RETURN!
Words that he holds on his lips
And bites till they bleed
coloring his memory
A shaken body
Devouring the parting
Delaying, cherishing it

And he wants to go to heaven with her
With her face and her beloved hair
And clasped to her body
To her mouth
To her breasts that are his home
Shredded by abandonment
Then suckled
With his damp company

Yesterday I didn't want to leave you
And I remembered that I needed
no excuses to have you
And I came here
And can feel your hands
Hanging from mine
Invading my body
That doesn't want to be buried
Without your breath

TO CARRY YOU with me
Has not been easy
Would that I could fuse myself with your poem
Free, misspent
And stain the earth with your fist
Hearing you nearby

But this house is not the same
The wind has erased your footsteps
And brought others
To fill the night
A daily occurrence.

Ahora había que inventarte
Y me enamoro de tu cuerpo
Así...como al principio
Cuando humilde me conquistaste

Salí a buscarte
Con tu palabra clavada en mi oído
Entre la gente
Entre tumbas y relámpagos
Pegado a mi sombra

Pero a tu regreso
Hasta las paredes me miran sorprendidas
Ya no dibujan mi silueta moribunda
Traspasando su espacio
Ni mis cabellos revueltos
Cerrando sus heridas

Adopté a la soledad por compañera
Y caminamos juntas
Aferradas a justificar las noches

Pero a tu regreso
Ya no eras el mismo
En silencio te lamentabas
De que fuiste prisionero de tu carne muerta

Escondías el gesto
Cada vez que me acercaba
Y yo
Acostumbrada a tu voz
tengo que irme con el tiempo
Y te veo abriendo la tierra

Voy más allá
Y puedo ver las milpas
Y entre la hierba con su florecilla azul

Tu promesa a la tierra

You have to be invented now
And I fall in love with your body
As I did...in the beginning
When humbly you conquered me

I sought you
Your word nailed to my ear
Among people
Among tombs and lightning
My shadow following me

Now you've returned
And even the walls are surprised
They no longer sketch my dying silhouette
Across their space
Nor my disordered hair
Healing their wounds

I took up solitude as a companion
And we walked together
Tenaciously vindicating the nights

When you returned
You were no longer the same
In silence you lamented
Your imprisonment in dead flesh

You hid the gesture
Each time you approached me
And I
Accustomed to your voice
Must leave with the passage of time
And I see you opening the ground

I travel onwards
I can see the cornfields
Among the grass with its blue blossoms

Your promise to the earth.

H.P.

Cuando Mexicali era un pueblo fantasma

Cuando Mexicali era un pueblo fantasma
no había nada sobre este páramo infinito
había sólo un manchón de casas abandonadas
flotando en el cruce de los vientos

La vida florecía a un lado del río lodoso
y bajo la luna el algodón encendía sus campos

El tren corría de Sesbania a Hechicera
y de Cuervos a Paredones

Cuando Mexicali era un pueblo fantasma
no había nada sobre este páramo finito
sólo este sol brillando en el lago
como una corona de espinas

Mi abuelo se llamó Hipólito Barrancos
y cuenta que cuando él llegó a la Colorado River Land Company
ya estaban los chinos

Dicen que llegaron por el mar
cargados de sueños polvosos

Mi abuelo llegó a estas tierras cuando San Felipe
y el Valle de la Trinidad no existían en los mapas

Cuando Mexicali era un pueblo fantasma
no había comunicación con el territorio
del Distrito Norte
México se escribía con jota
y el desierto era un abismo intransitable

Unos años después y en ocasiones
los discursos del general
Cárdenas se escuchaban en radios de onda corta

Hoy he oído contar la historia de Mexicali
en los tarros El Norteño y en El Gato Negro
y en algunos cafés de chinos

GERÓNIMO MACIEL

When Mexicali Was a Ghost Town

When Mexicali was a ghost town
there was nothing on this endless plain
except a large stain of abandoned houses
floating in the cross-winds

Life flourished next to the muddy river
and cotton burned its fields in the moonlight

The train ran from Sesbania to Hechicera
and from Cuervos to Paredones*

When Mexicali was a ghost town
there was nothing on this finite plain
only this sun shining on the lake*
like a crown of thorns

My grandfather was named Hipólito Barrancos
He tells me when he got to the Colorado River Land Company
the Chinese were already here

It's said they arrived by sea
laden with dusty dreams

My grandfather arrived before San Felipe
and Valle de Trinidad* were on the maps

When Mexicali was a ghost town
there was no communication with the territory
of the Northern District
Mexico was spelled with a "j"*
and the desert was an uncrossable abyss

A few years later sometimes one could hear
the speeches of General Cárdenas*
on short-wave radio

Now the story of Mexicali is told
in dives like El Norteño and El Gato Negro
and in some of the Chinese cafés

Hoy he visto vagar
las almas fatigadas
de quienes vencieron el desierto
abrazando la tarde
en los barcos del sueño

Cuando Mexicali era un pueblo fantasma
sólo una puerta rechinaba
empujada por el viento

Cuando Mexicali era un pueblo fantasma
sólo una carreta cargada de lunas y de soles
lloraba por sus calles polvosas.

Now I see the exhausted souls
of those who conquered the desert
wandering around
embracing the afternoon
in ships of dreams

When Mexicali was a ghost town
only a door creaked
pushed by the wind

When Mexicali was a ghost town
only a cart loaded with moons and suns
wept through the dusty streets.

Note: The agricultural development of the Mexicali area and the founding of the city were the result of the irrigation system built with imported Chinese labor by the U.S.-based Colorado Land Company in the earliest years of the 20th century; it was completed in 1905.

* *Sesbania, Hechicera, Cuervos, Paredones.* Small towns in the Mexicali area. The sense is that the train didn't stop in Mexicali.

* *the lake.* Laguna Salada, a large salt lake south and west of Mexicali.

* *San Felipe.* A fishing port and beach town 100 miles south of Mexicali.

* *Mexico was spelled with a "j."* Méjico, an archaic spelling.

* *Valle de Trinidad.* A farming community halfway between San Felipe and Ensenada.

* *Cárdenas.* Lázaro Cárdenas, President of Mexico from 1934 to 1940.

H.P.

Crepuscular

He salido a la terraza a contemplar
Los techos macerados de las casas
Por la lluvia de la tarde y las últimas
Nubes que se desgajan lentamente
Una bugambilia resplandece junto al muro
Pródiga de humedad y fortaleza
Si Turner viviera–me pregunto–con qué tonos
De luz pintaría este paisaje: enramada
De cables y antenas que el viento agita
Que la oscuridad da alcance y acompaña

La Chinesca

En estas calles el día lame sus heridas
Y los adolescentes parecen ángeles voraces
Dispuestos a proclamar una violencia
Que atosiga sus gargantas

En estos callejones la muerte baila
Con ancianos que sólo piden una botella
Para salvarse del naufragio: héroes abatidos
Por un tiempo al que ya no pertenecen

En estas noches de perpetua fiesta
Las muchachas aceptan orgasmos y caricias
Con displicente aburrimiento:
El amor aquí no es un veneno

En estas paredes abandonadas al insulto
Las palabras delimitan territorios
Dan fe de victorias callejeras y honran
El fin de guardadas virginidades

En esta soledad que es el alba
La basura se acumula entre cadáveres
Y por sus calles de luz sólo deambulan
Los inevitables   últimos fantasmas

Twilight

I've come out onto the roof to contemplate
The battered rooftops of the houses
Through the evening rain and the last
Clouds as they slowly come apart
A bougainvillea luminesces along the wall
Lavish with humidity and strength
If Turner were alive–I ask myself–in what tones
Of light would he paint this landscape: a snarl
Of cables and antennas whipped by the wind
That the darkness catches up with and accompanies.

Chinatown*

On these streets the day licks its wounds
And adolescents seem like ravenous angels
Ready to shriek out the violence
Tearing at their throats

In these alleys death dances
With old men who only ask for a bottle
To save themselves from shipwreck: heroes battered
By a time to which they no longer belong

On these nights of perpetual partying
The girls accept orgasms and caresses
With dispassionate boredom:
Around here love has no sting

In these walls abandoned to insult
Words mark off territories
Bear witness to street victories and celebrate
The end of well-kept virginities

In this solitude which is dawn
Garbage piles up among cadavers
Through streets of light stroll only
The last   inevitable ghosts

*La Chinesca. Mexicali's red-light district.

P.I., R.L.J. & G.S.

Ti Yei

Aquí comienza el mundo
Lo digo sin jactancia
Entre las casas viejas
Que suben hasta el cielo
Por una escalera interminable
De llantas de segunda

Aquí comienza el mundo
Cualquier mundo que imagines
O pretendas levantar
Con cajas de cartón
Y láminas podridas por el tiempo

Una ciudad de plástico y alambre
Una metrópolis que el sol fecunda
Que la lluvia disuelve o petrifica

Y ángeles cantan en todas las esquinas
Y demonios apuestan sus ganancias
Y trompetas farfullan querubines

Los confines

Qué luz cabe en esta luz
Hecha con la sustancia de los sueños
Cierro los ojos para que las imágenes
Invadan mis pupilas
                Para que el tiempo
Filtre las arenas movedizas
Entre sus manos descarnadas

Pocas cosas me pertenecen:
A lo más el agua que fluye
Por los canales de riego
O las palmeras que adornan el horizonte
Con languidez y parsimonia:
Pequeños tesoros escondidos
Entre la muchedumbre de los días

TJ*

The world begins here
I say it without boasting
Among old houses
That climb to the sky
On an endless ladder
Of used tires

The world begins here
Any world you can imagine
Or conjure up
Out of cardboard boxes
And sheets of tin corroding with time

City of plastic and wire
Metropolis fertilized by the sun
That the rain dissolves or turns to stone

And angels sing on all the corners
And devils wager their winnings
And cherubim sputter their trumpet calls

*TJ. Short for Tijuana. *Ti Yei* in Spanish.

Boundaries

What light fits into this light
Made of the substance of dreams
I close my eyes so that the images
Invade my pupils
So that time
May filter the sands trickling
Through their fleshless hands

Few things belong to me:
At most the water flowing
Through the irrigation canals
Or the stringy, langorous palms
That adorn the horizon:
Small hidden treasures
Amidst the mass of days

Aquí
En los confines marcados por la sombra
En la frontera ilusoria de una antigua
Civilización que crece y se despeña
Soy un hijo de nómadas que acampa
Bajo el toldo lacónico del cielo
Un hombre que viaja sin moverse
Con el tumulto de la noche a sus espaldas

Y una luna de plata
Y un sol que resplandece

Raymond Chandler, San Diego, 1958

Regatas: a lo lejos aviones que ascienden
El puente de Coronado: la historia que es
Viento y espuma y té de china: pido un café
El pasado es una partida de ajedrez
Un largo adiós que se demora: el sueño
De un tiempo ingenuo y glamoroso

Si al menos supiera a quién persigo
Cuál es mi sombra mientras la lluvia
Cae sobre el techo de madera: música
Del tiempo que sigue mis pasos y se esconde
En las esquinas como un detective mal pagado
Que porta su destino con desgana

La nostalgia es un baile a solas
Un sorbo de café entre dos aguas
Frente a un océano que sabe mi nombre
Frente a un mundo que carece de medidas
Razonables a la hora de devolver golpe
Por golpe: retribuciones: puertas falsas

Esto es lo que soy: un dibujo en tiza
Un cuerpo mal trazado en una oficina
Donde el teléfono suena sin parar
Sin que nadie conteste a su llamado: al menos
Si pudiera aclarar mi propia vida
Cuál fue el motivo de tanta sangre acumulada

Here
Within boundaries marked by the shadow
On the illusory border of an ancient
Civilization that grows and collapses
I am a son of nomads who camp
Under the laconic awning of the sky
A man who travels without moving
The turmoil of night at his back

And a silver moon
And a sun that shines

Raymond Chandler, San Diego, 1958

Regattas: in the distance planes climbing
The Coronado Bridge: history that is
Wind and spray and tea from China: I order a coffee
The past is a game of chess
A long, lingering good-bye: the dream
Of an innocent and glamorous time

If I at least knew who I follow,
That it's my shadow, while the rain
Falls on the wooden roof: music
Of the time dogging my footsteps and hiding
On street corners like a badly paid detective
Who reluctantly accepts his fate

Nostalgia is a solo dance
A sip of coffee between two options
Facing an ocean that knows my name
And a world that at the moment lacks the means
Of returning blow
For blow: retributions: back doors

This is what I am: a chalk drawing
A badly outlined body in an office
Where the telephone keeps ringing
Without anyone answering it
If at least I could explain my own life
What the the motive was
For the accumulation of so much blood

Ahora es tarde: regatas
Barcos que avanzan por la costa de oro
El tumulto del mar y el graznido
De las aves: una postal de apacible
Belleza: hoy he pagado mis deudas
Hasta la última: que la pesquisa termine

Que las damas fatales se pierdan
En la niebla de la madrugada: yo sólo creo
En el sonido inconfundible de las armas
En dar a cada quien su justa recompensa
No más: no menos: es tiempo de cerrar
El caso: de irse de juerga con la muerte

A lo lejos: en alguna parte
En algún callejón oscuro
Alguien sabe que miento

It's late now: regattas
Boats moving up the golden coast
The sea's turmoil and the squawking
Of birds: a picture post card of serene
Beauty: today I've paid my debts
To the last penny: may the investigation end

May the femmes fatales lose their way
In the morning fog: today I believe
Only in the unmistakable sound of gunfire
In giving to each his just deserts
Neither more nor less: it's time to close
The case: to go on a killing spree

Far away: somewhere
In some dark alley
Someone knows that I'm lying

H.P.

219

EDUARDO ARELLANO

Australopithecus Robustus

No te he vislumbrado en sueños como Jack London el de *Antes de Adán*
ni ando el Africa exhumando tus huesos para estudiarte,
no necesité de ello, otros lo hicieron por mí
y se los agradezco a ellos, a quienes debo el haberte conocido,
a quien hizo un filme llamado Missing Link
–el eslabón perdido–que me dio a entender,
que un primo mío,
un semejante de aspecto imaginable
por su robustez y su mirada curiosa
podría estar respirando conmigo de este mismo aire
o hablando en nuestro idioma de las cosas comunes.
Ahí te vi tal y como debiste haber sido
según han reportado los especialistas
y justo antes de desaparecer
a una edad
en la que ya no eras bestia y aún eras muy joven
para la historia.
Sólo huesos dejaste,
pura especulación para nosotros
los descendientes de aquella raza, tu contemporánea,
cuya tecnología de piedra te detuvo en el tiempo anterior al tiempo.
De un salto enorme me coloco en tu mundo,
entro en tu mente temprana y me sumerjo en tus sentidos,
soy el otro que va siguiéndote o se adelanta a ti,
el que rodea tus visiones de la vida salvaje que me haces sagrada,
aquél que acompaña tu soledad con su asombro,
tu inquietud con su tensión de ánimo,
tu vía a la desaparición con su desamparo civilizado.
Así voy siendo uno contigo
y te recupero para mí en la repentina desolación urbana
que hace a cualquier hombre sentirse el último de su especie
al lado de los miles que junto con él corren a sus lugares de trabajo,
o te hago partícipe de una época que hace acopio de todos los misterios
de los tiempos pasados y de todos los engaños también
para que tú veas–si es que tus huesos ven–por qué tu descenso
roza mi actualidad con esa hacha-talismán expropiada al enemigo
y la convoca en tu espera, en tu final espera
absoluta y elemental.

Australopithecus Robustus

I have never seen you in dreams as Jack London did in *Before Adam*
nor exhumed your bones in Africa for study,
I don't have to, others have done it for me,
and they also have my gratitude, to whom I owe our introduction,
a film called *Missing Link*
from which I have learned
that this cousin
whose likeness I could recognize
because of its strength and inquiring gaze,
would have been able to breathe the air with me
or speak of the everyday in our common language.
There I saw you as the experts say
you must have been
not long before your disappearance
when you were no longer completely animal although still very young,
at the edge of history.
You left only bones,
mere speculation for us,
descendants of that other race, your contemporaries,
whose technology of stone finished you in the time before time.
With a great leap I place myself in your world,
enter your primitive thoughts and submerge myself in your senses,
I am the other who follows or cuts ahead of you,
who circles your visions of savage life that you sanctify for me,
accompanies your solitude with his astonishment,
your uneasiness with his spiritual distress,
your road to extinction with his civilized helplessness.
I see myself one with you,
recover you for myself in the midst of the sudden urban desolation
that causes any man to feel himself the last of his species
among the thousands that run with him towards their workplaces,
or I make of you a participant in an era that collects all the mysteries
of past ages and also all the deceptions
so that you may see it's what your bones see–why it is that your fall
taps at my present life with the talismanic ax you stole from your enemy
and summons it to your last
absolute and elemental waiting place.

Amanecer de los amantes *(fragmento)*

Para vestirnos de hojas, para robar el fruto y darnos
un banquete de deliciosa prohibición, con dentada dulzura
probémonos, alma, mientras estemos vivos.

Este jardín florece contra el temporal,
labrándonos de cuerpo entero,
con la mirada en el abismo del otro,
cada vez más allá adentro de la sangre y del labio,
donde aún se oculta lo que nos rebela y nos alienta,
la fuente ciega de este minuto en que to reconoces mía
y algo nos dice que se ha rebasado el compás de los segundos.

No regreses aún a tu nombre, observa estos vestigios,
el campo que se abre ante los exhaustos cuerpos.
Prueba aún, suspendida como estás, de esta semilla
a punto de germinar para nosotros,
más allá de nosotros
en un paraíso donde nada es aparte
y un viento sin origen nos entrega su hálito.

Camino a Tecate

i
Por la ventana del ómnibus
el mundo me mira
                          cristal de lunas
oscilar de la tarde
              entre sueño y abismo
                          dibujo abandonado
a su suerte de fondo interminable
borrando mi margen como una niebla
                              como una sola y finísima nada
                                  (o como un soplo que deja
                                  en la alacena desierta
                                  su dispersión de pájaros)

Cuando lo veo traspaso
la oscuridad que soy
–huevo primitivo sellado como una piedra
por la fatal soledad de su perímetro–

from **The Lovers' Dawn**

So as to clothe ourselves in leaves, so as to steal the fruit and prepare ourselves
a banquet of delicious prohibitions, with toothy sweetness,
love, let us taste each other while we live.

This garden flowers despite weather,
carving out of our bodies
a view into each other's depths, each time further
into blood and lip where that which rebels,
that which breathes in us,
still hides, the blind well of this moment
when you know yourself mine,
and something tells us that we have exceeded the second's compass.

Wait, don't return yet to your name, observe these vestiges,
the field that opens before exhausted bodies.
Astonished as you are, taste this seed
about to sprout for us, beyond us
in a paradise where nothing is marginal
and a wind without origin delivers us its breath.

The Road to Tecate

i
Through the bus window the world
watches me
              window glass full of moons
swaying this evening
          between dream and the abyss
                    a sketch of a bottomless depth
left to its own devices, erasing
my boundaries like a fog
            like a solitary final nul
                   (or like a gust of wind that leaves
                        a scattering of birds
                    in the empty cupboard).

Crossing
the darkness of myself
–that primitive egg sealed like a stone
by the fatal solitude of its perimeter–

Lo veo destemplándose
hermosamente vibrar de sus heridas

                        lento

                                    unánime

                                                diverso

su cuerpo frente al mío
diferente en toda magnitud y materia al mío
me mira todo desde un tiempo imposible
desde otra profundidad que no adivino
y me regala toda su extranjería

En un minuto dos tres minutos
nos quedamos mirando

                        cuerpo a cuerpo
                        soledad a soledad
y en una forma desconocida
nos reconocemos
el mundo y yo
un mismo ojo

ii
Por la ventana
el mundo
su vasta gratuidad
                        su innominable faz
el terrible silencio del silencio
que desde siempre–un siempre que me mira
se libera en la piedra
                        se muestra
            en toda la materia visible de este ahora

Como presa de un súbito temblor que lo desnuda
frente a mis ojos viajantes
                        cuerpo
tendido a placer
                        oh mío mío
creándose
            saltando
al vuelo suspendido de un abrazo
                                    (la cadencia de un mar
                                        en dispersión
                                    siembra semillas de agua
                                            en la hora)

It appears excited and angry
quivering beautifully because of its wounds

                           slow

                                 unanimous

                                         diverse

its body the opposite of mine
different in every dimension and substance
watching me from an impossible age
another depth beyond my guessing
and giving me the gift of its otherness.

After a minute, two minutes, three,
we watch ourselves still

                        body to body
                        solitude to solitude

and in an unknown form
we know ourselves again,
the world and I
a single eye.

ii
Through the window
the world
its enormous gratuitousness

                           its unnameable face
the terrible silence of silence
that always–an always that watches me–
is loose in the rock

                        shows itself
             in all material things visible at this hour.

As if the prey of a sudden tremor that strips it naked
to my wandering eyes

                    body

                         oh my own

at ease
creating itself

              leaping
into the suspended flight of an embrace

                              (the rhythm of a sea
                                 spreading itself
                              sowing seeds of water
                                 at that instant).

Aquí despierto
de un sueño más antiguo que yo mismo
me dejo seducir
           Grieta del mundo
en tu vértigo
me deshabito
me lleno en el espejo de tu asombro

iii
Separado de mí
          pero continuo
por una vibración ya presentida
en el velamen último del cuerpo
lejano
      abierto
         intacto
fuera del cerco y sin conciencia apenas
de haber nacido al filo de esta luz
indómita
       sedienta
bandera de un sentido que se avienta al vacío
bucea en los espacios de la niebla
y se llena de hondura

iv
Ah la ligera travesía
por la madre tendida y protuberante
tostada por los soles
            paciente mirada desde
cada piedra y hierbajo
inmenso desamparo bajo el cielo
cúmulos para el Hades

Pero nos tenemos madre
después del mar y de las cosechas entre las estaciones
ciclos latiendo en tu corteza y mi tiempo
hacia afuera creciendo de este punto
en expansión que revienta
desde las venas del cuerpo el cúmulo del orbe

Sólo un instante dame
este trayecto de callado mareo y resplandor
en que se agita un aire que nunca mis ojos
mi piel extática la avidez de la sangre

Here I awake
from a dream older than myself
that I allow to tempt me
                          World's cleft
I empty myself
into your vertigo
and fill myself again
from the mirror of your astonishment.

iii
Separate from myself
                          but continuous
because of a stirring already at play
in my body's final sail
distant
          open
                    intact
beyond the boundary and almost unaware
of having been born at the edge of this light
untameable
                    parched
banner of a sense that expands into the void
dives into the foggy spaces
and fills itself from the deep.

iv
Ah the easy voyage
striding across the protruding mother
warmed by suns
                          the patient glance of
every rock and hummock
enormous helplessness beneath the sky,
the trove of Hades.

But mother we still possess each other
after the sea and harvests, between seasons,
cycles throbbing within your crust and this moment,
and finally exploding, expanding outwards, growing
from this dot
from the body's veins and the globe's accumulation.

Grant me this instant
this course of silence I navigate and the astonishing light
in which a breeze flutters, that my eyes
my ecstatic skin the greed of the blood

cruzarían hacia ti en caída libre
                          estanque
de mi exterioridad en que me baño

¿y si ahogándome ahí acaso diera
                          con el devenir
de mi sangre
con el hueso en la roca
y la desnuda desnudez de mi piel bajo el sol del principio?

Ah madre en que me miro viajante de la tarde
olas de tierra y de silencio ¿ya duermes? tierna
como virgen impúdica
                    inocente
                              satisfecha
ante tu propia carne constatada en el cabo
de mi pupila tu espejo más efímero
te muestras
            y estalla tu plenitud en mi conciencia

v
Polvo y fragancia
sales y polen
soledad y círculos retóricos en que se luce el viento
basuras ramas semillas
viajan tus nombres por tus faldas y llanos
marea imperceptible podría caminarte
hacer que con tu aliento me acaricies la greña
bandolear por las distancias agreste flor del planeta
modalidad del universo
sueño creado
ahí estás
me has mirado y ahora
tu nombre de paisaje no te salva de mis manos
de mi corazón hambreado en las distancias inundado
por la marea más vasta que un cuerpo no resista

Sólo déjame ver
tu ojo en el abismo

never drift in free fall towards you
                                    pool
of my outsidedness in which I bathe,

and if I were to drown there would I find perhaps
                                                my blood's
history and in the rock
my bones and the sheer
nakedness of my skin beneath the first sun?

Oh mother in whom I watch myself, evening traveler,
waves of the earth and silence, do you sleep? soft
as a flirtatious virgin
                        innocent
                                self-satisfied
before your assembled flesh, in the end
to my eye, your still more ephemeral mirror,
you show yourself
                    and burst your fullness into my awareness.

v
Dust and fragrance
salts and pollen
solitude and circles of rhetoric in which the brilliance of the wind shines forth
filth tree-limbs seeds
travel your names across your foothills and prairies,
imperceptible tide, I could make my way across you
causing your breath to smooth my disordered hair
to rampage across great distances, the rough flower of the planet
modality of the universe
a dream created
you are here
you have watched me,
your landscape name won't save you from my hands
or from my heart hungering in the distance, flooded
by a tide too large for flesh to resist.

Only let me see
your eye in the abyss.

                                                            M.W.

Elegía frente al mar

a Genaro Saúl Reyes

Bajo esta soledad he construido mi casa,
he llenado mis noches con la rabia del océano
y me he puesto a contar las heridas de mi cuerpo.
En esta casa de cuartos vacíos
donde las palomas son apenas un recuerdo
contemplo el cadáver de mis días,
la ruina polvorienta de mis sueños.
Fui el náufrago que imaginó llegar a tierra,
el homicida que esperó la presencia de la víctima;
la víctima que nunca conoció al verdugo.
Este día el remordimiento crece,
es la sombra que cubre las paredes de la casa,
el silencio agudo que perfora mis oídos.
Este día soy la sucia mañana que lo cubre todo,
el mar encabritado que inunda la sonrisa de los niños,
el hombre de la playa que camina contra el viento.
Soy el miedo que perfora el cuerpo de la tarde,
el llanto de las mujeres que alimentaron mi deseo,
aquél que no vuelve la mirada atrás para encontrarse.
No sacudo el árbol para que la desesperación caiga,
para que el fruto ya maduro se pudra entre mis piernas
y el grito surja a romper la calma de la muerte.
No, me quedo sentado a contemplar la noche,
a esperar los fantasmas que pueblan mi vida,
a cerrar las puertas, a clausurar las ventanas.
Me quedo en esta casa de habitaciones vacías.

"He visto a la corneja volar..."

He visto a la corneja volar siete veces sobre mi cabeza
y al caballo de la bruja merodear las fronteras del reino.
Mi sueño se ha poblado de serpientes y dragones,
he descubierto que me engañas con el mejor de mis espadas.
Ahora sé que la batalla no será en Worms ni en Wichester, como se había
        anunciado,
sino aquí, en los jardines de mi casa, en los pasillos,
en la terrible oscuridad de mi alcoba.

Elegy Facing the Sea

for Genaro Saúl Reyes

Beneath this loneliness I have built my house,
filled my nights with the ocean's fury
and set myself to count my body's wounds.
In this house of empty rooms
where doves are but a memory
I contemplate the corpse of my days,
the dusty ruin of my dreams.
I was the shipwrecked sailor who imagined reaching land,
the murderer who waited for his victim;
the victim who never knew his executioner.
Today remorse grows,
it is the shadow covering the walls of the house,
the sharp silence that pierces my ears.
Today I am the filthy morning that covers everything,
the angry sea that drowns the smiles of children,
the man on the beach walking into the wind.
I am the fear piercing the afternoon's body,
the cries of women who fed my desires,
I am he who never looks back to find himself.
I don't shake the tree so that hopelessness may fall,
the ripe fruit rot between my legs
and a shout burst forth to break death's calm.
Instead, I sit contemplating the night,
waiting for the ghosts that fill my life,
closing the doors, shuttering the windows.
I remain in this house of empty rooms.

"I've seen the crow fly..."

I've seen the crow fly over my head seven times
and the witch's horse plundering my kingdom's borders.
My sleep has been filled with serpents and dragons,
I have discovered that you've betrayed me with the best of my young
    swordsmen.
I now know despite the foretelling that the battle will not be at Worms or Win-
    chester,
but here, in the gardens of my house, in the passageways,
in the terrible darkness of my room.

A Clodia

Los ojos azules de los muertos vigilan desde lo alto de la noche.
Las aguas del Egeo, quietas, a la orilla de la playa;
y las mujeres, desnudas, en la oscuridad de su deseo.
Con octubre han llegado los hombres de corazón solitario,
han llegado a instalar sus tiendas, sus madejas de actos fallidos.
El cielo se tiñe con el color de estas calles, con el color de esta ciudad adormecida,
mientras las muchachas deambulan, de aquí para allá, con la tristeza de sus lunas
      perdidas.
Son el abandono, la rapiña y la usura el platillo fuerte de esta mesa,
la música que deleita a nuestro oído y marca el compás de los danzantes,
la tregua que marchita la flor de la victoria, y la herrumbre que muerde el filo de
      la espada.
Estamos aquí, en el banquete, saboreando los placeres de la carne,
gozando de los besos de Clodia y sus hijastras,
rodeados de mancebos de mirada hueca.
Pero es el mar quien nos entrega su tributo de cadáveres y demonios hambrientos,
es él
el que araña las paredes, el que abre las puertas e inunda la noche,
el de los jardines desolados; el asesino que recorre los cuartos de la casa.
No hay quien pueda detener su paso, su fuerte batir de alas encendidas,
ni quien cubra la herida que deja el navajazo de su vuelo.
El mar es, en realidad, el silencio que separa nuestros cuerpos.
. . .
El salón ha quedado vacío, sólo se oye el viento entre las hojas,
el canto lejano de las sirenas, y el lamento, apenas quedo, de los marineros
      perdidos.
Está amaneciendo en Mitilene bajo un cielo gris de lluvia y ángeles;
la ciudad se puebla de gente ordinaria, de gritos y extranjeros.
Clodia, te he vuelto a amar en esta ciudad de bárbaros.

En mañanas como ésta

He sentido la tristeza en tus ojos,
la luz de mi casa apagada a todas horas,
el jardín que duerme junto a tu olvido.
En mañanas como ésta, cuando miro fijamente el mar,
tu rostro desaparece de la ventana,
te empiezo a perder en la brillantez salada de la espuma.
Te sé sobre la arena envuelta en una soledad más que violenta,
en una madrugada de hombres solos y de playas desiertas.

To Clodia

From night's precipice the blue eyes of the dead keep watch.
The waters of the Aegean, calm, at the edge of the beach,
the women, naked, in the obscurity of their desires.
With October the lone-hearted men have arrived,
they have arrived to pitch their tents, their piles of vain efforts.
The sky is dyed the color of these streets, the color of this sleeping city,
while the girls wander, aimless, carrying the sadness of their lost moons.
Abandonment, theft, and usury are this table's main dish,
the music that delights the ear and sets the beat for the dancers,
the truce that withers victory's flower, and the rust that spoils the sword's edge.
Here we are, at the feast, savoring the pleasures of the flesh,
relishing Clodia and her stepdaughters' kisses,
surrounded by youths with empty stares.
But it's the sea that offers us its tribute of cadavers and hungry demons,
the sea
that scratches at the walls, that opens doors and floods the night
of disconsolate gardens; the murderer stalking the rooms of the house.
No one can stop it, the powerful beating of its flaming wings,
no one to bandage the wound left by the slash of its flight.
In truth, the sea is the silence that separates our bodies.
. . .
The room has remained empty, the wind in the leaves is the only sound,
the distant song of the sirens, and the almost imperceptible lament of lost
            sailors.
At daybreak in Mitylene beneath a sky gray with rain and angels
the town fills with ordinary people, shouts, and foreigners.
Clodia, I have come to love you again in this city of barbarians.

On Mornings like These

I have felt the sadness in your eyes,
the light in my house turned off all the time,
the garden that sleeps next to your oblivion.
On mornings like these when I stare at the sea,
your face disappears from the window,
I begin to lose you in the foam's salty brilliance.
I know you are on the sand wrapped in a more than violent aloneness
in a morning of solitary men and deserted beaches.

En mañanas como ésta
en que el amanecer no significa gran cosa
tu cuerpo invade mi cuerpo como la marea cansada de mojar la misma piedra.

Tijuana

a Roberto Castillo Udiarte

Esta ciudad nos duele como una espina en la garganta,
como el hombre que pasa con el miedo dibujado en el rostro.
Nos duele como el amor y sus ejércitos,
como los ángeles irremediablemente perdidos.
Es la mujer que nos desnuda frente al mar,
la lluvia de marzo y las dos tormentas del verano,
el golpe que nos hace abrir los ojos; el beso que nos cierra los labios.
Es el monumento de la infamia y del rencor,
el perro que nos asustaba cuando volvíamos del colegio,
el mismo que a veces vemos en la mirada del hombre más próximo.
Esta ciudad se levanta sobre el sudor y los sueños de nuestros padres,
sobre el cuerpo violado de la muchacha y la mano siempre dispuesta del asesino.
Crece como el odio, como el polvo y la rabia,
como un mar encabronado que se te escapa de las manos.
Es la mujer que pasó sin verte, la que no te recuerda,
esa que constantemente disfrazas, pero a quien siempre le escribes tus versos.

On mornings like these
in which the dawn doesn't mean much
your body invades my body like a tide tired of lapping the same stone.

Tijuana

for Roberto Castillo Udiarte

This city wounds like a fishbone stuck in our throats,
like the man passing by with fear written all over his face.
She wounds us like love and its armies,
like hopelessly lost angels.
She's the woman who strips us naked at the shore,
the rains of March and Summer's two storms,
the slap forcing our eyes open; the kiss that closes our lips.
She's infamy and rancor's monument,
the dog that frightened us on the way home from school,
the one we sometimes see in the stare of the man beside us.
This town is built upon the sweat and dreams of our parents,
over a girl's raped body and the murderer's always ready hand.
She grows like hate, like dust and rage,
like an angry sea that slips through your fingers.
She's the woman who walked right by without seeing you, who doesn't
        remember you,
the woman you always disguise, for whom you write your verses.

S.B.

San Andrés Cohamiata

Descubrí tu cuerpo de roca cuando el bosque se vestía de silencio. Tú me llamaste. Convocaste a tus hijos a trascender los mares de la memoria; al lugar donde las palabras nacen del sueño y el canto se hace perpetuo. Y he venido a danzar al ritmo del corazón de la tierra, al gran templo donde la danza se llama viento y mi cuerpo nube. Voy desnuda envuelta en el halo pertinaz de las palabras, para saber la pregunta que murmuran los copos de los árboles:
¿quién la de la sombra?
Cuando sea cómplice del sueño de la fronda y sienta que la Sierra Madre escucha mis pasos, al crujir de las hojas, al ladrido de los perros, sabré cómo prenderle fuego a la pregunta. ¡Solo tú, madre, puedes darme la sangre, la magia, el lenguaje, los signos que contengan mi nombre! Mi único alimento es tu raíz. El germen de este viento que aligera mis pasos. La savia de estos días que alumbran mis pupilas.

El poeta

El poeta no le teme a la nada.
El va con su paso descalzo escudriñando sombras, alcanza la luna y no toca su luz sino la sal. Vuelve el canto amargo, dulce,
el follaje del alma en un saber de ausencias. Oficiante que mira a lo lejos lo invisible, huésped de la fuente que es espejismo y sortilegio. Primitivo que descubrió el fuego y que le niegan.

El poeta no le teme a la nada ni a los sueños.

Flor de agua

Nada hay qué temer
pues esa flor luminosa que nace
en mis entrañas cuando entras en mí.
Es mi casa
es mi ciencia
es mi cielo.

San Andrés Cohamiata

When the forest was clothed in silence I found your stone body. You summoned me. You gathered your sons to call forth the seas of memory where words are born of dreams and song becomes eternal. And I've come to dance to the rhythm of the earth's heartbeat, to the great temple where dance is called wind and my body cloud. I go forth naked wrapped in the halo that belongs to words, so as to know the question that treetops murmur:
who belongs to the shadow?
When I have become companion to the dream of the foliage, knowing that the Sierra Madre hears my footsteps as I pass through the leaves and the dogs bark, then will I know how to set that question on fire. Only you, mother, can give me blood, magic, language, the signs that contain my name! Your root is my only nourishment. The seed of this wind that speeds my footsteps. The sap of these days that enflame my eyes.

The Poet

The poet is not afraid of nothingness.
Barefoot, he scrutinizes shadows, he reaches the moon not for its light but to touch its salt. The bitter, sweet, song returns,
the foliage of the soul in the knowledge of absence. Celebrant who sees the invisible from afar, guest of the fountain which is both mirror and sorcery. The primitive who discovered fire and was disowned.

The poet fears neither nothingness nor dreams.

Flower of Water

You have nothing to fear
from the luminous flower that is born
within me when you enter me.
It is my house
my science
my sky.

H.P.

Mujer de sal *(fragmentos)*

I

A la profundidad del mar
voy, madre.
En tus manos dejaré el molde de mi rostro,
litorales donde se fundan mis riberas
con las tuyas,
los cristalinos de mis ojos para verme al fin
en tus mareas.
Prestadme tu penacho de quetzal
olas marinas para mi falda
pulseras de caracoles y cascabeles
adornen mis pies
a cambio de esta ofrenda.
Que mis pasos por escalinatas y balcones
entonen un canto que las aves lleven
a los grandes señores de la luz salada
a los oídos de Neptuno
antes de que amanezca.

II

Me desvisto del traje de abandono
que iluminan las llamas de Sodoma.
La sal de mis lágrimas
me vestirá un río de luciérnagas,
tras el umbral sembrado de lirios y guirnaldas.
Por ti sea que reciba la luz de la montaña,
frente a tu vestido azul turquesa,
cuando mañana,
salga el sol solito.

from **Woman of Salt**

I

Mother I voyage
to the depths of the sea
to leave in your hands the cast of my face,
coastlines where my shores and yours are made,
the lenses of my eyes
seeing me in your tides at last.
Lend me your quetzal feather,
waves of the sea for my skirt,
anklets of snailshells and bells
adorning my feet
in exchange for this offering.
May my steps on staircase and balcony
intone a song that the birds carry
to the great lords of salty light,
reaching
the ears of Neptune
before he awaken.

II

I strip off the clothes of abandonment
that the flames of Sodom illuminate.
The salt of my tears
will clothe me in a river of glow-worms
beyond the threshold sown with lilies and garlands.
Thanks to your power I receive the mountain light
here, before your turquoise dress
when in the morning
the solitary sun rises.

M.W.

Para empezar

para Rubén

En la mañana escribí tu nombre
con mal tiempo y sin fecha.

El cielo es el mismo,
las ventanas no mienten.

De puntillas ando por la casa
rehaciendo tu imagen
en las cosas que no me pertenecen.

Nadie en casa te recuerda,
¿Quién fuiste?

En el espejo del baño
aún húmedo, gotoso e ilegible
tu nombre se evapora.

Epígrafe

Sí, ya sé
porque lo has dicho antes
que no es que me ames
que sencillamente soy la mosca
cautiva en tu cabeza
de ventanas cerradas

Sin agradarme del todo la imagen
te dejo por lo pronto creer que es cierto

To Begin

for Rubén

In the morning I wrote your name,
wrong time, no date.

The sky's the same,
windows don't lie.

On tiptoe I walk through the house
remaking your image
out of things not mine.

Nobody at home remembers you.
Who were you?

In the fog on the bathroom mirror,
dripping, illegible,
your name fades away.

Epigraph

Yes, I know
because you've told me before
it's not that you love me
I am simply the fly
trapped by the closed windows
inside your head.

Although I'm not crazy about the image
I'll let you believe it for now

S.B.

El fantasma del cine Curto

Baja del camión
chupa su cigarro
tose, escupe miasmas
tiene mañas populares este cabrón.

Viene del barrio
de los limbos de interés social
es un fantasma con los bolsillos rotos.

Pasa por la iglesia
compra semillas
las abre con su lengua pecaminosa
mastica los minutos
mira las piernas, mira los culitos
de las vírgenes que vienen a excitar a Dios.

Son las cinco de la tarde
hora hueca
la góndola de los boletos sigue vacía
el hombre de la puerta tampoco está.

El Fantasma del cine Curto viene del jale
es un peón de la chinga asalariada
su rostro es la protesta muda
sus manos, chalanes sin libertad
cumple el ritual de la cartelera:
"Hoy no habrá función en este cine".

El Fantasma es un adolescente nervioso
lleva sobre su espalda la carga moral de un milenio
entrega su boleto y entra a la sala
no se detiene a comprar palomitas
fruta prohibida es la atracción.

El Fantasma se sienta en la butaca cueruda
viene solo, lo acompaña su mujer
trae a su vieja pa' que aprenda posiciones
anda con una ruca que le gusta rebanar
lee basura bajo el letrero de "escape"
se echa una siesta porque a eso vino.

The Phantom of the Curto Cinema*

He gets off the bus
sucks his cigarette
coughs, spits out miasmas:
this fool has lousy manners.

He comes from the barrio
from an entry-level limbo
a phantom with ripped pockets.

He passes the church
buys sunflower seeds
opens them with his lecherous tongue
chews away the minutes
ogles the legs and asses
of virgins here to turn God on.

It's five in the afternoon
the hollow hour
the ticket booth still shut
the doorman missing.

The Phantom of the Curto Cinema arrives from work
a fucked-over wage-slave
his face a mute protest
his hands, bound apprentices,
he performs the billboard ritual:
"No show today."

The Phantom is a jumpy kid
toting the millennium's moral weight
he turns in his ticket and enters the theater
no popcorn for him
forbidden fruit's what he's here for.

The Phantom sits down on the leather seat
he comes alone, his woman comes with him,
he brings his woman so she can learn new tricks
he comes with a broad who likes to suck
he reads trash under the exit sign
takes a nap because that's what he came for.

El Fantasma es el dandy engominado
es el mecánico de fierros sin nada qué componer
es el agricultor del valle que nomás pasaba por el pueblo
es el lobo urbano que suele congalear.

La película es un churro o una obra maestra
todo depende del ojo que la ve.
El Fantasma es una ficha metido en problemas
el Fantasma es un artistete en busca de inspiración
(nalgas, tetas y panochas
pieles a flor de luz
besos y caricias de celuloide importado
todas las metáforas para el público albur:
"ya tienes películas en el Curto").

El Fantasma es un leandro cazador de mayatones
los sigue al baño o los espera ahí
tiene ojos de insecto, de babuino suplicante
le gusta la verga y le gusta mirar
es el señor del retrete oloroso a esmegma
aquél que todos miran con cierta repulsión
el ambivalente sayo que vive dos vidas
anda buscando aquí su verdadero yo.

El Fantasma es un actor de apellido siciliano
comparte la pantalla con un trasvestí francés
es el amante de la Fenech o la Mutti
alcalde culero en la prisión femenil
sadomasoquista con swástica, *dildo* y vibrador
cinemaescópica es su carne
jadea en Magnavox
pretende venirse cuando lo indica el script.

The End

Vuela sobre el cine abandonado
un viento caliente que enchina los genitales
remolinos de basura danzan entre las rejas
el reloj de neón marca las diez.
Es hora de cerrar
hora de irse
regresar sobre los pasos que lo trajeron aquí
el hombre de la puerta está cansado
la mujer de las golosinas ya no vende hot-dogs.

The Phantom is a greasy dandy
a tool mechanic with nothing to fix
a farmer from the valley who's just passing through
a city wolf with a taste for whores.

The movie's a dog or a masterpiece
depending on how you see it.
The Phantom is a two-timer in trouble
the Phantom is an artiste looking for inspiration
(ass, tits, cunts,
highlighted light-deep flesh,
caresses and kisses of imported celluloid
all metaphors for the public joke:
"He's got hairs on it").

The Phantom is a meat-hunting fag
he follows them to the bathroom or waylays them there
he has insect eyes, eyes of a begging baboon
he likes cock and he likes to watch
he's the lord of the toilet stinking of smegma
whom all regard with a certain revulsion
an ambivalent character who lives two lives
and comes here looking for his true self.

The Phantom is an actor with a Sicilian name
he shares the screen with a French transvestite
he's Fenech's or Mutti's lover*
ass-kicking warden of a women's prison
sadomasochist with swastika, dildo, and vibrator
his flesh is Cinemascope
he moans in Magnavox
he fakes it whenever the script says.

The End

A hot wind that curls the genitals
blows over the abandoned theater
eddies of trash dance among the grates
the neon clock says ten.
It's closing time
time to leave
retrace the footsteps that brought him here
the doorman is tired
and the woman isn't selling hot dogs any more.

El Fantasma del cine Curto regresa a la calle
siente la descompresión
afuera la vida es real en demasía
(nadie reza ya en la Catedral)
la ciudad bosteza y el Fantasma se va por donde vino
regresa al barrio
se mete a la cantina
se lo traga un camión.

Pasaporte caliente fuera del mundo frío
mañana otra película no rodará;
sólo queda chupar el clavo de la rutina
fantasmear por las calles y la sala de cine
junto a otros que mascan un chicle del mismo sabor
soñar por unas horas que la soledad no existe
que el amor se carnaliza aunque no se pueda tocar
sentirse satisfecho (fantasmalmente)
quitarle a la vida su poco de muerte
esperar en una esquina la próxima función.

The Phantom of the Curto Cinema returns to the street
feels the decompression
life is realer than real outside
(no one prays in the cathedral any more)
the city yawns and the Phantom goes back where he came from
returns to the barrio
plunges into a dive
a bus swallows him.

Steamy passport out of the cold world
another movie will not play tomorrow
all that remains is to chew on the bone of routine
go phantoming through the streets and the movie house
with others who eat the same shit
dream for a while that there's no such thing as solitude
that love becomes flesh even if you can't touch it
feel phantom satisfaction
his bit of death squeezed out of life
and hang out on a corner until the next show.

*Curto Cinema. One of the oldest theaters in Mexicali. It closed in 1988.

*Fenech, Mutti. Edwige Fenech, Ornella Mutti, erotic stars of the 70s and 80s.

H.P.

"Rayo..."

RAYO
Súbita fractura
en el muro absorto de la noche.

PAPALOTE
Volarlo es pescar en el cielo.

LLUVIA
Restos dc mar perdido,
en su regazo la melancolía crece.

MÚSICΛ
Cerámicas evanescentes
trepando el corazón de las horas.

ÁRBOLES
Correr tras ellos es inútil,
son inalcanzables.

DANZA
No hay movimiento sobre el mundo,
sólo abismo en la raíz del cuerpo.

SUEÑO
Se soltó el péndulo del reloj
y se fue corriendo.

NIEBLA
Agua sonámbula,
caen certezas de la mirada.

DESTINO
Tras la puerta, el azar:
quemar las naves, penetrar el día.

AVIONES
En temporada de patos
se les ve caer con frecuencia.

DESEO
Crees conquistar,
pero en verdad sucumbes.

"Lightning..."

LIGHTNING
A sudden fracture
in the distracted wall of night.

KITE
To fly it is to fish in the sky.

RAIN
Remains of the lost sea,
Melancholy grows in its lap.

MUSIC
Evanescent ceramics
climbing the heart of the hours.

TREES
Running after them is futile,
they're unreachable.

DANCE
There's no movement upon the earth,
only the abyss at the body's root.

DREAM
The clock's pendulum broke free
and ran away.

MIST
Water sleepwalks
certainties of the gaze fade.

DESTINY
Through the door, chance:
to burn the ships, to penetrate the day.

AIRPLANES
One often sees them falling
in duck season.

DESIRE
You believe you can conquer,
but in truth you succumb.

MAGRITTE
Pájaros sembrados al margen del río,
legiones de agua entre flores aladas.

MILAGRO
Bajo las vías del tren
los durmientes despiertan.

MEXICALI
Ante la soberbia del sol,
el orgullo de la resistencia.

OLVIDO
El dolor del parto,
la violencia del desierto.

MAGRITTE
Birds sown along the riverbanks,
watery legions among wingèd flowers.

MIRACLE
Under the train tracks
the sleepers awaken.

MEXICALI
The pride of resisting
the sun's arrogance.

FORGETFULNESS
The pain of birth,
the desert's violence.

H.P.

(a los muertos)

I

Fino cliente,
que paga bien y no debe,
soy; patrona muerte:
¡cómo has subido el precio del tequila,
de tu robusta carne, de tu café caliente!

(Vasto corazón abierto que te dí,
que te he dado,
que poco a poco recupero, para luego entregarlo).

La luz de tu pupila ¡cómo sube!
muerte, de tanto amar acomplejada.

¡Muérdeme un poco, morena!
deja tu marca cruel sobre mi espalda

II

Alta luna en la noche de Tijuana,
oronda, gorda, descarada.
Presumida ciudad:
si la miras que baja para buscar mi esquina,
si se acurruca–leve–bajo el alero de mi casa,
si desciende hasta el mar,
si se mete en mi cama y mete el pie en el agua,
ciudad, no te acongojes,
no quieras deslumbrarla,
no me quieras quitar esta cuchilla que abre la noche en dos,
que se desangra oronda, gorda, descarada,
alta luna en la noche de Tijuana.

ALFONSO GARCÍA CORTEZ

(to the dead)

I
A good customer,
I pay well and I'm
debt-free, landlady death:
how you've raised the price of tequila,
your tough meat, and your hot coffee!

(Huge open heart that I gave you,
that I go on giving you,
that little by little I'm getting back, to give away again).

How the light of your eye increases,
death, from so much complicated loving!

Bite me a little, my brown one,
leave your cruel mark on my shoulder.

II
Moon high in the Tijuana night,
round, fat, shameless.
Conceited city,
if you see it come down to look for my corner,
if it's huddled–a whisp–beneath the eaves of my house,
if it goes down to the sea,
if it gets into my bed and puts its foot in the water,
don't be distressed, city,
you don't want to dazzle it,
don't want to take from me this knife that cuts the night in two,
that round, fat, shameless, it may bleed
moon high in the Tijuana night.

H.P.

Mar, fin de la tierra

Hablar, déjame hablar
¿Qué hacemos aquí,
adoloridos de niebla al filo del reino
apedreando autos, de un perro a otro
camino a las muchachas del bar?

La colina se ha oscurecido como un hueco
y el sol ya es sólo una botella rota que brilla
sus fragmentos cn cl aceite del puerto

Hablar, déjame hablar
¿Qué hacemos ahora aquí,
ceremoniando la tristeza
de la cabeza del atún desprendida en la sanguaza?

Pescó así el anzuelo las uñas ardidas de la sal
y el muelle dejó al descubierto las costillas de su muladar
desastre

El marinero ocultó sus entrañas en el orgullo
y borracho aprendió el dolor de ser extranjero
en su natal colonia y en el río de su calle

Naufragó la gaviota un abstracto de heces en el tablón

La mujer del puesto dijo mi padre alguna vez quiso
hablar de amor conmigo...y sonrió.

Los niños en el Mirador no suspendieron sus delfines de
luna ni sus gritos de circunstancia almirante

Exiliada del vaivén, la barca dejó caer cáscaras de pintura
Y en el milagro del Mercado Negro el loco público
bajó el rostro al cielo sepultado del atracadero
y farfulló: Hablar, déjame hablar
     El fin de la tierra es el mar

               el mar

                  el mar...

The Sea, Land's End

Speak, let me speak
What are we doing here,
afflicted with fog at the edge of the kingdom
throwing rocks at cars, approaching girls at the bar
like dogs meeting dogs?

The hill has become as dark as a mine
the sun no more than a broken bottle
polishing its shards in the oil of the port

Speak, let me speak
What are we doing here,
making a ritual of the sadness
of the decapitated head of a tuna floating in its own gore?

That's how the hook caught fingernails, the wound burning with salt,
and the wharf revealed the ribs of its disastrous
filth

Out of pride the sailor hid his feelings;
drunk he learned the pain of becoming a stranger
to his own neighborhood, to the river of his street

Onto the deck the gull sank an abstraction of shit

The woman selling fish said that once my father
had tried to talk to her of love...and she smiled.

The children at El Mirador* didn't suspend their moon dolphins
nor those shouts like an admiral's orders

Exiled from the tides, the boat dropped husks of paint
And in the miracle of the Black Market the street crazy
inclined his face to the buried sky of the landing
and sputtered: Speak, let me speak
                Land's end is the sea

                        the sea

                                the sea...

*El Mirador. A cliff-top scenic lookout.
*Black Market. Ensenada's shorefront fishmarket.

A.P.

El paraguas del espejo

Somos laberinto de olas ordenadas, anteriores al tiempo y la palabra
Somos larga busca; sueño entretejido en casi una idea

por el mar que es un pájaro dormido que canta
por el mar que es un templo de ríos que descansan
por el mar que es un ángel marinero que se esfuma
por el mar que es un triste hombre que predica
por el mar que es un corazón de caminos que se orillan
por el mar que es un barco de alarmas que se elevan
por el mar que es un roca diminuta que se extiende
por el mar que es una flor despavorida que perdona
por el mar que es un cielo acariciado que se imagina
por el mar que es una lenta jirafa que se obsequia
por el mar que es una espesa valentía que no tiembla
por el mar que es una galaxia roja que se descarga
por el mar que es una mujer solitaria que se busca
por el mar que es un siglo multiplicado por las olas
por el mar que es un niño desconocido que se posesiona
por el mar que es un listón inmóvil por las fuentes
por el mar que es una oración derramada por un gato
por el mar que es un guerrero encarcelado en su crimen
por el mar que es un látigo movido por la dicha
por el mar que es un ojo viril que no reprime sus alegrías
por el mar que es un guante lívido que dobla su nieve
por el mar que es una isla rodeada de tierras
por el mar que es una vieja osamenta de lumbre
por el mar que es un hombre manoseado por escombros
por el mar que es un perfume de sombras argentinas
por el mar que es un llano de hundimientos necesarios
por el mar que es una fiebre picoteada por los pasos
por el mar que es una cruz divertida en el cielo
por el mar que es un muerto que flota entre diamantes
por el mar que es una tiniebla borrada por silencios
por el mar que es un simulacro de amantes en las redes
por el mar que es una nube de vidrios por el cuello
por el mar que es un paraguas frente a los espejos
por el mar que es un imán de chispas en verano
por el mar que es un abrazo de puñales rojos en lo blanco
por el mar que es un arte de pañuelos en el ojo
por el mar que es un decorado de vientres y de alas
por el mar que es salitre de cebras sollozando por las nubes

The Mirror's Umbrella

We're a labyrinth of ordered waves, prior to time and the word
We're a long search; a dream almost woven into an idea by the sea

that's a sleeping bird singing
that's a temple of resting rivers
that's a marine angel disappearing
that's a sad man who preaches
that's a heart of roads at its shore
that's a boat full of uppity alarms
that's a tiny rock stretching out
that's a terrified flower that pardons
that's a cherished imagined sky
that's a slow giraffe that one flatters
that's a thick valor that trembles not
that's a bursting red galaxy
that's a solitary woman who is sought after
that's a century multiplied by waves
that's an unknown boy who is yielded up
that's a ribbon immobile in fountains
that's a prayer poured forth by a cat
that's a warrior incarcerated in his crime
that's a lash moved by luck
that's a virile eye whose joy is untrammelled
that's a livid glove folding snow
that's an island surrounded by lands
that's an old skeleton of fire
that's a man pawed at by mackerel
that's a fragrance of silver shadows
that's a prairie of necessary cave-ins
that's a fever pecked at by footsteps
that's a cross entertained in the sky
that's a corpse floating among diamonds
that's darkness erased by silences
that's the appearance of lovers in the nets
that's a cloud of glass through the neck
that's an umbrella in front of mirrors
that's a magnet of sparks in summer
that's an embrace of red daggers on white
that's a trick of scarves in the eye
that's a décor of wombs and wings
that's saltpeter of zebras sobbing in the clouds

por el mar que es harina de perla ordenada en un gis
por el mar que es sexo diminuto en su oriental paciencia
por el mar que es estrella polar en un envase roto
por el mar que es silla turca en el pensamiento
por el mar que es molusco invisible del calor
por el mar que es hueco a través del día
por el mar que es inventario de asombros
por el mar que es desordenada es
por el mar que es
por el mar
por él
por
po
p

that's flour of pearl made up as chalk
that's a minute penis in its oriental patience
that's a polar star in a broken container
that's a Turkish chair in thought
that's an invisible mollusk of heat
that's a hollow in the day
that's an inventory of surprises
that's confused that's
that's
that
tha
th
t

H.P.

Aviso clasificado

Deje de fumar en 22 minutos
con el poder de su mente
puede lograrlo todo:
deje la pasión
los estados depresivos
las malas vibraciones   las putas
las ideologías extranjeras   la cerveza
los poetas malditos
las calles transitadas
le garantizamos que no escribirá
un solo poema por el resto de sus días
y si no es así
le devolvemos su dinero.

Shit blues

Sálvese quien pueda de ser una mierda
deje la puerta abierta
que se lo coman los perros
póngale escalera contra incendio a su vida
orille sus penas al borde de una aspirina
coleccione navajas de afeitar usadas
y no olvide sobre todo
pedirle consejo al bote de la basura.

Blues final

Estoy a punto de perder el corazón
lo deje en la casa de empeño
una noche que necesitaba ser otro.

Want Ad

Stop smoking in 22 minutes
with the power of your mind
you can do it all:
stop passion
depression
bad vibrations   whores
foreign ideologies beer
doomed poets
busy streets
we guarantee you won't write
a single poem for the rest of your days
if not
we'll return your money.

Shit Blues

Let he who can save himself
from being a piece of shit
leave the door open
may the dogs eat him
put up a fire escape against
the conflagration of his life
trim his sorrows at the edge of an aspirin
collect used razor blades
and above all don't forget
to ask advice of the garbage can

Final Blues

I'm about to lose my heart
I left it in the pawnshop
one night when I needed to be someone else.

H.P.

Perpetuo suicidio

Debo ponerme una máscara azul
y sentir un barco en las entrañas,
pelar una naranja a carcajadas
mientras el espejo vomita margaritas
sobre la alfombra casi eterna de un suspiro,
lavar mis manos de agosto
para poder ser pájaro,
para sentirme todo un espuma
o ahogar en un ósculo la maternidad de mis uñas,
como si el viento supiera la respuesta
de lo que nunca fue,
como si tu cuerpo fuera una bandera de lluvia
sostenida por diez obscuros cuellos de cisne,
o como si de pronto
la diferencia entre la vida y la muerte
estuviese sostenida en la ventana de este sueño,
como si la muerte germinara en tu vagina tibia
y sólo una lágrima de distancia
hubiese entre tú y yo:
incapaces de volvernos uno solo en la mañana
que toda enverdecida de guitarras
tocará tu pecho en una huérfana rosa,
o una navaja de viento;
tengo que desnudarme otra vez ante ti
y cantar otra vez mi canción de otoño
para ser de nuevo libre,
y morir de nuevo en algún reloj
que no se obscurezca con mi sangre de gaviota.

Perpetual Suicide

I wear a blue mask
and I carry a ship within me,
helpless with laughter I peel an orange
while the mirror regurgitates daisies
onto the almost endless carpet of sighs,
washing August from my hands
so as to become a bird,
so as to feel myself completely foam
so as to drown the motherhood of my fingernails in a kiss,
as if the wind knew the answer
to what never was,
as if your body were a flag of rain
held aloft by the necks of ten dark swans,
or as if suddenly
the difference between life and death
were held aloft in the window of this dream,
death germinating in your warm vagina
and only a distant tear
between us:
unable to blend into one in the morning
that, made verdant by guitars,
will touch your breast within an orphaned rose
or a knifeblade of wind;
once more must I make myself naked before you
and sing once more my autumn song
so as to be newly free,
and to die again within a clock
undarkened by my seagull's blood.

                                                                    H.P.

A orillas de la montaña

a Víctor Soto Ferrel

Cierta vez desperté ante la mirada silenciosa de un árbol
en la brisa de un día que comenzaba.
Su tronco era el cauce rebosante de un principio
que estremecía la copa
renovada en el aire, en la luz que colgaba de las ramas
y en las hojas que al brillar parecían hablarme.

También allí, en la amistad de sus raíces,
junté piedras para construir una casa.
No es que no tuviera a donde ir
pero mi voz y mis sueños
habían sucumbido en la descreación de la noche
y la memoria de un refugio era más real que mis pasos.

De vuelta en la ciudad tan poco es lo que avanzo
que a mis pies se hunde el suelo cuando creo recorrerla,
absorto en medio de la lluvia
que toca el fondo de los hombres,
sin sombra
pero en marcha al baldío de osamentas
y hierros infinitos:

Mi corazón es una piedra,
mi corazón es una piedra que respira
y marca el sitio donde hubo una montaña,
en este instante
o en otro
al pie de una columna solitaria como el humo
no otra cosa
que el aullido de la hierba muriéndose lejos.

"Hubo una vez un hombre…"

Hubo una vez un hombre que hablaba siempre de ti
y te quería.

Era un hombre sencillo e indiferente al dinero.
Alguien
que no tenía casi amigos,

MANUEL ROMERO

At the Foot of the Mountain

for Víctor Soto Ferrel

Once I awoke facing the silent stare of a tree
in the breeze of a new day.
Its trunk was the flooded stream of a principle
that shook its crown
transformed by the air, by the light that hung from its branches
and the leaves that shining seemed to speak to me.

In the community of its roots
stones to build a house were gathered.
It's not that there was no place to go
but my voice and my dreams
had succumbed to the night's entropy
and the memory of a refuge was more real than my footsteps.

On my return to the city I advance so little
that the ground sinks at my feet when I think to pass over it,
transfixed in the rain
which touches the depths of men,
shadowless
on the road to the wasteland of bones
and endless metal junk:

My heart is a stone,
my heart is a stone that breathes
and marks the place where a mountain was
at this or another moment
at the foot of a column as solitary as smoke
nothing more
than the distant howl
of dying grass.

"There was once a man..."

There was once a man who loved you and spoke of nothing else.

He was a simple man, indifferent
to money. He had
few friends

que rara vez iba a fiestas y a quien el sol alumbraba
si al final surgías tú, única entre todas;
si el breve nombre
que un día le dieras
lo pronunciabas.

Pero como nada es para siempre, o porque sí.
Por seguir una moda, o por costumbre,
un día exigiste el derecho
de decir que fue viernes
cierto lunes oscuro,
que esa tarde nevaba–cuando que llovía–
y que era odio y no amor
lo que ese hombre te daba.

Y una herida abriste en su costado.
Y sangrando lo dejaste.
Porque sí.

Porque así es la vida.

Porque un hombre que te amaba
fuese más innominado que Zutano.
X, o Zeta su apodo.
Su aspecto hoy el de un fantasma:
pálido y absorto entre la gente.

24 de diciembre

El silencio crece a tu alrededor.
Cuando se ha hecho tarde, finges dormir,
fijos los ojos en el techo, en la eternidad, en otra noche.
Quién eres tú nadie lo sabe.
A veces tu cuerpo te abandona:
otro calza tus zapatos,
viste tus camisas, sonríe con tus ojos.
Pero a ti, ¿quién te conoce?
Anuncian que ya estás aquí tus pasos
sobre la escalera rápida, en ciega caída
a un sótano, a los precipicios, y mienten.
Miente, quizás, el hueco de la puerta
cuando cruza alguien con tu rostro,
y el mundo afuera, veloz, sugiere en cada estallido
el nacimiento de un eclipse.

rarely went to parties, and the sun
only shone upon him when finally
you would emerge,
you and you only,
or if you called him
by the little name you had given him once.

But because nothing is forever, or just because,
for the sake of fashion or custom
one day you demanded the right
to say it was Friday
on a certain dark Monday,
that it snowed that afternoon, when in fact it was raining,
and that it was hate and not love
that he gave you.

And you opened a wound in his side
and left him bleeding.
Just because.

Because life's like that.

Because a man who loved you
was more nameless than John Doe.
X or Y was his name.
Now ghostlike he hovers
pale and withdrawn in the crowd.

December 24th

Silence grows around you.
Late at night you pretend to sleep,
your eyes fixed on the ceiling, eternity, another night.
No one knows who you are.
Sometimes your body leaves you:
another wears your shoes and shirt
another smiles with your eyes.
But you, who knows you?
They proclaim that now your path is here
on the the escalator, in free fall
to a basement, to cliffs, but they lie.
Perhaps the doorway is also lying
when someone with your face passes through it,
and the quick external world suggests
the birth of an eclipse in every outburst.

En la radio se escucha una canción.
Sobre los cristales un poco de relumbre
predice la llegada del nuevo día:
ya es veinticuatro.
Clara como el agua, y más fluida,
una hora plena te sostiene.
Y si después oscurece, menos débil
la luz vendrá a brillar contigo, transparente.

Paseante y humo

Desnudo,

oscuro
de silencio
y origen,

enciendo
un cigarro.

Un cigarro
y mi cuerpo
que ya se alejan
por donde
inadvertidos
llegaron;

pequeñitos
los pies
del hombre
que así
desaparece:

a tientas
bajo el humo.

¿O no es verdad
que algo de él
se quema
mientras fuma,

que el páncreas

A song is heard on the radio.
A small glow on the window panes
foretells the arrival of the new day.
Now it's the 24th.
As clear as water, and more fluid,
a full hour sustains you.
Even though afterwards it will grow dark, the light,
transparent and less feeble, will come to shine
where you are.

Passerby and Smoke

Naked,

uncertain
of silence
and origin,

lighting
a cigarette.

A cigarette
and my body
which now wander
from the place
they had arrived
by chance;

the tiny
feet
of the man
who vanishes

groping his way
beneath the smoke.

Or is it that
something of him
was burning
as he smoked,

that his pancreas

y el riñón
empujan fuerte
hacia la brasa
detrás de un brillo,

un destello
que ilumine
la turbia fisiología
de quien ama?

En una calle
un cigarro
y el caos:

los mundos al girar.

and kidney
struggled
toward the flame,
searching for a glow,

a flash,
illuminating
the turbid physiology
of one who loves?

On a street
a cigarette
and chaos:

the spinning of worlds.

M.W.

Tata Arturo (otros fragmentos)

Era un eucalipto grande como mi niñez
Entre sus hojas se desparramaba el sol
y caía hecho sombra en mi abuelo

Es un eucalipto grande pero triste
de sus ramas se desprendió la noche
y ocupó el patio   la casa   y algo de nuestras vidas

*

¿Qué mirará mi abuela
cuando no mira nada?

¿En quién pensará
cuando piensa en ti?

Esta ausencia tuya
ahora de polvo
nos ensucia

*

La miro jugar
Cinco años
Graciosa y ágil
debajo del eucalipto
parece una mariposa

La miro brincar
ríe
saca la lengua

Después de todo
abuelo
tu muerte aún es niña

*

Habría que verte
a través de la tierra que ya eres
para saberme nieto de la tierra
Para saber que tu nombre
es una piedra más con nombre en un cementerio

*

Tata Arturo (Other Fragments)

It was a eucalyptus as big as my childhood
The sun was scattered among its leaves
and shade fell upon my grandfather

It's a large sorrowful eucalyptus
the night unfolded from its branches
filling the yard   the house   and something of our lives

*

What will my grandmother look at
when she looks at nothing?

Of whom will she think
when she thinks of you?

Now that your absence
covers us
with dust

*

I watch her play
a five-year-old
sure-footed, graceful,
like a butterfly
beneath the eucalyptus

She skips
laughs
sticks out her tongue

Despite everything
grandfather your death
is young

*

Perhaps I must see you
through the earth you've become
to know myself a grandson of this land
To know that your name
is one more named stone in the cemetery

*

No sé cuántas misas
te han mandado decir
ahora
que ya no oyes

*

En el panteón
–dicen todos–que estás ahora

¿A quién se le ocurrió
esconderte entre tanto muerto?

Debieron haberte enterrado en el mar
y dejar la tierra
para que nos ahoguemos los vivos

*

Amanece

¿Qué sentido tendrá para ti
este estruendo de alas anunciando el día?

*

Vuelvo a ser el hombre de sonrisa franca. El niño que mira reír a su abuelo.
Vuelvo a ser el viejo venerable que escribe versos. El poeta que se ahoga con su
llanto. Vuelvo a ser el fantasma de mí mismo: la sombra de un árbol triste.

*

Reincidencias

I
Salgo a caminar las viejas calles de este barrio. Echo a andar por la Morelos hasta
la Belisario Domínguez. Busco la casa de mis abuelos. Por fin–después de exigirle
mucho a mi memoria–doy con la fachada de ladrillo sin número. En el patio, un
niño distraído me pregunta a quién busco; a Don Arturo, contesto; soy yo, me
dice, y dejo a mi hijo mayor jugando con él.

II
En medio del patio
hay un niño distraído
jugando con las sombras

How many masses
have been said for you
now
that you can't hear them

*

Now–everyone says–you are in
the cemetery

Whose idea was it
to hide you among the dead?

They should have buried you at sea
and left the earth for those of us alive
in which to drown ourselves

*

It's dawn

This noise of wings announcing day
what meaning could it have for you?

*

Once again I become the man with the open smile. The boy watching his grand-
father laugh. I become again the old man writing verses. The poet who drowns
in his own tears. I become again my own ghost: the shadow of a sorrowful tree.

*

Echoes

I
I walk the old streets of this quarter, down Morelos towards Belisario Domínguez,
searching for my grandparents' house. Finally, memory exhausted, I stumble
upon its unnumbered brick facade. In the yard a mischievous boy asks me who
I'm looking for; for Don Arturo, I answer. That's me, he says, and I let my oldest
son play with him.

II
In the middle of the yard
there's a mischievous boy
playing with shadows

275

Otro niño se acerca
No se conocen
Sólo se parecen en la voz
y en la extraña manera
de inventar juegos

III
Mi abuelo quedó atrapado
en el patio de su casa
un jueves lejano
en que se acabó el tiempo

Su abuelo   Ignacio Cienfuegos
salió a las calles a buscarlo
Hace un rato estuvo aquí preguntando por él
y tuve que mentirle
que sí   que se fue
que yo lo vi
que sólo llevaba
un par de maltrechos remos
y un presagio en la mirada

"La noche se alarga en el desierto..."

La noche se alarga en el desierto
ángeles y demonios
luchan por California
¿Quién ha de quedarse con las almas?
¿Quién inventó esta isla
de cerros de oro
y salvajes amazonas?

En la parte más septentrional del país
se prepara la venganza
El grito de guerra es el alba
Alguien no volverá a despertar
Alguien quedará hundido en el sueño

Another boy approaches him
They don't know each other
Only their voices
and the peculiar way
they invent new games
are similar

III

My grandfather was still trapped
in the yard of his house
on a distant Thursday
when time ran out

Ignacio Cienfuegos   his own grandfather
searched the streets for him
A while ago I was here asking after him
and I had to lie to him
that yes
that he'd left
that I'd seen him
that he carried only
a pair of battered oars
and a look of foreboding

"The night grows long in the desert..."

The night grows long in the desert
angels and demons
struggle for California
Who shall win the souls?
Who invented this island
of golden hills
and savage Amazons?

In the northernmost part of the country
Vengeance is prepared
Dawn is the cry of war
Someone will never awaken again
Someone will remain sunk in a dream

M.W.

FLORA CALDERÓN

Marea de brujas *(fragmentos)*

1

Me niego a recordar
Por eso aquí me quedo
En el baile de sordomudos
En la arcilla de tu nariz
En esta copa de vino
Que lava heridas
Embriaga tu imagen
Te hace besarme
Morir por mí
en un abrazo de ceniza
en años de taquicardia

Pero no
No es verdad
Sólo mi embriaguez es absoluta
La tuya
¡Dios la tuya!
es una locura que invento
según el camino por donde pasas.

5

para Antonio Mejía

Hombre de fuego verde y uñas de sal
Prófugo del desamor
Ríes
Eres martillo y canto
Rompes

Sonaja del otoño
siervo de la furia
Me enclaustras en tu castillo
de lagartijas y escarabajos
Lloras
Con el embrujo de un beso
con la fe de los necios
decides abrigar tu temor
en el sudor de mi cuerpo bajo el tuyo
Átame

FLORA CALDERÓN

from **Witches' Tide**

1

I refuse to remember
So I remain here
In the dance of the deaf mutes
On the clay of your nose
In this glass of wine
That cleanses wounds
Intoxicates your image
Makes you kiss me
Die for me
in an ashen embrace
years of tachycardia

But no
That's not it
Only my drunkenness is absolute
Yours
God   yours!
is a madness I invent
depending upon which road you take.

5

for Antonio Mejía

Man of green fire and fingernails of salt
Fugitive from indifference
You laugh
You are hammer and song
You break

A small autumn bell
I serve up rage
I'm cloistered in your castle
of lizards and beetles
You cry
At the haunting of a kiss
with the faith of fools
you decide to cover your dread
with the sweat of my body beneath yours
Tie me down

Contigo dentro soy fuego eterno
Calcíname.

10
Señora de los delirios y ramajes de miel
Señora del zacate y la penumbra
He aquí el alma indómita que me habita
Protégenos   no   nos abandones

Si he de matar
Que sea con la mano que escribo.

15
Viene la noche partida en soles
a desmembrar embrujos

Aquí nadie es lo que fue
Ni vino
Ni agorero
Ni dioses

Todos venimos a ser cantos
de los recuerdos más antiguos
a ser voz para milenios

Somos esclavos y amantes
a quienes nadie puede matar
Tambores del mar
enredaderas de carne.

With you inside I'm eternal fire
Burn me

15

Lady of frenzies and branches of honey
Lady of the grass and shadows
The untamed soul lives in me here
Protect us   do not   abandon us

If I must kill
Let it be with the hand that writes.

15

The night comes split into suns
to undo curses

Here no one is what he was
Neither wine
Nor prophet
Nor gods

We all become chants
of the most ancient memories
become millennial voice

We are slaves and lovers
whom no one can kill
Drummers of the sea
lianas of flesh.

H.P.

Cartas de Averroes

V

En el desierto invierno donde pastan mis fuerzas
hay detalles de puentes, tronos y palacios
ajadas las columnas por el sol y los vientos
restos de lo pasado en las lanzas del sueño.

Cenizas del Islam me recorren el cuerpo
Alá todo lo sabe, lo mira y nunca duerme
de su boca sabré lo profundo del tiempo
Torre o Sepulcro el seno de la hierba.

IV

Caracol en madera labrada por los ojos
camino de huesos, máscaras y clavos
al colmillo de bronce lo roen los tridentes
en las puertas de un arco cruzan las golondrinas.

Yunque veleta en la urna del cráneo
ángel tejiendo un piano funerario
solenoide del tímpano molusco vítreo
desde el ojo la tierra muda de aspecto.

III

Desenfadado lirio que no oculta sus quejas
nenúfares airados contra hormigas y arenas
aguapé isla vegetal de ranas y de sapos
al borde del estanque una flor más se inquieta.

El árabe o el ángel corta el filo del agua
se humedecen las carnes tras el viento de enero
danzan en el reflejo los colores inciertos
leves ondas describen fragilidad de cuerpos.

II

Cetro de oro en la mirada del ángel
desnuda la espada vigorosa rompe en llanto
la roca del violento cristal corta las manos
por el ojo transita la noche y el abismo de sangre.

Letters from Averroes

V

In the winter desert where my forces pasture
there are details of bridges, thrones and palaces
their columns wasted by sun, by wind
the remains of the past caught on the lances of dreams.

The ashes of Islam spill over my body
Allah knows all, sees all, never sleeps
from his mouth I will learn the depths of time
Tower or Sepulcher the bosom of the grass.

IV

Snail etched in wood by the eyes
pathway of bones, masks and nails
tridents gnaw at its bronze tusk
swallows sweep across an arched doorway.

The anvil in the urn of the cranium
angel weaving a funerary piano
solenoid of the tympani vitreous mollusk
to the eye the earth appears mute.

III

Carefree iris which doesn't hide its complaints
water lilies exposed to ants and sand
watery vegetal islands of frogs and toads
one more flower worries at the edge of the pond.

Arab or angel cuts the edge of the water
flesh grows damp with January's wind
uncertain colors dance in the reflection
gentle waves outline the fragility of bodies

II

In the angel's eye a gold scepter
a naked sword breaks into tears
the rock, violent crystal, cuts the hands
night passes through the eye and the abyss of blood.

Tendido bocarriba el ángel flagelando al cielo
nada hay detrás del muro y de la estrella
lo negro del silencio reina en la vasta ciencia
el espejo es un templo donde las formas duermen.

I

El árabe descubre una cuerda en el tiempo
hay un arriba y un abajo y una concha de cielo
cuevas oscuras donde el silencio es miedo
vano esqueleto del espacio pensado.

El árabe es un ángel que ha volado hasta el fondo
en su viaje excentrado descubrirá lo opuesto
temerarias sus alas arrancarán el nombre
lo profundo, recóndito, inmirable, se llamará NADIR.

"Hay un viento que sopla..."

Hay un viento que sopla

        humores florecidos

atmósfera del miedo

        temblor donde estremecen

nervaduras del agua.

        Hay un soplo en el viento

donde residen frutos

        maduros de inocencia.

Hay un viento que sopla

        entre los dedos vivo

una hoguera compacta

        con estruendo de rayo.

Hay un soplo en el viento

        que llama al barro, ola

se sumerge y asciende

        hasta besar su borde.

Hay un soplo y un viento

        desprendidos del aire

buscando entre las cosas

        sus verdaderos nombres.

Stretched out on its back the angel whips the sky
there is nothing behind the wall or the star
the blackness of silence reigns over the vast science
the mirror is a temple where the forms are sleeping.

I
The Arab discovers a chord in time
there is an up and a down and a shell made of sky
dark caves where silence is fear
vain skeleton of imagined space.

The Arab is an angel who has flown to the depths
in his off-centeredness he discovers his opposite
his reckless wings will uproot the name
the deep, the recondite, the unseeable, will be called NADIR.

"There is a wind blowing..."

There is a wind blowing

        flowery moods

atmosphere of terror

        a quaking where the nerves

of water tremble.

        There is a breath in the wind

in which reside fruit

        ripe with innocence.

There is a wind blowing

        alive between fingers

a bonfire dense

        with the sound of thunder.

There is a breath in the wind

        calling to the clay, the wave

that rises and falls,

        to kiss its edge

There is a breath and a wind

        detached from the air

they search among things

        for their true names.

"El barro es una cosa…"

El barro es una cosa

un objeto del mundo

vana materia, flujo

que no siente ni piensa.

El barro es elemento

sustancia sin esencia

sólo una mezcla adúltera

de la tierra y el agua.

"El pie no tiene un nombre…"

El pie no tiene un nombre

es órgano activado

sin voluntad ni cuerpo.

El pie es lo que sostiene

un edificio vasto

de incontables texturas.

El pie es sólo parte

partícula del polvo

sin valor aparente.

"Clay is a thing..."

Clay is a thing

an earthly object

mere matter, flux

that thinks not, feels not.

Clay is an element

sustenance without essence

an adulterous mix, no more,

of water and earth.

"The foot has no name..."

The foot has no name

with neither body nor will

is an active organ

it's the foot that sustains

a vast edifice

of countless textures.

The foot is only a part

a particle of dust

of no apparent worth.

J.L.

287

"En mi memoria..."

En mi memoria
ondea tu bandera
ese rostro
que ahora escribo
y tiene los colores
de la ausencia

esta ceremonia es el silencio
voz apagada del olvido
no hay oraciones
                    no hay himnos

a partir de hoy
mi cuerpo tiene un héroe dibujado
una herida que sangra
por todas las guerras del amor

"Escribo de ti..."

Escribo de ti
para tocar con palabras
ese cuerpo que no tuve

la carne de tu alma
que brilla en cada acento
de la hoja

"¿Cómo es el interior del árbol?..."

¿Cómo es el interior del árbol? Responde: adentro sólo oscuridad, gritos de raíces. De vez en cuando, un insecto en sus travesuras deja entrar algo de luz, pero poco se ve. Del mundo recibimos agua; de pronto un murmullo, mil hormigas hablan al mismo tiempo, todo se vuelve a un lado, caemos. Cuando despertamos alguien escribe en nosotros: "¿Cómo es el interior de un árbol?"

"In my memory..."

In my memory
your flag waves
this face
that I now write
has the colors
of absence

this ceremony is silence
voice of oblivion extinguished
there are no prayers
                              no hymns

starting today
a hero is sketched on my body
bleeding wound
of all of love's wars

"I write of you..."

I write of you
to touch with words
this body I never held

flesh of your soul
shining in each accent
on the page

"What is the inside of the tree like?..."

What is the inside of the tree like? It answers: inside there is only darkness, the
crying of roots. Once in a while a mischievous insect lets some light in, but little
is visible. We receive water from the world; soon a murmur, a thousand ants
speaking at once, everything turns to one side, we fall. When we awake some-
one is writing on us: "What is the inside of a tree like?"

H.P.

CARLOS MARTÍNEZ VILLANUEVA

"Bajo las frutas que la miel olvidó..."

Bajo las frutas que la miel olvidó
se extiende muda la mesa
y el mantel sucio de presencias
multiplica vacíos indeseados.

Crujen los muebles obesos de tristeza
la ausencia se refleja
En todo espejo
el silencio se peina de lado.

Un musgo ha nacido sobre la sopa
el vaso clavado a la mesa
es un pájaro de vidrio
un punto de luz
una luciérnaga a lo lejos.

"Son las seis en punto..."

Son las seis en punto
hoy no me ha estafado el reloj
con su maligno juego de la espuma.

Mi madre cocina
hace lo mismo en cualquier sitio
espanto las moscas en estos pensamientos
mi padre celebra la victoria de su equipo favorito.

El vello púbico ha invadido a mis hermanas
he soñado mi última día
mis testículos llenos de amargura.

Sé que una especie de huevo metálico
nos separa
tras la ventana miro al cielo
cruzar a la misma gente
Algún día no estaré aquí.

"Mute, the table extends..."

Mute, the table extends
Beneath the fruit that the honey forgot
and soiled by presences the tablecloth
multiplies the unwanted spaces.

The heavy furniture creaks with sadness
reflecting absence
In all the mirrors
silence parts its hair to the side.

Moss grows on the soup
the glass stuck to the table
is a crystal bird
a point of light
a distant glowworm.

"It's six o'clock sharp..."

It's six o'clock sharp
today I haven't cheated the watch
with its vicious play of spume

My mother is cooking
she does the same thing everywhere
in these thoughts of mine she chases away the flies
my father is celebrating the victory
of his favorite team.

Pubic down has invaded my sisters
I've dreamed of my last day
my testicles full of bitterness.

I know that a kind of metallic egg
separates us
through the window I see
the same people cruising through the sky
Some day I won't be here.

"Acaso no es éste el mundo del hombre…"

Acaso no es éste el mundo del hombre
no hemos sido niños aquí
no son ciertos los besos hollados
la frescura de los pozos
tu sexo rosado frente a mis ojos
y ahora el tiempo se adelgaza
los instantes en su anemia
palidecen las horas y los rostros
Una manada de otoños
se oye
en estampida venir desde el recuerdo
no viví aquí, no pisé aquí
no es el cielo un vestigio
negarse no es tan fácil
he visto los muertos dorarse al sol sobre las tumbas
una lágrima desbordar presas
la catedral del silencio hundida
una botella vacía
una cicatriz   el mapa del mundo.

"Perhaps this isn't the world of man..."

Perhaps this isn't the world of man
we haven't been children here
the kisses of humiliation may not be real
the coolness of wells
your rosy sex before my eyes
and now time grows slender
the moments in their anemia
the hours and faces turn pallid
A flock of autumns
can be heard
stampeding from memory
I didn't live here, didn't walk here
the sky is not a vestige
to deny oneself is not so easy
I've seen the dead on their graves
browning themselves in the sun
a tear overflows its bank
the cathedral of sunken silence
an empty bottle
a scar   the map of the world

H.P.

Anclaje I

La misma pregunta todos los días
la miseria convertida en fe
la débil anarquía.

Niños que revientan por comer
viejos sin alma ni cuerpo
mujeres sin sentido que se aburren
hombres sentados sobre su propia ternura.

Nos arrastramos a partir de la primera célula
jóvenes desde la prehistoria
curiosos de la cara oculta de la Luna
tras la ilusoria promesa de un callado vientre.

Anclaje,
oficio de las almas extenuadas;
acto de olvidar, de morirse,
de ignorar a la conciencia,
partir para siempre y quemar las naves.

Anclaje II

Éste es tan sólo un momento,
sólo un segundo que casi llega
cuando ya se ha ido;
no hay ayer ni después y el hoy se desvanece.

Lo que queda es el vacío de la esperanza perenne,
la decisión de continuar a la deriva o anclarse:

el anclaje es la muerte y es siempre una tentación;

el ancla renuncia a dejarse llevar
aunque se estanque,
aunque se entierre
como se entierran los cangrejos en la arena
                              (para no ver)
como se entierran los muertos
a las lombrices de tierra.

Anchorage I

The same question every day
misery changed into faith
a feeble anarchy.

Boys wracked by hunger
old men without soul or body
senseless women boring each other
men seated on their own gentleness.

We drag onwards from the first cell
youths since before time
curious about the hidden face of the Moon
beyond the illusory promise of a silent womb.

Anchorage,
the business of emaciated souls;
the forgetting, the dying,
the ignoring of conscience,
departing forever and burning the boats.

Anchorage II

This is no more than a moment
only a second that's hardly arrived
before it's gone;
no yesterday no tomorrow, today already vanishing.

What remains is the emptiness of perennial hope,
the decision to drift or drop anchor;

the anchorage is death and a constant temptation;

the anchor gives up being carried
even if it snags
even if it's buried
like crabs buried in the sand
                              (so as not to see)
like corpses buried
to feed the worms.

Luces al fin

Desaparece la luz al final de la brecha,
nuevamente, sin giro inusitado
simplemente se desvanece.

Y caemos hacia el obscuro precipicio infinito lleno de agua.

En suspensión, segmentos de mar
estropean la vertiginosa caída.

A ciegas, un cardumen de luminosos peces abisales
se perfilan al acecho.

Una boca de dragón arroja fuego
al fondo del oceánico despeñadero.

Una nueva luz se prende al final del camino
luz de fuego de dragón hambriento,
brillantez de luminiscentes peces en jauría:
luces al fin en los extremos de la caída.

Hale-Bopp

Año 5397...
trazos al fondo de un acantilado
celebran con el viento tu regreso.

En su memoria:
ojos azorados con telescopio,
polvo de estrellas, Laguna Salada, Luna ausente.

Desierto y noche:
perfección suspendida en puntilleo de tinta.

Hale-Bopp: elipse difusa
cauda oblicua, densidad imprecisa.

Escupes polvo de ti mismo congelado,
lluvia silente en tu agonía.

Falsa penetración a un Sol inerte
lumbre asciende, no desistes,
y el corazón te llama en su guarida.

Lights at the End

The light disappears into the opening
once more, nothing unusual
just gone.

And we fall towards the dark endless water-filled chasm.

Suspended, chunks of the sea
spoil our vertiginous fall.

Blindly, a luminous school of deep-sea fish
wait in ambush.

At the base of the cliff
a dragon breathes fire.

A new light ignites at the end of the road
the flame of a starving dragon,
the brilliance of a school of luminescent fish:
lights at the end at the base of the slope.

Hale-Bopp

The year 5397...
lines at the bottom of a cliff
celebrate your return with the wind.

In your memory:
eyes excited by the telescope,
stardust, Laguna Salada,* the absent Moon.

Desert and night:
perfection suspended in a drop of ink.

Hale-Bopp: hazy ellipse
oblique flow, imprecise density.

In your agony you spit
congealed dust, silent rain.

False penetration to an inert Sun
splendor ascending, you don't stop,
and the heart calls you to its haunt.

Estéril invernal nuevo paisaje:
desierto helado,
Luna tripartita;
iniquidades de la vida extinta.

Nadie sospecha de ti o de tus adentros
ningún suspiro anuncia tu partida.

Al fondo del acantilado un claroscuro,
vestigio final de tu pasada visita.

El poema alude a varios dibujos de la exposición "Paisajes bajacalifornianos", de Cuauhtémoc Rodríguez Piña, artista mexicaliense. El cometa Hale-Bopp visitó nuestro sistema solar en 1997.

sterile new wintry landscape:
frozen desert,
tripartite Moon;
iniquities of extinct life.

Nobody suspects you or your innermost being
no sigh announces your departure.

At the bottom of the cliff a chiaroscuro
the final remnant of your past visit.

Author's Note: This poem alludes to various drawings in the exhibition "Paisajes bajacalifornianos" (Baja California Landscapes), by the Mexicali artist Cuauhtémoc Rodríguez Piña. Hale-Bopp visited our solar system in 1997.

*Laguna Salada. A salt lake south of Mexicali, B.C. The reference is to the light glinting on salt crystals.

H.P.

Puntillas

¿Qué corazón avaro
cuenta el metal de los instantes?

Xavier Villaurrutia

Soy un laberinto instantáneo,
interminable
combate de los tiempos.
Un ave amanece por mi costado izquierdo
sugiriéndome el elíxir de la espera,
cierro el puño
y la ligerísima escapa.
A lo lejos me veo haciéndome señas
que no logro entender.
En un cerrar de ojos despierto,
me incorporo
y el aire, mi andar de aire
es un espejo de palabras que me levita.
No, no existe engaño alguno,
voy tejiendo los silencios
hasta crecer una telaraña
en que queda atrapado el mundo.
¡Cuántas edades de desnudez
guardo bajo este muelle amigo!
El presente es un *iceberg*
que se derrite
entre mis dedos ávidos de certezas.
El ayer un mar inconcluso
en perpetua ebullición bajo mi pecho.
Del futuro sólo preservo su aroma
a sal de muerto,
sazón de este andar a tientas,
eterno imperio de la duda.

Cuadro de un pintor que te mira

No respires, no.
¡Muérete mejor
así como estás!

Xavier Villaurrutia

Un santo se acuesta a los pies de tu sombra.
Las frases son mariposas que revolotean
ligeras en tu entorno.

Lace

> To what greedy heart
> does metal recount the moments?
>
> *Xavier Villaurrutia*

I'm an instantaneous labyrinth,
the weather's
endless combat.
A bird emerges from my left side
implying the elixir of waiting,
I close my fist, but agile, it escapes.
I see myself in the distance making signs
incomprehensible to me.
I awake in a flash,
bolt upright,
and the air, my airy pace
is a mirror of words I rise on.
This is no swindle,
I weave silences
into a spider web
to catch the world.
How many ages of nakedness
I keep beneath this tender friend!
The present is an iceberg
melting
between my fingers eager for certainties,
and yesterday is an unfinished sea
boiling ceaselessly in my chest.
Of the future I only keep the smell
of the salt of death,
the flavor of this groping
eternal empire of doubt.

Painting of a Painter Who Looks at You

> Don't breathe.
> Better to die
> as you are!
>
> *Xavier Villaurrutia*

A saint reclines at the feet of your shadow.
Phrases are butterflies revolving
around you.

Ves árboles, tocas un fruto.
Por tus cabellos
desciende,
cadenciosamente,
un canto de fuego.
Tocas ese canto,
cantas ese fuego.
Te quedas quieta y el pintor de atardeceres
te coloca más allá de las nubes.
El fruto cae,
el niño levanta el vuelo.
Elevas tus cabellos,
el sol
y toda transparencia.
Te suspendes,
de tus pies llueven estrellas,
granadas que son ojos,
ojos que son ángeles.

Espuma *(fragmento)*

Mis sueños espantan
a los cuatro demonios que huyen
por las ventanas de mi cuerpo.
Un verano se abre
punta a punta,
se puebla de silencios inacabados.
Un meteoro voltea
y encuentra en sus huellas
el rostro terrible de Dios.
Volvemos a inventar nuestra existencia.

Álgebra urbana

Como un ángel
de su nube
cae
el último grano
de arena:
dos ayeres
no suman
cuatro soledades.

You see trees, you touch a fruit.
Rhythmically
a song of fire
descends
from your hair.
You touch this song,
you sing this fire.
You stay calm, and the painter of sunsets
positions you beyond the clouds.
The fruit falls,
the boy takes flight.
You lift your hair,
the sun
and all transparency.
You suspend yourself,
stars rain from your feet
pomegranates are your eyes,
eyes that are angels.

from Foam

My dreams frighten
the four demons, and they flee
out the windows of my body.
A summer opens
point by point,
is peopled by unfinished silences.
A meteor turns
and finds in your footsteps
the terrible face of God.
We return to invent our existence.

Urban Algebra

The last grain
of sand
falls
like an angel
from its cloud:
two yesterdays
don't equal
four solitudes

H.P.

Alfa y omega

I

Esta mañana
volví a ser el polvo del que surgió Adán
(quien ayuntándose con el resto de los seres creados
los encontró impropios para su abrazo)
Y fui costilla
Y fui hembra
hecha para copular.

II

Mas también estuvo en mí el soplo divino
Hecho Adán a su imagen y semejanza
Dios me hizo a mí
del tamaño de su concupiscencia.

III

He recorrido, como quien deslinda un baldío,
la circunferencia de mis senos
Pienso en el día de la Creación
Descubro el tamaño de las manos de Dios
              sobre mi cuerpo.

IV

Estoy viendo mi cadera
la oquedad perfecta de mi vientre
el pubis tibio y acolchado como el mítico
              vellón de oro
los muslos blanquísimos y llenos.

He palpado la humedad entre mis piernas
hasta tocar el fondo
he tocado con mis manos el límite del infinito.

Alpha and Omega

I
This morning
I became again the dust from which Adam emerged
(hungering after the rest of creation
he found it unsuitable for his embrace)
And I was rib
And I was female
fashioned to copulate.

II
But the divine wind was also in me
Adam he made in his image and likeness
God made me myself
but scaled to his lust.

III
I've surveyed, like one who charts a wasteland,
the circumference of my breasts.
I think of the day of Creation
I discover the size of God's hands
          on my body.

IV
I'm looking at my hip
the perfect hollow of my belly
the pubes warm and padded like the mythical
          golden fleece
the thighs white and full.

I've felt the moisture between my legs
even touched its depths
I've touched with my hands the edge of the infinite.

H.P.

Arenario

Reptarte, arenario
Serpiente nohayarena surcada por tu paso
                  que no escurra
      reloj
          de mano a mano
                retenerte
 *

      Apenas lo tocas, el desierto se abre,
se entrega curva escurridiza de arena, que aprisionas entre las manos;
se desborda   se derrama   huye y tú
lentamente reconstruyes sobre la superficie nuevas fisionomías
castillos, fortalezas, cuevas profundas, oscuros abismos salados,
secos, no secos, mojados, cálidos.

 *

      No hay aves, no hay cantos,
sólo el rumor seco de la piel contra la arena;
el paso del reptil es sutil zigzagueo,
el árido ronroneo del reptil que barre la piel del desierto
Y el reptil va barriendo la piel del desierto
Y el reptil va, barriendo la piel del desierto
Y el reptil, baba riendo, la piel del desierto
Y el reptil baba, ríe en do la piel del desierto
que es curva y honda, y es seda y se da.

 *

      El sol calienta sobre la piel del desierto
descubre su geografía de mujer incierta
las dunas   los abismos   hendiduras y huellas
          huellas del reptil

      Serena   resbala por los granos de arena
la piel del reptil sobre la piel del desierto.

 *

      El reptil surca la piel del desierto
la descubre, busca, corre y recorre sobre, bajo y tras la arena abierta
que se desploma y se recompone
se da, se quita, se abre y se cierra.

      Conforme el paso del reptil se va adentrando
entre las dunas, entre las piedras,
se goza, se regodea,

Sandbook

       Slither, sandbook
Thereisnosand snake stopped by your step
                         you slide away no longer
      hourglass
                  from hand to hand
                              holds you back.
   *

       You barely touch it and the desert opens,
surrenders itself slippery crescent of sand imprisoned between your hands;
it overflows   runs over   slips away
slowly on its surface you build new faces
castles, fortresses, caverns, dark salty depths where it's
dry, not, wet, warm.

   *

       There are no birds, no songs,
only the dry sound of skin against sand,
the reptile's trail a subtle zigzag
the reptile's arid purr sweeping the skin of the desert
and the reptile is going to sweep the skin of the desert
and the reptile goes, sweeping the skin of the desert
and the reptile, laughing slime, the skin of the desert
and the reptile froths, laughs on the skin of the desert
which is sway and sling, and silk, and surrenders itself.

   *

       The hot sun on the skin of the desert
finds its geography of uncertain womanhood   dunes
depths   clefts and tracks
               tracks of the reptile

       Serene   the skin of the reptile slides through grains of sand
across the skin of the desert.

   *

       The reptile streaks through the skin of the desert
finds it, searches, again and again runs over, beneath and across the open sand
which unseals itself and pulls itself together
gives itself, withdraws, opens and closes.

       Like the path of the reptile it dives inward
among dunes and stones,
rejoices, luxuriates,

con la piel del reptil que es acero y escama
y la cama que no para
y sube y baja, como el reptil
que alcanza tan merecida presa, y la apresa.

*

El reptil crece y descrece bajo la caricia
el roce de la piel
lo turba, lo estremece,
lo vuelve líquido, profundo (mar)
y va a desembocar sobre la arena
que se expande, se realiza
y en su vasta extensión
se sabe arena, se sabe nada
(pero amada)

*

       No es silencio el desierto
es murmullo de mareas secretas, internas;
el reptil recostado sobre la piel del desierto escucha:
hay ríos, hay lluvias;
bajo la piel del desierto viven aves, corren bestias
se eternizan.

*

La arena escurre
brota
grano a grano se desliza
corre
en tu mano, si la cierras
agua

*

       El desierto se mueve, sube y baja lentamente
es tan extenso que sólo el reptil basta para conocerlo
lo recorrerán las aves, y no bastarán
lo recorrerán las bestias, y no bastarán
lo recorrerán mil hombres, y no bastarán
lo recorrerán el viento, el sol, el frío de la noche, la tristeza y no bastarán
porque es tan extenso, que sólo el reptil basta para conocerlo y es que el
                desierto quiere
quiere ser conocido y se deja, se despoja de sus vestiduras,
toma al reptil de la mano y le muestra el camino,
lo lleva de la mano hasta el oasis para que el reptil beba a sus anchas

with the skin of the reptile which is courage and fear
and the bed that never stops
but rises and falls like the reptile
that finds its prey and grasps it.

*

The reptile grows and shrinks beneath the caress
the scraping of skin
disturbs it, troubles it
turns it to liquid, a deep (sea)
and it will spill onto the sand
which expands, fulfilled,
and in its vast expanse
knows itself to be sand, to be nothing
(but loved nonetheless)

*

     The sand is not silence
it's the murmur of secret internal tides;
the reptile listens, reclining on the skin of the desert:
there are rivers, there is rain;
birds live and beasts run beneath the skin of the desert
and become eternal.

*

The sand drains away,
drips,
grain by grain, slips
runs
in your hand, and if you close it
water.

*

     The desert moves, slowly rising and falling
it is so large that only the reptile can know it
the birds will fly over it, but it won't be enough
the beasts will run through it, but it won't be enough
a thousand men will walk through it, but it won't be enough
the wind, the sun, the cold of night, sorrow, will not be enough
because it's so large that only the reptile can know it and the desert wants
wants to be known and surrenders, is stripped of, its garments
it takes the reptile by the hand and and shows it the way,
it leads the reptile by the hand to the oasis that it may drink its fill

y el reptil también se deja y va y bebe de frente, de cara al oasis
y todo él es agua, es sal, humedad, tibieza que tiembla nosaber
si es el desierto o el reptil quien tiembla
o ambos
o ninguno.

*

     La caricia del reptil roza la piel del desierto
se desvanece, rezuma-azota explorando sensaciones:
subir una curva hasta la cima suavemente
descender hasta un abismo amenazante
desbordarse desde un muslo una rodilla y deshacer la geografía del
desierto con un soplo para después rehacerla con las manos;
esculpir nuevos paisajes, una duna más alta, un oasis más lleno,
más fragrante; llenar el desierto de huellas, de cuevas para reptiles,
casas
llenar de calor la piel del desierto.

*

     El desierto arde en la espera,
sin su amante, es como marea seca
un antiguo ir y venir de olas lo confirma
el rumor habla de peces, de geografías húmedas ya extintas.
     Poco queda de ese adorno desertario
        unas conchas
la huella de un molusco en una piedra.

*

     De noche, la piel del desierto resplandece
la luna la borda con sus rayos de plata
la arena/ ayer oro, amarillo, brillante/ polvo
hoy es de agua
el calor del día la ha fundido
es cristal.

*

     Un desierto sin reptil no tiene vida
piensa
se extiende y resplandece bajo el paso del sol
ondula
busca imitar el paso del reptil sobre su piel
añora.

and the reptile surrenders and goes and drinks before, in the face of, the oasis
and it is all water, salt, humidity, warmth, trembling notknowing
if it's desert or reptile trembling
or both
or neither.

*

      The reptile's caress scrapes the skin of the desert
evaporates, ooze-whips, exploring sensations:
smoothly it climbs a curve to the summit
descending threateningly to the abyss
overflowing onto a thigh a knee undoing the geography
of the desert with a breath and remaking it with its hands;
sculpting new landscapes, a higher dune, an oasis more plentiful,
more fragrant; filling the desert with traces, caves for reptiles,
houses
to fill the skin of the desert with heat.

*

      Without its lover the desert burns
with expectation, it's a dry tide
an ancient coming and going of waves corroborates it
its murmuring speaks of fish, of damp geographies now gone.
      Little remains of that desert adornment
                some shells
the trail of a mollusk in stone.

*

      At night the skin of the desert glitters
the moon embroiders it with its silver rays
the sand/ yesterday gold, yellow, shining/ dust
today is water
the heat of the day has melted it
it is glass.

*

      A desert has no life without a reptile
it thinks
it expands and glitters beneath the sun's passage
it undulates
it seeks to imitate the reptile's passage across its skin
it is filled with longing

Llega el reptil
reptil-abrazo, reptil-beso, reptil-mano, reptil-caricia
y la abraza, la besa, la toca y la acaricia
a ella
desiertomar, desiertoarena, desiertoaire
que se desdobla, se entrega, se deja.

The reptile arrives
reptile-embrace, reptile-kiss, reptile-hand, reptile-caress
and embraces, kisses, touches and caresses it
seadesert, sanddesert, airdesert
that unfolds, surrenders, yields itself.

M.W.

Cortejo de la musa

Amiga mía, el tiempo nos acerca
y nuestras voluntades cada día
se acomodan mejor, amiga mía,
al martilleo de la hora terca.

Alfonso Reyes

Uno

Muéstrame el geranio de tu casa.
Déjame entrar por vez primera,
curioso, atento a detonantes
que señalen la que fuiste cuando aún
no te intuía ni sospechaba.
Me grabaré desde el recibidor
a la cocina, incluyendo esos pasillos
tapiados de acuarelas orientales
que tu madre ha pintado.
Para acoplarme a tus recuerdos
te tomaré por la cintura y viajaré
contigo cabalgando tu pasado
entre sillones y retratos sesenteros:
corolas de tus nalgas, cáliz de tus mieses.

Dos

En playas de silencio
montaré tus pensamientos
tal como venimos pretendiendo
en estas dos semanas.

Ninguno hablará por el otro
ni tratará de resolver
el acertijo de la premonición.

No debemos permitir malentendidos.

Tres

Ni aforismos ni sentencias.
Las citas de Montaigne
para cenas con amigos.

JORGE ORTEGA

Courting the Muse

> My love, time draws near
> daily our wills
> grow more accustomed
> to the hammering of the implacable hour.
>
> *Alfonso Reyes*

One

Show me the geranium of your house
Let me enter for the first time,
curious, careful of the explosives
that signal what you were even before
I imagined or suspected your being.
I'll engrave in memory the path from entry
to kitchen, as well as these corridors
lined with oriental watercolors
that your mother painted.
To join myself to your memories
I'll encircle your waist and travel
with you riding through your past
between armchairs and portraits from the 60s:
corollas of your cheeks, calyx of your fields of grain.

Two

On beaches of silence
I'll mount your thoughts
as we assumed we would
for these two weeks.

Neither will speak for the other
nor try to resolve
the riddle of premonition.

We should not allow misunderstandings.

Three

Neither aphorisms nor maxims.
Quotations from Montaigne
for dinners with friends.

Divagaré por tu confianza
y al sorber una cerveza
leeré nuestra ignorancia
en la veracidad de tu sonrisa.

Así comenzaremos a pulsar
en la doncellez de la memoria
el párrafo primicio, la sangría.

Cuatro

Anda, descorre la tiniebla
confesando tus andanzas.
Quiero oírte decir
"Por ti es revalorado
mi talle de fuga moderada".
Codifica en mis desplantes
artilugios de tu frase.
Colma con anécdotas mi escucha.
Has de la duda una ceguera
revertida en la creencia del presente.
Ya meces la franqueza
en el trapecio de la plática
y cada respuesta es obelisco,
es una fuente.

Cinco

La tarde se te pone al hombro;
tu hombro es paraje discurrible,
resolana plegada hasta tu ropa
pues el verano anda aún tras sucursales.
Por eso al hablarte de mis cosas
presiento en el ambiente radiaciones,
estrategia solapada de bochornos
traficados en el carro de mi escucha.
Violentando cuanto duerme bajo prenda
busco entrar orbitado a pulmón lleno
y ordenar por urgencia tus sentidos
y claudicar pergolados en el gozo.
Habrá que distraer las manecillas
para no cancelar citas postreras.
Mas pronto decidamos,
pues la tarde es ave asoleada
tocada por las hélices del sueño.

I'll wander through your confidence;
sipping a beer
I'll read our ignorance
in the truth of your smile.

In this manner we'll begin to play
within the maidenhood of memory
its first paragraph and the space before it.

Four

Go, retrace the darkness,
confessing your wanderings.
I want to hear you say
"The scope of my modest flight
is reassessed for you." My boasts codify
the little tricks of your phrase.
My hearing overflows with anecdotes.
You are blind to doubt
returning to present belief.
Even now you swing frankness
on the trapeze of chatter
and each response is an obelisk,
a fountain.

Five

The evening settles on your shoulder;
your shoulder is a place for travel
a sunny space enfolded in your clothing
because summer seeks its branch offices.
So it is that when I speak to you of my concerns
I foresee radiation in the atmosphere,
a cunning strategy of blushes
conveyed illicitly into the car of my hearing.
Doing violence to whatever sleeps beneath the pledge
I look to enter orbited with lungs full
urgently demanding your meaning
limping pergolaed with joy.
The hands of the clock must be distracted
so as not to cancel final dates.
Immediately we'll decide
that the evening is a sun-bronzed bird
touched by the helices of dream.

Seis

Paseamos por la colonia en automóvil
esperando que mamá abandone casa;
remonte a su trabajo el asfalto vespertino.
Ya deambula el otoño entre los fresnos,
lo denotan los sahumerios de la calle
con apariencia de cristal pulverizado;
así los arrullos del ramaje
destellando por el brío de quien disfruta
ascua dilatada en atmósfera violeta.
Podríamos tendernos sobre el pasto
y olvidar las tareas por media hora,
poseer con el ojo el crepúsculo del rumbo
haciendo del ocio un levitar de sinfonolas
para la soltura de los ánimos.
Volvámonos motivo de polémica,
blanco digno en torno a habladurías.

Siete

No hay mejor retribución ni buena suerte
que coincidir contigo en la piscina;
se ensancha el patrimonio del instinto
y soy tímido estudiante bajo el agua.
Tela inútil untada a lo probable
eres tú tras la vitrina de los gogles,
suculencia intangible pero viable
más allá de paredes sumergidas.
Ni sirena, ni pez, ni paralelos:
arponcillo infalible es la metáfora
para obtener la hermosura que se impone
retocada por la natación.
Femenino roquedal que posa altivo
mojado en diamantina de canícula
a ojo de caimán deshidratado.

Ocho

Mientras te allegas de sustento
profesando matemática
yo estoy sentado en la pausa de un ensayo
rodeado de pichones que nunca alimenté
pero se han arrimado al escritorio

Six

We glide through the neighborhood by car
hoping that mother has left the house,
climbing the evening street to work.
Autumn wanders among the strawberries,
the smells of the street announce it
with the appearance of crushed glass;
thus the lullabies of branches
sparkling because of the spirit of whoever enjoys
an ember postponed in violet atmosphere.
We could stretch out on the grass,
forgetting our chores for half an hour,
controlling with the eye the dusk of pomp
making of idleness a raising of jukeboxes
for the release of joy.
Let's make ourselves the topic of small talk,
a proper target for gossip.

Seven

No reward nor luck could improve
upon being with you in the pool;
the patrimony of instinct is proud
and beneath the water I'm a timid student.
Useless cloth smeared with the probable
it's you through the panes of the goggles,
untouchable but possible succulence
beyond the submerged walls.
Neither siren, nor fish, nor parallels:
a small harpoon that never fails is the metaphor
for obtaining beauty that commands attention
retouched by swimming.
Feminine field of stones perched aloft
drenched in the diamond-hard dog days
with the eye of a dehydrated alligator.

Eight

While you approach your livelihood
the professing of mathematics
I'm surrounded, seated during a moment's rest
from writing, by pigeons I have never fed
but they've moved closer to the desk

regocijados por estar amenizando
la suerte de los signos que trazo en torno a ti.

Planeando como plumas
                              alebrestan los papeles
en actitud de comensales
cual si hubiese algo escondido en los cajones.
La penetrancia de su canto
tan escaso a este lado de la urbe
se me anuncia tentación indeclinable.

Son las doce del día con seis minutos.
¿Será oportuno alcanzarte en la puerta del colegio
con una onza de maíz
y una afición por las palomas de la plaza?

Nueve

Allá en tu ribera me descifras
la voz que te doy y ya conoces,
alfombra invisible que aletea
nombres de las cosas por su nombre.
¿Cuáles nuestras citas de costumbre
si vicios a mi voz no conocieses?
Así con el tenor de mi propuesta
elucidas que de mí se va tratando.
Aflojas la ofensiva y desafanas
la tensión de tu delirio, relegando
el motivo esencial de la llamada.
Adrede te apoderas de la plática.
Nos sabes ahí y eso te ensancha.

Diez

Ocupo tus labios con mis ojos.
Los acerco hacia mí:
calistenia hipnótica, huelga de razones.
Te afronto, pues, con afinidad.
Podo la neblina de tu carne,
su flotante languidez de espejo.
Apago con besos tus preguntas.
Médico soy de tus ademanes.
Cirujo tus nobles vestiduras
desempapelándote de nimbos.

delighted to be pleasant
the fate of the signs that I trace around you.

Gliding like feathers
                              the papers quiver
in the posture of dependents
as if something had been hidden in the drawers.
Their song's penetration
unusual in this part of the city
speaks to me of irresistible temptation.

It's six past noon.
Will I find you now at the school door
with an ounce of corn
and a fondness for the plaza's doves?

Nine

There on your shore you decipher me
the voice that I give you (you already know it),
invisible carpet that flutters
the names of things by their name.
Which of our customary dates
if you didn't know the vices of my voice?
The tone of my proposal makes clear to you
that it has to do with me.
You ease up on the offensive, relaxing
the tension of your frenzy, banishing
the call's essential motive.
Deliberately you seize the sermon.
You swell, knowing us there.

Ten

I busy your lips with my eyes.
I draw them towards me:
hypnotic exercise, reason on strike.
So I defy you with affinity.
I prune the mist of your flesh
your floating looking glass languor.
I extinguish your questions with kisses.
I'm the physician of your gestures.
I make an incision in your noble vestments
stripping away your halos.

Digna de operaciones secretas
te dejas tomar por el arrobo,
cedes la porción amenazada.

Once

Mi derecho es ahora protegerte
y proteger significa aligerar,
esterizar tu salud con mi palabra
rociándote con temas epifánicos.
Por eso al volver del sanatorio
confíate al tenor de mi discurso;
franela encerada para el vientre,
rosicler contra el sopor del rostro.
Un vistazo echarás a tu suplicio
hallando en su lugar el aura intacta
de ciudad jalonada por la fiesta.

Doce, y último

Pásame, Amor, algo de esófago
para juntos mitigar esta dolencia,
compartir ventura tuerta
en el galope rutinario de la tarde.
Alvéolo de tu aguante soy, amor en vía
de quejidos y gemidos donde fija
coyuntura de humor el entusiasmo;
alvéolo de tus aspiraciones
por cual asientes la ruta decidida
sin pronunciar palabra o aludir el tema.

(No suena el alba al despuntar sobre la costa,
ni cruje el litoral bajo la vara de la luz.)

La empatía sella hemisferios.

Worthy of secret operations
you let yourself be carried away with ecstacy,
you surrender what's threatened.

Eleven

My right is now to protect you,
and to protect means to ease,
to sterilize your health with my word
sprinkling you with epiphanic themes.
So returning from the sanitarium
you trust in the tone of my discourse;
flannel polished by the womb,
rosy against the face's drowsiness.
A glance you'll discharge at your punishment
finding in its place the intact aura
of a city staked out for the fiesta.

Twelfth, and last

Pass me, Love, something of the esophagus
that together we might mitigate this sorrow,
share crooked happiness
in the afternoon's routine gallop.
I am the alveolus of your endurance
love on the path to moans and groans
where inspiration establishes
the articulation of humor;
alveolus of your aspirations
by which you agree to the determined route
without word or allusion.

(Dawn doesn't dream of beginning on the shore,
nor does the coastline creak beneath the bar of light.)

Empathy seals up hemispheres.

M.W.

Epístola

Vivo en un mundo de infancias
enterradas,
de manitas olvidadas en la nieve,
de frágiles pupilas
adheridas al concreto.
Cada noche voy cortando
las pestañas de tu cara,
mis sueños son lluvias
cayendo de un nublado espejo
y mis días los suelos del océano
bajo el agua de los sueños,
y estoy de más
porque soy deforme
tengo la mirada
como raíz en unas venas
brisa de mar
entre la espalda y el pecho,
y estoy de menos
por ser un hueco
entre la puerta de la casa
y los pasos en el cemento,
como la llaga
que sangra miel en la puerta,
nos cuenta de un niño
que desapareció en la madera
con taciturnos vuelos
de gaviotas en su garganta
quiso entrar o salir
al jardín de su espalda
su sangre era de oro
y de cristal sus venas.
Todos los días lamo
la puerta ensangrentada
y me asomo a los colores
que vienen de la calle,
por la banqueta
una muchacha lleva del brazo
a su novio
lo besa
y la tarde se vuelve

Epistle

I live in a world of buried childhoods,
tiny hands forgotten in the snow,
fragile eyes
stuck to the concrete.
Every night I trim
the eyelashes from your face,
my dreams are showers
falling from a clouded mirror
my days the bottom of the ocean
beneath the water of dreams,
and I am out of place
because of my deformities
I'm like
a root growing from a vein of rock
the sea-breeze
on back and chest
and I am too unimportant
to become even the space between
the door of the house
and footsteps in cement,
like the wound
bleeding honey in the doorway,
it tells us of a child
who disappeared into its wood
with quiet flights
of gulls in his throat
he tried to enter or emerge
into the garden of his back
his golden back
his veins of crystal.
Every day I lick
the bloodstained door
amazed at the colors
streaming from the street,
across the sidewalk
a girl strolls arm in arm
with her boyfriend
kisses him
and the evening

una cavilación de sombras
sacudidas por estrellas
Mira:
A mí nadie me lleva.

Vía-Síntesis

No aguanto más...
¡como ansias!
¡¿ansias?!
ya voy, como ansias que se filtran
en los poros de la mesa
–blanca
–opaca
–marca
de la carrera del Sol y las estrellas
en lo que no es
y se toca del viento...

Como ansias
el explorador de puentes y drenajes,
recorre su inconciencia
el animal veloz
rápido
marchita que renueva:
¡Zoom...va!
al rasgar
y corre la iluminación mecánica
sobre la ruta humana,
y brilla el ojo de la rata
sobre el agua,
Animal,
       hombre,
              Máquina
marcha
       pronto
mancha
(mil veces perro
mil veces carro   mil atropella)
         la sangre del perro
y sangra manchando pronto la máquina al perro

becomes a deep thought of shadows
shaken by stars
Look:
nobody comes to carry me away.

M.W.

Via-Synthesis

I can't bear it...
what longing!
longing?
I'm going, like longing filtered
through the table's pores
–white
–opaque
–trademark
of the track of Sun and stars
through what it's not
that's touched by the wind...

Like longings
the explorer of bridges and drainages
crosses his unconsciousness
the swift animal
quick
wilting that renews
Zoom...it works!
slashing
and the mechanical illumination runs
along the human route
and the rat's eye shines
on the water,
Animal,
          man,
                    Machine
it leaves
          right away
stain
(thousand times dog
thousand times car   thousand hustle)
blood of the dog
and bleeds staining quickly from machine to dog

y maquina su sangre pronto manchándose
                              y
                 saluda
con su sangre.

Rojo
rojo
ya viene
ya viene——————@*?!

                    Caracol del ojo
                    que se clava en el alma.

Al final del cuento

Al final del cuento
El héroe se suicida y la princesa le da un beso para que no despierte.

Nos dijeron que nada en este mundo nos hará llorar.

El dragón era mi padre, caemos demasiado lento como para recordarlo.

El brujo me entregó la espada menos ágil,
nada en este mundo nos hará reír.

Volviste tarde, las nupcias no te quisieron esperar.

Al principio del cuento no hablamos con el trino
Entendiendo nada, diciendo todo.

Una caravana recorre el pueblo
Y tú no escapas.

Y porque las mujeres rasgan por un lugar donde nos amen
Nada en este mundo nos hará reír.

Y abrazan y abrazan, intento lo que tiembla en mí!

Y porque sus verdugos incendiados cortan nuestros cantos gritan:

Nada en este mundo nos hará llorar.

and machines its blood quickly staining itself
                          and
              greets
with its blood.

Red
red
he's coming
he's coming—————————@*?!

                        Snail of the eye
                        nailed to the soul.

                                                    H.P.

At the End of the Story

At the end of the story
The hero commits suicide and the princess kisses him so that he won't awaken.

They said that nothing in this world would ever make us cry.

The dragon was my father, we understood too slowly to remember him.

The wizard gave me his slowest sword,
nothing in this world will make us laugh.

You came back late, the wedding refused to wait for you.

At the beginning of the story we didn't warble
We understood nothing but said everything.

A caravan passes through town
and you don't escape.

And because the women fight for a place to love us
Nothing in this world will make us laugh.

They embrace and embrace, and I seek what trembles within me!

And because their burnt headsmen cut our songs they shout:

Nothing in this world will make us cry.

                                                    K.A.E.

Lunáticas

–el lunar del cielo
        (las estrellas son las pecas)
            –el hoyo blanco del universo
–la pupila de la noche
            –una nube encerrada en sí misma
–el globo que se me fue cuando cumplí cinco años
            –un chicle de menta pegado en el techo más alto
–la nostalgia del amanecer
            –la huella digital de algún marciano
–una salpicadura de luz de la pared del día
            –el calendario celeste
–una moneda de plata tirada al aire cuando nadie hizo apuestas
            –la chapa del paraíso
–la agujeta de los tenis de dios
            –un piercing celestial
–un tatuaje nocturno
            –el graffiti del sol
–la Ostia Mayor en la misa del sueño
            –la tumba del primer conejo del universo
–el mejor blanco para cazadores de conejos
            –el pelo del Hombre Lobo y los colmillos de Drácula
–la luciérnaga petrificada
            –la salida de emergencia en la película del sueño
–la ampolla de Lucifer
            –el sello de recibido en la oficina del día
–el ombligo de Andrómeda

"Al llegar al oasis…"

Al llegar al oasis que conocemos
escribiré dos poemas:
el primero extinguirá la sed de sueños
        y cuando eso sucedo
el segundo ya lo habré desperdiciado

Lunacies

–the moon is the sky's beauty mark
      (the stars are its freckles)
           –the white hole in the universe
–the pupil of night's eye
         –a self-contained cloud
–the balloon I lost on my 5th birthday
         –a piece of mint gum stuck to the ceiling
–nostalgia at dawn
         –a Martian's fingerprint
–a spattering of light on the wall of day
         –the celestial calendar
–a silver coin tossed in the air when no one called it
         –the coin toss of paradise
–the lace in God's sneakers
         –a celestial "piercing"
–a nocturnal tattoo
         –the sun's graffiti
–the Ghost Host in the Dream Mass
         –the tomb of the first rabbit in the universe
–the perfect target for rabbit hunters
         –the Wolf Man's fur and Dracula's fangs
–the petrified firefly
         –the emergency exit at the cinema of dreams
–Lucifer's light bulb
         –the in-stamp at day's office
–Andromeda's navel

"On arriving at our familiar oasis…"

On arriving at our familiar oasis
I will write two poems:
the first will quench the thirst for dreams
      and when it's finished
I will already have squandered the second

"Sonoros tiros anuncian..."

Sonoros tiros anuncian
a predadores de plomo
y *Tayé** solo desea
       la aridez de nuestro desierto
       el viento de la montañaz
       y la hierba que ya no ramoneará
jamás.

**Tayé:* borrego en lengua cochimí.

Soledad a los 24 años (mi abuela)

Esa muchacha
ha de haber estado muy loca
para mudarse
a una ciudad
donde tu
iría a nacer

Habrán de pasar
       algunos años
para que otra vez
yo sea mi abuela
fundando ciudades
surgidas de sueños.

1932

Jamás imaginó el migrante
que esa ciudad cruce
iría a ser su tumba
40 años más tarde

"Ringing shots announce..."

Ringing shots announce
lead predators
and *Tayé** only wishes for
      our desert's aridity
      the mountain wind
      and grasses it will never graze
again.

*Tayé: "sheep" in the Cochimí language.

Soledad at 24 (My Grandmother)

That girl
must have been pretty crazy
to move
to a city
where you
would be born

Years would have to pass
before I would become again
my grandmother
founding cities
born of dreams

1932

The migrant never imagined
that this crossroads city
40 years later
would be his tomb

Encuesta nóm. 8,456
central camionera, 12:34 a.m.
de una noche medio húmeda

¿Datos?
6to. de primaria
siembro maíz
mil pendientes
ocho en casa
tempranito, amaneciendo
...primera vez

¿Qué busco?
Vida,
señorita,
la vida.

Survey No. 8,456
Bus Station, 12:34 a.m.
on a moderately humid night

Personal info?
6th grade education
I plant corn
a thousand chores
eight kids at home
early, early, waking up
...my first time

What am I looking for?
Life,
señorita,
life.

P.I.

"Hoy tu voz..."

Hoy tu voz
no tocó mi alma
moribunda;
hoy tu voz
sonó como tantas otras;
agonía
riéndose a carcajadas.
Tu voz
se libró de mi alma,
ya no es infinita
en la mía.

"Superfluo..."

Superfluo
catastrófico
amargo
CORAZÓN
abierto
obscuro
ansioso

"Era un gusano..."

Era un gusano
devorando
mi jardín
de pequeñas
flores plásticas
Estúpido y hambriento
Fugaz

"Casi dentro..."

Casi dentro de mí
besos
desvanecientes angustias
Días fríos

"Today your voice..."

Today your voice
did not touch my
tired soul;
today your voice
sounded like so many others:
agony
loud with laughter.
Your voice
broke free from my soul,
no longer bound
completely to mine.

"Superfluous..."

Superfluous
catastrophic
bitter
HEART
open
obscure
anxious

"It was a worm..."

It was a worm
devouring
my garden
of plastic flowers
Stupid ravenous
Ephemeral

"Almost inside me..."

Almost inside me
kisses
dissipating anxieties
Cold days

Una vez más
dentro de mí,
imposibles de plasmar
sobre estas líneas
inútil siquiera intentarlo.

"Pulverizando..."

Pulverizando
el vacío infinito
de mis ojos
todos mis anhelos
resplandecen
broto
(como varicela)
sobre el tiempo,
aunque no exista
una respuesta
termino suspendida
en el cielo
en medio de la nada
en medio de lo obscuro
....de lo subterráneo
....de lo común
....¡aterrada!

"Sólo ruido..."

Sólo ruido
cuando mi cabeza
pide pensar,
taladrando
hasta el último rincón
de mi mente.
Allí está;
más intenso
e insistente;
maldito,
ignorante,
perfecto.

Once more
inside me,
impossible to capture
in these lines
futile even to try.

"Shattering..."

Shattering
the infinite emptiness
of my eyes
all my desires sparkling
I break out
(it's like chicken pox)
over time,
though there is
no answer
I end up suspended
in the sky
amid nothingness
amid darkness
....the hidden
....the everyday
....terrified!

"When my head..."

When my head
asks for thought
only noise,
drilling
into my mind's
deepest corner.
There it is:
more intense
more insistent;
cursed,
ignorant,
perfect.

P.I.

Arte poética

Homenaje a Altazor *de Vicente Huidobro*

Altazor desciende desde una rebelión de estrellas;
en la punta de mi cigarro coloca sus dos piernas,
ha caído desde lejos y su trayectoria es bienvenida.

¿Existirá la rosa de cien mil pétalos,
el fuego de dulce quemadura,
el viento de agujas invisibles,
el aire de piedra que lo golpea todo?

¿Existirán días con agujeros colgados como aretes,
noches violadas por resplandores íntimos,
mujeres pubis-magnético, hombres lengua-de-hierro?

¿Existirá la criatura que nunca muere,
el cadáver pálido del tiempo,
el embrión de polvo en la placenta del espacio?

Se puede existir el paraguas, tanto puede existir el paraluces;
los poetas del desierto necesitamos un paraluces lírico,
que nos proteja de espejismos, y del exceso
de la palabra *luz* en nuestros versos.

Quiero contemplar un mar de flores, un desierto de olas;
una luna alegre, un sol de carcajadas,
¡planetas diminutos como átomos enormes!

Quiero contemplar cometas donde sólo veo pájaros o aviones;
contemplar estrellas al mediodía o soles a media noche,
quiero contemplar eclipses ordinarios, como beber hormigas o dormir sobre
        un lagarto.

Quiero conocer potros enormes como montañas,
cabalgar el mundo a lomo de un terremoto,
¡saltar indómito en las praderas del atardecer!

Las bestias enormes son más eternas que las obras de arte;
si yo fuera inmenso mi sed de infinito tal vez cesara;
quiero conocer escarabajos místicos,
arañas beatas, abejas eruditas;
conocer al Dios con más súbditos del planeta,

Ars Poetica

Homage to Vicente Huidobro's Altazor

Altazor comes down from a rebellion of stars;
he alights on the tip of my cigar,
he has fallen far and his trajectory is welcome.

Will there be the rose of a hundred petals,
the fire of sweet burning,
the wind of invisible needles,
the stone air that beats down on everything?

Will there be days with holes hung like earrings,
nights violated by intimate radiances,
magnetic-crotched women, iron-tongued men?

Will there be one that never dies,
the pale corpse of time,
the dust embryo in the placenta of space?

There can be umbrellas, and dark glasses;
desert poets, we need lyric shades
to protect us from mirages, and from the excessive
use of the word *light*.

I want to contemplate a sea of flowers, a desert of waves;
a joyful moon, a sun bursting with laughter,
planets as small as enormous atoms!

I want to contemplate comets where now I see only birds or planes;
to contemplate stars at noon or suns at midnight,
I want to contemplate ordinary eclipses, like drinking ants or sleeping on a
        lizard.

I want to know colts as big as mountains,
to ride the world on the back of an earthquake,
to jump untamed in the pastures of evening!

Huge beasts are more eternal than works of art;
perhaps if I were immense my thirst for the infinite would cease;
I want to know mystical beetles,
beatific spiders, erudite bees;
to know the God with more subjects on this planet,

al Dios insecto en su trono de sumbidos
al Dios oscuro de pequeñas alas,
al gran Dios en su trono de zumbidos;
al padre creador, al verdadero,
único y omnisapiente,
Dios mosquito.

Eco nerudiano

Soy una estatua
pero no de piedra
pero no de lluvia
pero no de flores
Soy una estatua
de cristales

Soy un camino
pero no de tierra
pero no de hielo
pero no de luz
Soy un camino
de caracoles

Soy un convento
pero no de polvo
pcro no de viento
pero no de insectos
Soy un convento
dc azucenas

Soy una imagen
pero no de poema
pero no de poeta
pero no de Rimbaud
Soy una imagen
de telescopio

the insect God on his mosquito throne
the dark God of small wings,
great God on his buzzing throne;
father creator, the true one,
unique and all-knowing,
the mosquito God.

Nerudian Echo

I'm a statue
but not of stone
but not of rain
but not of flowers
I'm a statue
of crystal

I'm a road
but not of earth
but not of ice
but not of light
I'm a road
of snails

I'm a convent
but not of dust
but not of wind
but not of insects
I'm a convent
of tiger lilies

I'm an image
but not of the poem
but not of the poet
but not of Rimbaud
I'm an image
of a telescope

H.P.

Naranja

y la mirada sigue
viciada
como dos culebras en el lecho
como un ave macabra

ángel o artefacto

*

en nuestra tierra el paisaje

el cielo es una befa
los árboles escasos y las piedras muchas

junto al seco regajo
los muertos borregos danzan

en un desfiladero
las voces de otro mar se acendran
aguardan el solsticio de los tiempos
y no dudan en perturbar a los viajeros

camino adentro
el repentino incendio de un suspiro y un cirio nos alumbran

*

nada es posible
cuando el bermellón satura el horizonte
y el cielo es cándido
y una sola línea la fuga
          de la mirada

*

nos despojaron del elixir
nos cambiaron las líneas de la mano

somos el alivio de la madre

*

CARLOS ADOLFO GUTIÉRREZ VIDAL

Orange

and the glance follows
corrupted
like two snakes in bed
like a gruesome bird

angel or artifact

*

in our country the landscape

the sky is a taunt
trees scarce and rocks abundant

alongside the dry watercourse
dead lambs dance

in a gully
voices from another sea are purified
expecting the solstice of the times
and they don't hesitate to disturb travelers

down by the road
the sudden fire of a sigh and a cirio cactus illuminate us

*

nothing is possible
when vermilion saturates the horizon
and the sky is white
the gaze's flight
        a single line

*

they kept the elixir from us
they changed the lines on our hands

we are mother's consolation

*

somos choque   la voz perdida

somos los signos de los tiempos
un archipiélago
un continente trazado sobre el aire
manos que dicen lo que el viento

*

otro mundo nos espera en la mañana
una mansa vida
la hermandad de siempre
más allá de la agripnia

las ruedas de la santimonia

la arrebatada puericia

*

los coyotes nos salieron del costado
y el corazón se nos llenó de agua
muy cerca estaba el despeñadero de las almas

dijiste: *la luna es el sol de los ciervos*
la voz el pozo de los hombres
en el preludio de la muerte

yo dije: *nos hace falta una silla*
algunos tiestos

pero un amplexo obstruyó nuestros plurívocos ruegos
luego un mutismo de postal
los cardos
la demencia y el planto

una línea continua postergando el encuentro de la carne

*

errar es un solaz como cualquiera
como lanzar perdigones a las aves

*

y los chopos vanos
y las llagas deslumbrantes

we are shock   the lost voice

we are the signs of the times
an archipelago
a continent traced on the air
hands that say what the wind says

*

another world awaits us in the morning
a calm life
the endless brotherhood
beyond the agripnia

sanctimony's wheels

innocence wrenched away

*

coyotes came out of our sides
and our hearts filled with water
the cliff of souls was very close

you said, *"moon is sun to the deer,*
voice is the well of men
before death"

I said: *"we need a chair*
some flowerpots"

but an embracing obstructed our many-voiced prayers
then a postal silence
the thistles
madness and the flood of tears

a continuous line postponing the meeting of the flesh

*

to make a mistake is a solace like any other
like shooting at birds with a shotgun

*

and the useless poplars
and the dazzling wounds

Tierra prometida

para Max Llanes

primero fuimos la niebla
trepando en el alambre la niebla
alumbrando su trayecto
reflejo antagónico del mundo

primero el principio de la sombra
de un espacio recorrido
sin esfuerzo   de cierto parpadeo
en la velocidad aciaga   y el transcurso
daba fe de un tiempo
que no correspondía a nuestro deseo

¿cómo alcanzarnos en el rumbo?

¿cómo tentar materia y alma
sin percibir la diferencia
otra sonrisa calándonos el rostro?

primero otros fuimos raíces sin abono
aliciente de un cosmos repentino
¿cómo hermanarnos sin asombro?

habíamos de traspasar otra frontera
y nada nos era tan distinto
habíamos de cruzar una autopista
de contraria dirección a nuestra vista
y hacerlo nos era placentero

cierto era el mundo y nuestro
cierta la hora del arribo y libre
el paso hacia la incertidumbre inmensa

la música nos trajo otro misterio
nada tan cercano a la gracia
como contemplarnos los dedos en la sombra

era la tierra un cariño tan sincero
como el alba era la tierra
una sonrisa postergada
en los brazos de todos de lo ausente
era la tierra más tierra que otras veces
nos obsequiaba a cada paso una vereda

Promised Land

for Max Llanes

first we were the fog
climbing the wire the fog
illuminating its path
antagonistic reflection of the world

first the beginnings of the shadow
of a space crossed effortlessly
of a certain blinking
in the unlucky speed   and its course
yielded the faith of a time
that didn't correspond to our desire

how can we overtake ourselves along the way?

how can we touch matter and spirit
without perceiving the difference
another smile drenching our faces?

first we were others roots without security
attraction of a sudden cosmos
how can we become brothers without fear?

we had to cross another border
and nothing could have been more different
we had to cross a highway
in the direction opposite to our line of sight
and it pleased us to do so

the world was certain and it was ours
certain the time of arrival and free
the passage toward an immense uncertainty

music brought us other mysteries
nothing closer to grace
than contemplating our fingers in the dark

the land was a tenderness sincere
as the dawn the land
was a smile postponed
in the arms of all the absent
the land was more land than at other times
at every step a pathway entertained us

era la tierra un templo descifrado
perpetrábamos la danza y el sacrificio
los dedos se clavaban en los ojos para nada

la voz del aire clavada en el contento
la voz del ojo perpetrando su silencio
la voz del can el cálido embalaje del cuerpo

eran los dedos partículas de sombra
aclamábamos la luz en el delirio
bastaba la piel de otros tan certera

las lenguas se clavaban en el aire
las lenguas nos llamaban cada hora
revelando una sed incontenible
las lenguas parpadeaban en el tronco
puesto encima de nosotros sin motivo

la piel perpetraba cada paso
la piel era un vértice
de sombras   una historia
contenida en el asombro
de algún vértigo hallado sin esfuerzo

la piel nos traía de vuelta a casa

la piel a contraluz detrás del templo

After Hours

para Iván Díaz Robledo

Aquella era la luna de septiembre,
inmóvil, luminosa,
eje eterno de los astros.
Tocabas el agua con la palma de la mano;
las olas, coronadas de una espuma fluorescente,
parecían que iban a tragarte de un bocado.

–La humanidad es un prejuicio–,
dijo alguien perdido entre las rocas.
–La humanidad es nuestro juicio–,
pensé mientras frotaba con arena mi frente.

the land was a deciphered temple
we perpetrated both dance and sacrifice
fingers plunged into eyes for nothing

the voice of the air held fast to joy
the voice of the eye committing its silence
the voice of the dog the warm wrapping of the body

fingers were particles of darkness
in rapture we applauded the light
the skin of others was enough that sure

tongues pierced the breeze
tongues called to us at every hour
revealing an unquenchable thirst
tongues flickered on the trunk
placed over us for no reason

the skin committed each step
the skin was a vertex
of shadows   a history
contained in the astonishment
of some vertigo found effortlessly

the skin brought us back home

the skin against the light behind the temple

After Hours

for Iván Díaz Robledo

That was September's moon,
motionless, bright,
eternal axis of the stars.
You touched the water with the palm of your hand;
the waves, crowned with fluorescent foam,
seemed about to swallow you whole.

"Humanity is a prejudice,"
someone said, lost among the rocks.
"Humanity is our judgment,"
I thought as I rubbed sand on my forehead.

Y así, sintiéndonos prehumanos,
pioneros de nuestra propia historia,
tratábamos de hallarle
nuevas formas a las constelaciones.

El cielo era una playa inmensa
que había que recorrer,
nosotros dos láminas empotradas en la arena.
Fui el espejo de la danza ulterior;
entonces recordé que de niño
me gustaba contemplar el horizonte,
presentir el punto exacto
en que la tierra daba vuelta.

De súbito las voces,
arrebatándose palabra tras palabra.
De súbito un pelícano
diciéndonos que uno
es la primera sílaba del nombre.
Fuimos monosilábicos entonces,
pronunciamos monosílabos
en un idioma nuevo,
un punto medio entre la risa
y aquello que precede a la palabra.

–Me gustaría tener hijos con las flores–,
dije en silencio,
tú dijiste que hacía tiempo
no veías alguna y te hacía falta.

A veces hablo con los muertos.
A veces las flores charlan
con las piedras y se callan.

Horas antes la autopista
bailaba en nuestros brazos;
habíamos olvidado
de dónde provenía tanta luz.
Mi mano se cerró
como un destello sobre la arena,
y caí de nuevo frente al cielo,
con el corazón lleno de desierto.

Thus, feeling ourselves prehuman,
pioneers of our own history,
we tried to find new shapes
in the constellations.

The sky was an immense beach
that we had to walk down,
we, two engravings embedded in the sand.
I was the mirror of the subsequent dance;
then I remembered that as a boy
I liked to contemplate the horizon,
to anticipate the exact point
on which the earth was spinning.

Suddenly the voices
were being swept away, word after word.
Suddenly a pelican
was telling us that one
is the first syllable of the name.
We were monosyllabic then,
pronouncing monosyllables
in a new language,
a midpoint between laughter
and what comes before words.

"I would like to have children with flowers,"
I said in silence;
you said it had been a while
since you'd seen any and you missed them.

Sometimes I talk with the dead.
Sometimes the flowers chat
with the rocks and they fall silent.

Hours before the highway
danced in our arms;
we had forgotten where so much light
came from.
My hand closed
like a sparkle on the sand,
and once again I fell before the sky,
my heart overflowing with desert.

¿Quién nos obligaba, criaturas de la noche,
a intercambiar palabra y pensamiento?
Nuestra moneda era el verbo
en aquella feria improvisada.
Casi desde la ingravidez, hablábamos del este y del oeste
como dos cuerpos paralelos,
improbables, perseguidos.

Habíamos de construir un escudo
contra tanta inocencia revelada,
uno que sirviese para cruzar la distancia
entre el deseo y la palabra.
Aquel escudo sería el vértigo.

Miles de kilómetros a ras del suelo
habrían de mostrarnos una puerta.
¿De cuál de los dos lados veníamos?
¿Qué nos hacía cuestionar
el orden y el nombre de los astros?

Neonatos. Delirantes.
Tal vez debíamos morir
para clarificar el sueño de los otros,
olvidar un verso apenas presentido
porque era demasiado tarde para pronunciarlo.
Pero era el tiempo justo
y la risa una proeza que no nos era ajena.

Y los objetos huían de nuestra vista,
y el cielo se abrió sobre el desierto de las manos.
La violencia del cuerpo
se nutría de aquellas verdades.
Y nada podía detenernos.

La historia estaba sumergiéndose en las aguas.

Orión estaba colgado en el vacío,
preferimos evocar el alba
antes que la noche terminara.

Who forced us, creatures of the night,
to exchange word and thought?
Our currency at that improvised fair
was the word.
Since almost before gravity we spoke of east and west
as two parallel bodies,
improbable, pursued.

We had to build a shield
against so much revealed innocence,
a shield that would cross the distance
between desire and word.
That shield would be vertigo.

Thousands of kilometers at ground level
would reveal a door to us.
Which side did we come from?
What made us question
the order and names of stars?

Neonates. Frenzied.
Perhaps we should die
to purify the others' dream,
to forget a verse that was scarcely foretold
because it was too late to recite it.
But it was the right time
and laughter was a familiar exploit.

And the objects escaped our sight,
and the sky opened above the desert of our hands.
The violence of the body
nurtured itself on those truths.
And nothing could stop us.

History was submerged beneath the waters.

Orion hung in the void.
We preferred to conjure the dawn
before night ended.

S.B. & M.W.

Maníacos y locos

rencos ubicuos con las greñas tiesas y la ropa
puerca y desgarrada
deambulan por las calles atoradas
hurgan entre los monotones de basura colectiva, los desperdicios
afuera de las escuelas, comen la escamocha de los restaurantes
    meten la mano y el hocico en las capitaneadas cajitas de comida china y
        revuelta,
recogen la lechuga rancia tirada alrededor de las taquerías
        permanecen cerca de los puestos de comida callejera
porque esa es su única esperanza de comida tibia,
pero huyen de los taqueros porque sus delantales blancos embarrados
de sangre y pellejos les recuerdan los horrores de las enfermerías,
los maníacos pepenan las verduras pachichis afuera de la central de abastos,
comen gatos y palomas que asesinan y calientan
en los callejones y luego alacenan en los sobacos,
beben aguas negras en los parques públicos
y en los charcos que se anidan en los baches de asfalto,
rejuntan frascos, buscando latas entre las alcantarillas calamitosas
pordioserando botellas y alambres,
en sus rostros se extreman los rasgos del mundo externo
y la catacumba interior,
monjes locos
        limosneros poseídos
ciegos embrutecidos, lisiados cínicos,
salen al paso
        en la avenida
piden monedas aventando su mal aliento en la cara
de los cuerdos,
deformados por los días tronando
          un vaso de plástico en la acera cicatrizada
por los pasos,
        acosan escaparates y taxistas,
se mean en postes fálicos
        e hidrantes estupefactos,
cruzan la calle desnudos enseñando la quemadura extensa,
tocan a secretarias semana inglesa y horas extras,
molestan a estudiantes a punto de titularse
de muerte por hambre, hacen caras
a ejecutivos esperando la luz verde del semáforo sobornado
por el reglamento municipal,

Maniacs and Crazies

ubiquitous gimps with matted hair
    and greasy clothes
walking down bottleneck streets,
digging through piles of garbage   the remains
of school lunches and restaurant scraps   plunging
their hands and muzzles into boxes of mixed leftovers of chinese takeout,
harvesting half-rotten lettuce tossed into the street by taco stands,
hovering around food vendors,
          their only hope for a mouthful of warm food,
although the taco makers' blood-spattered aprons terrify them
reminding them of the horrors of psych wards.
Maniacs recycling dried-up vegetables outside cut-rate markets,
eating cats and pigeons that they kill and cook
on dead-end streets, using their armpits as cupboards, drinking water
from gutters in public parks or puddles
in the asphalt's potholes, gathering soda bottles,
searching the manholes of despair for aluminum cans,
panhandling for empty bottles and scraps of bailingwire,
their features a mockery of the face of the world outside
and of the catacomb
                within.
Crazy monks
        possessed mendicants
the brutish blind and the disabled who calculate
the profits of disability
encountered on the avenue asking for coins
        in exchange for foul breath blown into the faces
of the sane, the deformed tapping
their plastic cups all day on the cracked sidewalk,
pressing grotesque faces to shop windows,
pissing on phallic telephone poles and dumb fire hydrants,
crossing the streets naked, their skin
                      burned and blistered,
fondling secretaries from high-class companies and the others
        who work to exhaustion in sweatshops,
hassling students about to graduate into god-knows-what,
making faces at executives waiting for the light to change
according to the government schedule of corruption.

                    son incurables
los maníacos
            jalan la camisa de los tanseúntes, raspan
la ventanilla de los conductores,
se dejan crecer la barba hasta que una infección los deja
molachos y sin cejas,
empujan carritos de mercado
                            pandeados y ruidosos,
hacen muecas y oraciones
                        engendros de la ingenería social
sordomudos heroinómanos
exigen su limosna
                los más depravados se esconden
en algún sitio, una parada de camión,
un tiradero, una banca, los techos bajos
para aguardar benefactor o victima,
los recoge la policía y la gerencia del hospital psiquiátrico local
no quiere saber nada de ellos, los dementes
son inmigrantes que enloquecieron
por el calor del pavimento,
drogadictos que se quedaron arriba,
extranjeros enajenados,
desempleados que a los pocos meses
de perder su escritorio, también perdieron la cabeza,
hombres y mujeres expatriados de su familia
apestados sociales
vociferan denuncias y estupideces
mientras se sostienen el transfigurado trapo
que usan de pantalones,
                    locos urbanos por todas las calles
gritando, arrastrándose,
                        llagados, apestosos,
pervertidos sexuales, vendedores de mercancías
robadas, carteristas, asalta indígenas y turistas,
sacos de golpear, criaderos de gangrena,
robachicos, violadores, desaparecidos
tostados por el sol, arruinados por el ruido de los
automóviles, muertos de escalofrío nocturno,
más asustados que cualquier otro ciudadano
de los tiroteos en la vía pública,
                    los locos caminan sin parar
se tropiezan con el gentío, los atropella el tráfico
maníacos y locos de una ciudad
que sólo les escupe baños de agua fría, golpizas
y monedas borradas por la codicia digital de los dedos contables,

Incurable maniacs tugging at the shirt-sleeves of passersby and scratching at
        windshields,
letting their beards grow as their teeth fall out
                            because of infections,
losing even their eyebrows,
pushing precarious shopping carts with broken wheels,
grimacing, addressing orations
                  to the streets at large,
these products of social engineering,
deaf-mute heroin addicts
        demanding alms,
the more depraved in hiding
anywhere, in bus shelters,
empty lots, on a bench beneath the eaves, in wait
           for victim or benefactor.
The police gather them in, but the authorities at the local psychiatric hospital
don't want to know anything about them–the deranged
migrants who lost it because of the sidewalk's heat
drug addicts who've never come down
foreigners
        cut off from home
unemployed workers who a few months back
lost jobs and minds, men and women
divorced from their families, social outcasts
shouting nonsense and denunciations
while clutching the transfigured rags they wear in place of pants,
street crazies on every corner
screaming, crawling,
suppurating, stinking
perverts   fences   pickpockets   muggers
      of tourists and Indians,
punching-bags nurseries of gangrene
abductors of children
rapists   runaways
roasted by the sun   wrecked
by the noise of cars   and at night
chilled to the bone.
Even jumpier than the rest of us from the sounds of gunshots
in the streets   they're always
in motion, bumping
through crowds, run down
by traffic
      the maniacs and crazies of a city
that spits at them cold showers beatings
and coins rubbed thin by avarice–which is why

para que se retiren de la vista
                    y no asusten
cuando la noche se desploma y los edificios abandonados
se vuelven espantosos, las farmacias apagan sus luces
exteriores, las zapaterías mandan a casa a sus
empleadas, y sólo queda el ruido de otros locos,
repegándose contra los pocos comercios donde al tocar la cortina de hierro no
exclama la alarma,
los maníacos callejeros comienzan a golpearse la cabeza,
se esconden unos de otros,
se meten a dormir en cajas de cartón desechadas por los consumidores
y las pizzerías,
                    tambos o cobijas arañadas,
repasan en la mente el mundo de los empleados y los cuerdos
(los hombres que pagan renta o lavan su auto),
y caen en la segunda parte de un viaje moribundo
pues
        cuando la ciudad amenaza con hacerse noche
sus locos mueren
                    en cierto porcentaje.

La vida de una mujer cucapá

Ahora tengo estufa de gas.
Y ya mi casa no es mi cuerpo enroscado
a un lado del fuego que puso mi abuelo.
Mi casa actual está amueblada.
Tengo estufa integral,
pero me ahoga y prefiero hacer la comida
en el fogón de afuera.
Rete a gusto en la noche
haciendo mi quehacer.
Desgraciadamente, no hay manera
de conservar las costumbres de los indios
¿quién las va a usar ya?
Rete a gusto en la noche
haciendo mi quehacer.
Mucha gente me dice "¿qué estás haciendo?
¿qué, no tienes gas? Sí,
sí tengo, pero si me traen leña
más a gusto hago los frijoles.
Rete a gusto en la noche
haciendo mi quehacer.

no longer frightening
they hide from view at nightfall
when abandoned buildings become terrifying and the drugstores
have shut their streetlights, the shoestore clerks
have left for home and there's no sound
but the other crazies, and they huddle against the gratings of the few stores
whose alarms don't go off at the merest touch.
Then the street crazies beat their heads with their fists they hide
from each other they sleep
in cardboard boxes discarded by consumers and pizzerias,
in barrels, or wrapped
in shredded blankets,
the world of the employed, the normal
          (those who pay the rent and wash their cars)
rehearsed in their minds as they fall
into the second part of a dying voyage,
       because each time the city's day threatens
to turn to night
a certain proportion
          of its crazies die.

                                 M.W.

The Life of a Cucapá Woman

Now I have a gas stove
And my house is no longer this twisted body
beside the fire
my grandfather made.
My new house is furnished.
I have a store-bought stove, but it suffocates me,
and I prefer to cook
outside, on an open fire.
I love doing my chores
at night.
It's too bad, there's no way
to save the Indian ways
Who would use them?
I love doing my chores
at night.
Many people ask me,
"What are you doing? What,
you don't have gas?" I do, but cooking beans
makes me happier if they bring me wood.
I love doing my chores
at night.

No, pero deveras, señor,
aquí nadie de nosotros conserva
sus costumbres.
Yo cocino en la noche, nada más.
A veces, cuando otro indio me visita,
ese día lo aprovecho hasta llenarme de
hablar cucapá.
Porque a mí me gusta mi idioma,
            cuando lo hablo
parece que viera
                y reviviera
toda mi gente que ya se fue.

(Poema construido con las palabras de Adela Portillo (n. 1923), hija de madre cucapá, en entrevista con Everardo Garduño)

Del estilo de vida "poco común" de los indios cucapá citados por R.W. Hale Hardy, teniente británico explorando del Golfo de California

Entre nosotros
existe la tendencia a no discutir o arrebatar
la propiedad de otros hombres.
Vivimos contentos en grupo
nuestros vecinos están felices con nosotros.
En la guerra somos invencibles
en la paz somos corteses.
Nuestras mujeres cuidan a los niños.
Conocen la valentía, no la venganza.

¡Entre cristianos qué diferente!

Ellos beben fuego
consideran esa bebida como nosotros
consideramos a nuestros dioses
el fuego que beben los convierte en locos
Apuestan a sus familias
Asesinan a sus amigos
Se roban ellos mismos
Son capitandeados por tiranos crueles
Bajo el signo de la cruz persiguen a los que se defienden
Engañan a los fuertes

¡Entre cristianos qué diferente!

In truth, sir, no one
maintains our ways here
any more. It's just
I cook at night.
And sometimes, when another Indian
visits me I gorge myself on
speaking Cucapá.
Because I love my language,
            when I speak it
I seem to see
            and see again
all of my people who now are gone.

(after Adela Portillo, as interviewed by Everardo Garduño)

On the "Unusual" Lifestyle of the Cucapá Indians as Recorded by R.W. Hale Hardy, British Lieutenant, while Exploring the Gulf of California

We tend not to argue among ourselves,
nor do we steal the property of others.
We live contentedly together,
our neighbors are happy with us.
In war we are invincible
in peace affable.
Valiant, not vengeful, our women
care for the children.

How different the Christians are!

They drink fire
they think of this drink
as we think of our gods
the fire they drink makes them crazy
They wager their families
They murder their friends
They rob one another
Their leaders are tyrants
The cross gives them authority
To persecute the weak
And deceive the strong

How different the Christians are!

Sus ancianos no son buenos para dar consejo.
Sus hombres jóvenes nos han hecho sufrir sólo
con venir hacia nosotros.
Nuestro pueblo está dispuesto a estar en paz
con ellos, pero nuestros guerreros
han jurado que no van a sufrir
viviendo entre los blancos.

¡Entre cristianos qué diferente!

[*Construido a partir de una cita contenida en Robert William Hale Hardy en* Travels in the
Interior of Mexico in 1825, 1827, and 1828, *(Londres, 1829)*]

Cada verano

de vez en cuando
se ve una seca planta
rodando por el boulevard
de Tijuana
una bola epinosa
casi dos metros de diámetro
metiéndose entre el tráfico
desconcertados
automovilistas paran
en seco dejan
una raya más negra
en el pavimiento
chocan
alguien hace una broma
sobre la revancha
de la naturaleza
cada verano
de vez en cuando
una bola espinosa
baja de algún cerro quizá
de un baldío perdido
en las afueras
rueda por las calles
señal chusca
del inminente
regreso
del desierto

Their old men give bad advice
and the young men have made us suffer
merely by approaching us.
We are prepared to make peace,
but our warriors have sworn
never to allow themselves
to live among white men.

How different the Christians are!

> [After *Robert William Hale Hardy*, Travel in the Interior of Mexico in 1825, 1827 and
> 1828, *(London 1829)*]

H.P.

Each Summer

Once in a while
a tumbleweed
rolls down the boulevard
in Tijuana
a spiny ball
just shy of 6 feet wide
interrupting traffic.
Surprised, drivers
stop short
leaving
a line of skid-marks still darker
than the pavement,
rear-ending
each other.
Joking, someone calls it
nature's revenge.
Once in a while
each summer
a spiny ball
descends a hill, perhaps
from an empty lot
lost in the outskirts, and rolls
down the streets
like a sly intimation
of the desert's
imminent return.

M.W.

"Ha encontrado su reflejo..."

Ha encontrado su reflejo en la ventana, su cara
sobre el vidrio confundiéndose entre eso que ve afuera y que parece estar tan
       lejos y aún tan cerca de tocarse

su mano seguramente terminará
en-friada por el contacto con la superficie.

"Ésta no es tu amante..."

a H.M.E.

Ésta no es tu amante es
una reproducción de tu amante
no...ésta es una fotografía de tu amante. Ésta es una vieja
fotografía de tu amante raspada de tanto uso, dije: "El reflejo
de tu amante
ésta es una persona soñando con tu amante
ésta es una mujer soñando ser tu amante
ésta es una inscripción en la pared que dice 'amante' al lado
de un número telefónico de alguien que dice ser tu amante y no es
más que alguien idéntica a tu amante
el retrato de tu amante
una muñeca inflable a la figura de tu amante
la gemela de tu amante ésta
es alguien a quien todos dicen conocer como tu amante
ésta es alguien que ni tú ni nadie sabe excepto ella que es tu amante.
Ella termina siendo tu amante.

"He aquí un amante..."

a H.M.E.

He aquí un amante: guapo, carita y bien fornido,
poeta, perfil de modelo y con dinero y un letrero en el pecho que dice: "Adelante"
       y adelante
ya adentro he ahí una mujer: tan chula, inteligente y de
buenos sentimientos (buenísima para el sexo) y portando un letrero
sobre sus blancos senos rezando: "Adelante" y adentro
a su vez adentro de ella
su amante, una vez más, con sus ojos perdidos sobre el trópico del deseo
portando un letrero que dice: "Adelante" y adelante ya

JUAN REYNA

"He found his reflection in the window..."

He found his reflection in the window, his face
on the glass getting lost between what he saw outside and what seemed to be
        still further off but close enough to touch

His hand would surely end up chilled
by its contact with the surface.

"This is not your lover..."

for H.M.E.

This is not your lover it's
a reproduction of your lover
no, a photograph of your lover. It's an old
photograph of your lover, worn from use, I said: "The reflection
of your lover
is someone who dreams of your lover
a woman who dreams of becoming your lover
a scribble on the wall that says 'lover' next to
the telephone number of someone who claims to be your lover but is only
someone identical to your lover
the image of your lover
an inflatable doll with your lover's figure
your lover's twin someone
to whom everyone says that they understand her to be your lover
someone who neither you nor anyone else knows is your lover except her.
And in the end she becomes your lover."

"Here's a lover..."

for H.M.E.

Here's a lover: good looking, sweet face, well-built,
a poet with a model's profile, money in his pocket and he wears a sign on his
        chest that says: "Step right in," and
inside there's a woman: cute, smart,
nice (and great in bed), wearing a sign
on her white breasts proclaiming "Step right in," and inside
and within her once again her lover, his eyes lost in the tropic of desire,
wearing a sign that says "Step right in" and inside

adentro está otra vez ella, su amante: una mujer
perdiéndose en los hemistiquios de su amado y portando
entre su ombligo y su barbilla (a quién sabe cuántos centímetros del sexo)
un letrero que dice: "Adelante" y adelante ya adentro él y adentro de éste ella,
        así
repitiéndose sucesivamente y reduciendo cada vez más su tamaño a fin de que
        pueda uno caber dentro del otro y el otro caber dentro del uno infinita-
        mente y viceversa
haciéndose cada vez más pequeños hasta que
el letrero que cada uno porta se hace cada vez más difícil de leer
las letras poco a poco se disuelven
ante los ojos, los cuerpos cada vez más pequeños hasta existir
sólo en la imaginación:
he aquí dos amantes vacíos.

"Casi ya no hay camas…"

a H.M.E.

Casi ya no hay camas, casi ya no hay sueños, ¿entiende? Ya no hay tiempo
ya se acaba casi el número de puertas, de ventanas, de salidas
disgustándonos. Ni modo
ya será otro día
de pronto ya casi no hay diccionarios, ¿escucha?
Ya cómo explicarlo casi ya no hay carros (¿o será que ella no tiene lugar o más
        asientos restantes?)
casi ya no hay cuentos es
que casi ya no hay más poemas y ya no hay acción
casi
nos quedamos sin padre, ¡madres!, o sin madre (¡qué padre!)
"Ya no hay primas casi–dije–. Ya no hay acción. ¿Sí sabe usted?
Deje que le explique
de pronto parece que ya no hay mujeres, sí: tampoco que hubiera deseo y no hay
        manera de evitarlo
pues casi han quedado prohibidas las golosinas. Ya casi
nos quedamos sin paraíso
es que casi ya no hay chocolate y prohibido
esculcar los botes de basura en busca de comida. Será que casi ya no hay
        tiempo, aguánteme
deje le digo: ya casi no hay recuerdos y se me aguanta que ya
casi no hay memoria
ya casi no hay esquinas, ya casi no hay callejones, casi ya no hay noche
ya no hay comas–casi ya no hay coca casi–ya no hay mañas.
¿Qué se han hecho nuestros nervios?
casi ya no hay vergüenza. ¿Entiende lo que digo?

there she is again, his lover: a woman
losing herself in her beloved's verse and wearing
between her navel and her chin (who knows how near her genitals) a sign
that says: "Step right in" and inside and within her he, then she,
successively repeated, each time smaller, so that each can fit within the other and
        so on and vice versa
each time the sign that each one wears
becoming smaller and more difficult to read
bit by bit the letters dissolving
before their eyes, their bodies each time smaller until they remain
only in imagination: and here we have
two empty lovers.

"There are almost no more beds now..."

for H.M.E.

There are almost no more beds now, almost no more dreams–get it? No more
        time,
the number of doors, windows, exits, is almost exhausted
annoying. No matter
there will be another day
but suddenly the dictionaries are almost gone. Do you hear me?
How to explain it–there are almost no cars (or is it that she has no reservation
        and there are no seats left?)
Almost no stories
almost no poems no plot
we are left
almost no fathers (oh, momma!) no mothers (oh, daddy!)
"Almost no cousins," I said. "No plot." Do you understand?
I'll spell it out:
suddenly there seem to be no women, yeah, no lust, and there's no way out
even sweets are almost forbidden. Almost no paradise
is left for us
there's almost no chocolate and it's illegal
to paw for food through trash cans. It's as if there's almost no time, hold on
I'm not finished: there are almost no more recollections, I can't stand it
almost no memory
almost no corners, no alleyways, no night,
no commas–almost no coke, almost, almost no quirks.
What's become of our minds?
There's almost no shame. Do you hear me?

Ya casi no hay momentos, espéreme tantito
ya casi termino
ya casi no hay cines, ni plastilina o vibradores o pleitesía
y las orejas, los ojos ¡ay! es que ya casi no hay palabras.
¿Le dije que casi ya no hay tiempo?
oh sí: y casi ya no hay nadie. Escuche: sólo
ilusiones al estar solo frente a un espejo.

Almost no moments, hold on,
I'm almost done,
no movies, no play dough no vibrators no deference
nor ears, eyes, oh almost no words,
Did I say that there's almost no time?
Yeah, and almost nobody. Listen: when you're alone
in front of the mirror there are only illusions.

M.W.

BIOGRAPHIES

Note:

We have listed individual poets' names in the manner in which they most commonly sign their work. For those who follow the traditional Spanish convention, in which the father's precedes the mother's family name, we have alphabetized by the former.

Because of limitations of space we have provided full bibliographic information only for sources of selections in the anthology.

Abbreviations

CECUT	Centro Cultural Tijuana
CONACULTA	Consejo Nacional para la Cultura y las Artes
ICBC	Instituto de Cultura de Baja California
IMAC	Instituto Municipal de Arte y Cultura–Tijuana
UABC	Universidad Autónoma de Baja California
UABCS	Universidad Autónoma de Baja California Sur
UIN	Universidad Iberoamericana Noroeste
UNAM	Universidad Nacional Autónoma de México.

Ernesto Adams (Tijuana, B.C., 1954). Resident of La Paz, B.C.S. since childhood. Studied economics at UABCS, where he is professor of library and information sciences. His book *Thurnera Aphrodisiaco* (La Paz: UABCS, 1994), from which "Maldición" and "Preceptos de la antigua y verdadera religión" were drawn, was published in 1994.

Elizabeth Algrávez (Mexicali, B.C., 1972). Currently a resident of Tijuana, where she is director of IMAC (Municipal Institute of Arts and Culture). Graduate of Centro de Estudios Literarios del Instituto de Cultura de Baja California, where she majored in literature. She has published *Cantos buranos. Traducción de los Carminas Burana* (1993), and three poetry collections: *La mujer habitada* (1994), *Arenario* (1994) and *Trilogía de arena* (Guerrero: Monte Gargano, 1999), from which "Arenario" was drawn. "Alfa y omega" was published in the journal *Tierra adentro* (San Ángel, D.F.: CONACULTA, 1997, v. 97).

Eduardo Arellano (Zacatecas, Zacatecas, 1959). Resident of Mexicali and Tijuana since 1988. Graduate of Universidad Autónoma de Nuevo León in Spanish literature. Teaches at UABC–Tijuana. He has published *La revolutión del desierto* (1990, translation. Author: Lowell L. Blaisdell), and three poetry collections: *Diáspora o pasión* (1984), *Desierto de la palabra* (1994) and *La tierra destinada* (Monterrey: Libros de la Mancuspia, 1999), from which "Amanecer de los amantes" was drawn. "Australopithecus Robustus" and "Camino a Tecate" are previously unpublished.

Mario Bojórquez (Los Mochis, Sinaloa, 1968). Resident of Baja California since 1989. He has published eight poetry collections: *Pájaros sueltos* (Mexicali: ICBC, 1991), from which "Cartas de Averroes" was drawn; *Penélope revisitada* (1992); *Los domésticos* (1993); *Bitácora de viaje de Fortum Ximénez, descubridor y conquistador de la isla de la California* (1993); *La mujer disuelta* (1995); *Contradanza de pie de barro* (Mexico City: CONACULTA, 1996), from which "Hay un viento que sopla," "El barro es una cosa" and "El pie no tiene un nombre" were drawn; and *Diván de Mouraria* (1999).

Flora Calderón (Mexico City, 1967). Resident of Baja California since the mid-80s. She has published *Montes de espuma sanguínea* (1989), *Ventana* (1991), *Pasión y canto de Estefanía de la luz* (1993), and *Marea de brujas* (Mexicali: La Rebelión de las Musas, ICBC, 1998), from which all of her poems in this anthology were drawn.

Noé Carrillo Martínez (Frasnillo, Zacatecas, 1970). Resident of Tijuana since early childhood. Director of Cultural Relations at CECUT, in charge of literary events and publications. He has published *El tiempo cada día* (1996) and *Aquí debería estar tu nombre* (Chimalistac, D.F.: Fondo Editorial Tierra Adentro / CONACULTA, 1999), from which all of his poems in this anthology were drawn.

Roberto Castillo Udiarte (Tecate, B.C., 1951). Resident of Tijuana. Teaches at UABC–Tijuana. He has published a volume of translations of the poetry of Charles Bukowski, two books of nonfiction, and one of short stories, and four poetry collections: *Blues cola de lagarto* (Mexicali: Gobierno del Estado de Baja California, 1985), from which "La última función del mago de los espejos" was drawn; *Cartografía del alma* (1987); *Nuestras vidas son otras* (1994); and *La pasión de Angélica según el Johnny Tecate* (1996).

Elizabeth Cazessús (Tijuana, B.C., 1960). Poet and performance artist, she has published four poetry collections: *Ritual y canto* (Mexicali: ICBC, 1994), from which "San Andrés Cohamiata," "El poeta" and "Flor de agua" were drawn; *Veinte apuntes antes de dormir* (1998); *Huella en el agua* (2000); and *Mujer de sal* (Mexicali: La Rebelión de las Musas, ICBC, 2000), from which "A la profundidad del mar..." and "Me desvisto del traje de abandono..." were drawn.

Rosina Conde (Mexicali, B.C., 1954). Resident of Tijuana since 1958. Poet, fiction writer, editor, jazz and blues singer and television director. Studied language and literature at UNAM. She has published five books of stories, one novel, and three poetry collections: *Poemas de seducción* (Mexico City: La Máquina a Escribir, 1981), from which "En secreto" was drawn; *De amor gozoso, textículos* (1992); and *Bolereando el llanto* (1993). "Mary Key" was published in the anthology *Baja California. Piedra de serpiente* (Mexico City: CONACULTA, 1993).

Luis Cortés Bargalló (Tijuana, B.C., 1952). Studied at UNAM. Resident of Mexico City since 1975. He has published, among others, volumes of translations of the poetry of William Carlos Williams and Gary Snyder, the anthology *Baja California. Piedra de serpiente* (1993), and four poetry collections: *Terrario* (1979); *El circo silencioso* (1985); *La soledad del polo* (Mexico City: Ediciones Toledo, 1990), from which "Dream song," "Prenda de amor" and "Tijuana moods / Ch. Mingus" were drawn; and *Al margen indomable* (Mexico City: CONACULTA, 1996).

Raúl Antonio Cota (La Paz, B.C.S., 1949). Literary journalist, editor, anthologist and poet. Founder of *La cachora*, the first, and for many years the only, literary journal in Baja California Sur. Editor of *Baja California Sur. Otro mar, otro desierto* (1991), an anthology of the literature of Baja California Sur. He has published six poetry collections, *De los viajes en general* (1984), *Refugio de ballenas* (1985), *Del fuego y del cuerpo* (1985), *La antigua California* (1986), *Para que la madrugada cante* (1990), *Temer el mar* (1992), and the compendium *Antigua California* (Mexico City: UNAM, 1994), from which all of his poems in this anthology were drawn.

Juan Antonio Di Bella (Ensenada, B.C., 1961). Resident of Mexicali. Fiction writer, rock musician and poet. "El fantasma del cine Curto" was published in the journal *Trazadura* (Mexicali, 1990.)

Tomás Di Bella (Ensenada, B.C., 1954). Brother of Juan Antonio. Resident of

Mexicali. Radio producer, composer, rock musician, translator and poet. He has published two poetry collections, *Cristalazos* (1985) and *La poética genealógica* (1999). "Aliteral poema elástico para linotipistas" was published in the journal *Trazadura* (Mexicali, 1990).

Marco Vinicio Félix Lerma (Culiacan, Sinaloa, 1971). Resident of La Paz, B.C.S., since early childhood. For the last ten years he has been studying for a doctorate in physics at UNAM and at the Universidad Autónoma de Querétaro. He has published numerous scientific papers. His poems in this anthology were drawn from an unpublished manuscript, *Estaciones oníricas*.

Ana María Fernández (Mazatlán, Sinaloa, 1947). Resident of Mexicali. Studied architecture at the Instituto Tecnológico de Estudios Superiores. She has published one poetry collection, *Amores últimos* (1987). Her poems in this anthology appeared in the anthology *Baja California. Piedra de serpiente* (Mexico City: CONACULTA, 1993).

Katery Mónica García (Monterrey, Nuevo León, 1960). Resident of Baja California since 1982. She has published one book of poems, *Para empezar* (Mexicali: UABC, 1985), from which both of her poems in this anthology were drawn.

Alfonso García Cortez (Tijuana, B.C., 1963). Graduate in communications of UIN, where he teaches. He has published three poetry collections, *Recuento de viaje* (1991); *Elegías postergadas* (Toluca: La Hoja Murmurante, 1994), from which "(a los muertos)" was drawn; and *Llanterío* (2001).

María Edma Gómez (Mexico City, 1945). Resident of Mexicali since 1970. She has published four poetry collections, *Las voces del silencio* (1988), *Imágenes de luz* (1993), *Canto de muerte* (1993), and *Yo no soy Eva* (1996). "Minutario" was published in the journal *Tierra adentro* (San Ángel, D.F.: CONACULTA, 1999).

Julieta González Irigoyen (Chihuahua, Chihuahua, 1939). Resident of Tijuana since 1971. Editor, journalist, essayist, fiction writer and poet. Studied literature and journalism at the Universidad Femenina de México. Teaches at UIN. She has published two novels, a collection of short stories and a book of essays, and one poetry collection, *En la rutina del vivir* (Tijuana: CONACULTA/CECUT, 1995), from which "Cuando muere septiembre" was drawn.

Daniel Gutiérrez Pedreiro (La Paz, B.C.S., 1964). Visual artist and poet. Studied Spanish language and literature at UNAM. He has published two poetry collections, *Ángel de una sola noche* (Mexico City: Cronopios, 1993), from which "Perpetuo suicidio" was drawn, and *Danza de los lagartos* (1994).

Carlos Adolfo Gutiérrez Vidal (Mexicali, B.C., 1974). Fiction writer and poet. Graduate in communication sciences of UABC–Mexicali, where he teaches, as well as at UABC–Tijuana. He has published one book of short stories and four poetry collections: *Once poemas para ser leídos en lata* (1992), *Sarcófagos* (1994), *Nortes* (1995) and *Befas* (Tijuana: CONACULTA/CECUT, 2000), from which "Naranja" was drawn. "After hours" and " Tierra prometida" are previously unpublished.

Óscar Hernández (Mexicali, B.C., 1955). Journalist, fiction writer, playwright and poet. Graduate in sociology of UABC–Mexicali. He has published an anthology of short stories by Baja California writers, a collection of plays, a collection of short stories, and two poetry collections: *Caldo de pollo* (Mexicali: ICBC, 1979 and 1995), from which "Carta" was drawn, and *Nubes* (1985).

Víctor Hugo Limón (Tijuana, B.C., 1958). Studied at UABC–Tijuana. He has published one book of poetry, *Nombre en blanco* (San Ángel, D.F./Tijuana: Hotel Ambosmundos/Imago Ediciones, 1997), from which all of his poems in this anthology were drawn.

Edmundo Lizardi (La Paz, B.C.S., 1953). Editor, journalist, fiction writer and poet. Graduate in law of UNAM, where he also studied literature; he studied journalism at the Centro Internacional de Prensa in Barcelona. Has taught at UABC–Tijuana. He has published a collection of journalistic pieces, a book of short stories, and four poetry collections: *Y después del crepúsculo* (1980), *Mar en sombra* (1986), *Azuvia* (1988), and *Preludio de las islas* (Tijuana: IMAC, 1999), from which "Baja Times" was drawn.

Luz Mercédes López Barrera (Mexicali, B.C., 1959). Editor and poet. She has published one book of poetry, *Letras* (1985). Her poems in this anthology are previously unpublished.

Estela Alicia López Lomas (Tlaquepaque, Jalisco, 1944). Also publishes under the name Esalí. Resident of Tijuana since 1957. Fiction writer, essayist and poet. She has published three books of fiction, one collection of essays and six poetry collections: *Esalí I* (1985), *Aprendiz de humano* (1987), *La visitación de eros* (1989), *Quincunce* (1995), *Mi tambor mentiroso* (1995), and *Alicia en la cárcel de las maravillas* (Bacalar, Quintana Roo: Nave de Papel, 1995), from which her poems in this anthology were drawn.

Gerónimo Maciel, pseudonym of Arnulfo Guzmán (Morelia, Michoacán, 1958). Resident of Baja California since the early 1980s. Resident of Mexicali. Journalist and poet. He has published two poetry collections, *Sueños de polvo* (1985) and *Campanas del desierto* (Mexicali: Voz de Arena, ICBC, 1993), from which "Cuando Mexicali era un pueblo fantasma" was drawn.

Javier Manríquez (San Antonio, B.C.S., 1952). Resident of Mexico City since 1971. Graduate in Spanish language and literature of UNAM, where he is editor for the Institute for Historical Research. He has published one collection of poetry, *Cuaderno de San Antonio* (La Paz: Colección Cabildo, 1982), which is included in its entirety in this anthology.

Carlos Martínez Villanueva (Mexico City, 1970). Resident of Tijuana since the early 1990s. He has published one book of poetry, *Nada queda por arder* (Tijuana: La Espina Dorsal, 1997), from which all of his poems in this anthology were drawn.

Francisco Mendoza (Morelia, Michoacán, 1964). Resident of Baja California since 1966. Graduate in law of UABC. He has published one book of poems, *Ahora no, señor blues* (Tijuana: Ediciones del XIII Ayuntamiento, 1992), from which all of his poems in this anthology were drawn.

Alicia Montañez Hinojosa (Mexicali, B.C., 1970). A surgeon by profession, she is currently a resident in internal medicine at Mount Sinai University Hospital in Chicago. She has published one book of poems, *Edades primeras* (Mexicali: Cuadernos del Taller de Literatura, UABC, 1998), from which all of her poems in this volume were drawn.

Karla Mora Corrales (Mexicali, B.C., 1974). Fiction writer and poet. Graduate in communications of UABC–Mexicali. She has published one book of poems, *Ciudadestufa* (Mexicali: Editorial Sintétika, 1998), from which all of her poems in this anthology were drawn.

Francisco Morales (Cananea, Sonora, 1940). Resident of Tecate from 1950 to 1969 and of Tijuana thereafter. He has published nine poetry collections, *La muerte adentro, al lado...conmigo* (1985); *La ciudad que recorro* (Mexico City: Panfleto y Pantomima, 1986), from which "Para echar los orines en tus postes...," "Pienso a veces, ciudad...," "No es muy fácil burlar tus horas flacas...," and "¡Nos quedaron tan grandes las palabras, ciudad!" were drawn; *Desencuentros del blues, de los amores* (1991); *Tijuana tango* (1992); *El día moridor* (1993); *Poemas del hogar y sus orillas* (1994); *Amanecida* (1994), *Poemas del mesón* (1994); and *Desolado amor* (Tijuana: Colección La Maldita Palabra/Editorial Aretes y Pulseras, 1999), from which "Arte poetica," "Blues de la esquina," "Hombre en azul" and "Oda al suicidio" were drawn.

Marco Morales (Tecate, B.C., 1952). Studied literature at UNAM. He has published one collection of poems, *Tijuana rifa k/z...y qué y otros poemas* (1986). "A padre" was published in 1987 in the anthology *...y todos tiramos piedras* (Tecate: Cuchumá, 1987).

Raúl Navejas Dávila (Mexicali, B.C., 1956). Researcher in history at UABC–Mexicali. He has published three poetry collections, *Palabra perdida* (1984), *Los dominios del ave* (1993), and *A través del cristal* (Mexicali, no publisher, 1999), from which "Hora cautiva" was drawn.

Jorge Ortega (Mexicali, B.C., 1972). Professor of Hispanoamerican literature at UABC–Mexicali. Essayist, cultural journalist and poet. He has published two books of essays and seven poetry collections: *Crepitaciones de junio* (1992), *Tierra cálida* (1994), *Rango de vuelo* (1995), *Deserción de los hábitos* (1997), *Cuaderno carmesí* (1997), *Baladas para combatir la inanición* (2001), and *Mudar de casa* (Mexicali: Fondo Editorial de Baja California, 2001), from which "Cortejo de la musa" was drawn.

Horacio Ortiz Villacorta (Tijuana, B.C., 1973) Graduate in Hispanoamerican language and literature of UABC–Tijuana. He has published two poetry collections, *Elocuencias de un loco* (Chimalistac, D.F.: Fondo Editorial Tierra Adentro / CONACULTA, 1994), from which "Epístola" was drawn, and *Bajo el ciclo de la esfera* (Mexicali: La Rebelión de las Musas, ICBC, 1998), from which "Vía-Síntesis" was drawn. "Al final del cuento" is previously unpublished.

Bibiana Padilla (Tijuana, B.C., 1974). Resident of Mexicali. Visual artist and poet. She has published one book of visual poetry, *Los demonios de la casa mayor* (1999), and one poetry collection, *Equilibrios* (1994). Her poems in this anthology were published in 2000 in the journal *Aquilón* (Mexicali).

Juan Reyna (Tijuana, B.C., 1980). Currently studying communications at UIN. He has published one poetry collection, *Vuelta al agua* (2001), and, in *Antología de jóvenes creadores* (Mexicali: Fondo Editorial de Baja California, 2001), the book-length selection *Próximo estoy a descubrir un tumor en la lengua de los hombres*, from which all of his poems in this anthology were drawn.

Raúl Jesús Rincón Meza (Tijuana, B.C., 1948). Studied literature at UNAM. Translator, anthologist and poet. He has published a volume of translations of English-language poetry, an anthology of Japanese poetry, and two poetry collections: *Poemas de santo y seña para descubrir un rostro* (Tijuana: Ediciones Amerindia, UABC, 1974), from which "Baja la lluvia" was drawn, and *Guardar todo* (Tijuana: Imago Ediciones, 1998), from which "Volver a casa," "Nocturno," "El pensamiento de la zorra," "Casa vacía" and "El hueso del mundo" were drawn.

Manuel Romero (Tijuana, B.C., 1964). Graduate in biochemical engineering of the Instituto Tecnológico de Tijuana; a chemical engineer for the San Diego water department. "Nocturno" and "24 de diciembre" were published in the journal *La hoja de poesía* (Tijuana), in 1991 and 1994. "No soy nadie..." was published in the anthology *Un camino de hallazgos. Poetas bajacalifornianos del siglo XX* (1992), "A orillas de la montana" in the anthology *Baja California. Piedra de serpiente* (Mexico City: CONACULTA, 1993). "Paseante y humo" and "Hubo una vez un hombre..." are previously unpublished.

Dante Salgado (La Paz, B.C.S., 1966). Graduate in law and in Spanish language and literature of UNAM. Teaches at UABCS. Editor and poet. He has published three poetry collections: *Mar de lejos* (1990), *Balandra* (1992), and *Agua del desierto*

(Chimalistac, D.F.: Fondo Editorial Tierra Adentro/CONACULTA, 1997), from which "Tata Arturo (otros fragmentos)" was drawn. He was also one of the four poets included in *La piel del desierto* (Mexico City: UNAM, 2000), from which "La noche se alarga en el desierto" was drawn.

Rael Salvador (Ensenada, B.C., 1963). Editor and poet. He has published six poetry collections, *Pandemonium* (1991), *Nieve izquierda*, *El libro de las cosas sencillas*, *Ciudad abierta, Te metes, tiras y sales* (1995) and *Ensenada. Instrucciones para hacer fuego con el mar* (Ensenada: Colección Pavía/Sinmuros Ediciones, 1999), from which both of his poems in this anthology were drawn.

Alejandro Sánchez (Mexicali, 1974). Graduate in psychology of UABC–Mexicali. He has published one poetry collection, *Entre la girasol y la sombra* (Mexicali: La Rebelión de las Musas, ICBC, 1998), from which all of his poems in this anthology were drawn.

Víctor Soto Ferrel (San Miguel del Cantil, Durango, 1948). Resident of Tijuana since 1953. Physician and professor of Spanish literature at UNAM. He has published two poetry collections: *Sal del espejo* (1982) and *La casa del centro* (Mexicali: Fondo Editorial de Baja California, 2001), from which all of his poems in this anthology were drawn.

Enrique Trejo Moreno (Tijuana, B.C., 1946). Anesthesiologist and graduate in literature of UABC–Tijuana. Photocollagist, translator and poet. He has published two poetry collections: *Los labios húmedos de la mañana* (Mexicali: ICBC, 1993), from which "Tijuana Border" was drawn, and *La otra realidad* (1997). "¿Qué pasó, 'ése'?" was published in the anthology *La virgen no llama tres veces* (Mexicali: UABC, 1997).

Gabriel Trujillo Muñoz (Mexicali, B.C., 1958). Professor of literature at UABC–Mexicali. Editor, fiction writer and poet. He has authored or edited over one hundred books, among them the anthology *Un camino de hallazgos, poetas bajacalifornianos del siglo XX* (Mexicali: UABC, 1992) and twelve poetry collections: *Poemas* (1981); *Rituales* (1982); *Bitácora* (1983); *Percepciones* (Mexicali: UABC, 1983), from which "Crepuscular" was drawn; *Moridero* (Mexicali: UABC, 1987), from which "La chinesca" was drawn; *Tras el espejismo* (1989); *Recapitulaciones* (1989); *Mandrágora* (1989); *Atisbos* (1991); *A plena luz* (Chimalistac, D.F.: Fondo Editorial Tierra Adentro/CONACULTA, 1992), from which "Los confines" was drawn; *Don de lenguas* (Mexicali: ICBC, 1995), from which "Ti Yei" was drawn; *Alfanjes* (1997); *Constelaciones* (1997); *Cirugía mayor* (1997); and *Rastrojo* (Mexicali: Plaza y Valdes/UABC, 2001), from which "Raymond Chandler, San Diego, 1958" was drawn.

Ruth Vargas Leyva (Culiacán, Sinaloa, 1946). Studied at UABC–Tijuana and the Universidad de Guatemala. She has published one poetry collection, *Celeste y ocho* *poemas* (1987). "Escena" was drawn from *Baja California. Piedra de serpiente* (Mexico City: CONACULTA, 1993).

José Javier Villarreal (Tijuana, B.C., 1959). Resident of Tecate from early childhood until 1976; since then he has been resident in Monterrey, Nuevo León. Began his studies at the Universidad Autónoma de Nuevo León in 1978 and joined the faculty, as a professor of medieval and baroque literature, in 1985. Editor, literary scholar, essayist, translator and poet. He has published eight poetry collections: *Historia de la coronación* (1982); *Estatua sumergida* (1982); *En torno a monumentos* (1983); *Poemas bajacalifornianos* (1984); *Mar del norte* (Mexico City: Joaquín Mortiz, 1988), from which "Elegía frente al mar," "Tijuana" and "En mañanas como ésta" were drawn; *La Procesión* (Mexico City: Joaquín Mortiz/ Ayuntamiento de Monterrey, 1991), from which "He visto a la corneja volar..." and "A Clodia" were drawn; *Portuaria* (1994); *Noche de fundaciones* (1996); and *Bíblica* (1998).

Rubén Vizcaíno Valencia (Comala, Colima, 1919). Resident of Mexicali from 1952 to 1959; thereafter, resident of Tijuana. A tireless promoter of the arts of Baja California. Novelist, playwright, essayist and poet. "Perdón por tener todavía mis ojos" was drawn from *Baja California. Piedra de serpiente* (Mexico City: CONACULTA, 1993).

Fernando Vizcarra (Mexicali, B.C., 1961). Studied communications at the Universidad Autónoma Metropolitana; has taught at UIN and at UABC–Mexicali. Editor, essayist and poet. He has published one book of essays and two poetry collections, *Días de salvación* (Mexicali: UABC, 1992), from which "Rayo..." was drawn, and *Raíz de luna* (1992).

Heriberto Yépez (Mexicali, B.C., 1974). Lifelong resident of Tijuana. Essayist, literary journalist, translator and poet. Graduate in philosophy of the Escuela de Humanidades of UABC–Tijuana. He has published three collections of essays, a volume of translations of the poet Jerome Rothenberg, and one book of poetry, *Por una poética antes del paleolítico y después de la propaganda* (Tijuana: Editorial Anortecer, 2000), from which all of his poems in this anthology were drawn.

Gilberto Zúñiga (Tijuana, B.C., 1955). Studied psychology at the Universidad Estatal de California. He has published one poetry collection, *Nightfields* (Mexicali: UABC, 1991), from which "Amata," "25 de diciembre," "Nightfields," and "La bailarina del balcón" were drawn. "Junto a la hora" and "Alabar el circulo" are previously unpublished.

THE TRANSLATORS

Elizabeth Bell is an award-winning translator based in San Francisco. Her work has appeared in the journals *Kenyon Review* and *Fiction,* and in the anthology *Light from a Nearby Window: Contemporary Mexican Poetry,* among other publications.

Scott Bennett is a translator and literary scholar resident in Santa Barbara, California. He received his M.A. in Spanish from San Diego State University and is completing his doctorate in Hispanic languages and literatures at the University of California, Santa Barbara. He is currently translating the Mexican novelist David Toscana's collection of short stories *Historias del lontananza* (1997).

K.A. Eherenman is chair of the Department of Languages and Literature of the University of San Diego. Scholar, translator and poet. She has published translations of Alberto Blanco, among others, and numerous scholarly articles. Her current project is *The Face of God in Latin American Poetry,* a book-length study.

Patricia L. Irby, after a brief incursion into the world of training assistance dogs, has returned to translating Latin American press for the Foreign Broadcast Information Service. She lives in San Diego county.

Robert L. Jones (1945-1996) taught at San Diego State University. He co-founded the transborder journal *El último vuelo* (1979) and published numerous translations of Tijuana poets and his one poetry collection, *Wild Onions* (1985), which was subsequently published in Spanish translation.

Michael Koch is a painter, poet and translator of French and Spanish. His translations have appeared in *Light from a Nearby Window: Contemporary Mexican Poetry,* and in the journals *Soup, Durak,* and *Compages,* among others. He lives in San Francisco, where he teaches school.

Joan Lindgren has lived on the border for over forty years; a former Fulbright Border Scholar, teaching cross-border translation workshops at UABC. Her essays, poems, stories and translations have been widely anthologized. She has translated three major poetry collections, *Letters to an Owl,* by Magda Santonostasio (1985), *The Task of Telling,* by Francisco Morales Santos (2000), and *Unthinkable Tenderness: Selected Poems of Juan Gelman* (1997).

Armida Polkinhorn's translations in this volume mark her debut in print.

Harry Polkinhorn (B.A. English, UC-Berkeley; M.A. English, M.A. Studio Arts, San Diego State University; Ph.D. English, New York University; M.A. Counseling Psychology, Pacifica Graduate Institute) is a permanent visiting professor in the Ph.D. program in Semiotics and Communication of the Pontifical Catholic

University of São Paulo, Brazil and Director of San Diego State University Press. He has published, as author and editor, over thirty books of visual poetry, poetry, fiction, translation, and scholarship. As a scholar his primary interests have been the international avant-garde and the culture of the U.S-Mexico border region. He has translated works from Italian, Portuguese, German, and Spanish.

Gustavo Segade has been a faculty member at San Diego State University since1967 in Spanish language and Latin American literature, comparative literature, Latin American Studies and Mexican American Studies. He is the former director of the Spanish-English Certificate Program in Translation Studies and Chair of the Translation Studies Committee of the College of Arts and Letters. He has published translations of numerous poems and stories in journals and anthologies as well as three book-length translations: Sergio Elizondo's poetry collection *Perros y antiperros* (1972), Rosina Conde's collection of short stories *Women on the Road* (1994), and *Points of Departure: New Stories from Mexico* (2001). He is currently translating a book of selected short stories by Mexican writer Eduardo Antonio Parra, forthcoming from City Lights Books.

Mark Weiss (B.A. English, Johns Hopkins; M.A. English, Columbia University; M.A. Social Work, Yeshiva University; Certificate in Family Therapy, The Ackerman Institute) is the publisher of Junction Press. He is currently editing the bilingual anthology *The Revolution in Cuban Poetry: 1944 to the Present,* and translating *Stet,* a bilingual selection of poems by Cuban poet José Kozer, both due in 2003. He is the author of five books of poems.

COVER ARTIST

Hugo Crosthwaite (Tijuana, B.C., 1971). Lifelong resident of Rosarito, B.C. Studied graphic design at San Diego State University. Among his numerous solo exhibitions in Mexico and the United States have been "Tablas de una novena" at Tijuana's Centro Cultural and "Urbe Tenebrosa" at Tijuana's State Gallery. He recently participated in the collective show of Tijuana artists "Pintura Fresca," at California State University–Los Angeles, and in the major exhibition "The Perception of Appearances: A Decade of American Contemporary Figurative Drawing," at the Frye Art Museum in Seattle.